BOOKS BY DANIEL FORD

Three-Mile Island: Thirty Minutes to Meltdown
Energy Strategies (with Henry Kendall and Steven Nadis)
The Cult of the Atom
The Button

THE BUTTON

The Pentagon's Strategic Command and Control System

by Daniel Ford

SIMON AND SCHUSTER
New York

Portions of this book appeared originally in *The New Yorker*.

Copyright © 1985 by Daniel Ford
All rights reserved
including the right of reproduction
in whole or in part in any form
Published by Simon and Schuster
A Division of Simon & Schuster, Inc.
Simon & Schuster Building
Rockefeller Center
1230 Avenue of the Americas
New York, New York 10020
SIMON AND SCHUSTER and colophon are registered trademarks of
Simon & Schuster, Inc.
Designed by Eve Kirch
Manufactured in the United States of America

10   9   8   7   6   5   4   3

Library of Congress Cataloging in Publication Data
Ford, Daniel F.
    The button.
    Bibliography: p.
    Includes index.
    1. Command and control systems—United States.
2. United States—Military policy.   3. First strike
(Nuclear strategy)   4. Missile attack warning systems—
United States.   I. Title.
UB212.F67   1985   355.3′3041′0973   84-27616
ISBN: 0-671-50068-6

ACKNOWLEDGMENTS

A Qantas flight across the Pacific in December 1982 provided the opportunity to catch up on some reading, and I spent much of the trip transfixed by a technical paper—"Can Nuclear War Be Controlled?"—written by Desmond Ball of the Australian National University. With the oversupply of literature on the nuclear problem, it is rare to find new and interesting information, but Ball's article contained startling data. If his extensively documented account of how "the button" works (or, in some cases, may not work) was correct, all the common assumptions about U.S. capability to retaliate after a Soviet attack were suspect. The very foundation of the nation's nuclear deterrent had a set of cracks that, while apparently well known inside the military, had never been revealed in public or reflected in official defense policy.

As it happened, I was en route to Australia on an unrelated assignment for *The New Yorker* and did not have the opportunity during that trip to talk with Ball. I didn't regret this very much, however, because instead of interviewing him, I wanted to return home as quickly as possible to try to obtain the source material on which he based his analysis. I also wanted to search out the other experts in the field to see what they thought of his conclusions. With the indulgence of William

Shawn, the editor of *The New Yorker*, I put aside my other project and began to investigate what Ball had to say.

During the course of my research I have received extensive assistance from military and civilian experts in command, control, communications and intelligence. John Steinbruner of the Brookings Institution—like Ball, one of the few independent analysts to study this problem—provided a great deal of background information as well as a long list of others with whom I should talk. Those on his Who's Who of people in the field were extremely helpful and I would like to thank them individually, although since they mostly work for the Pentagon or different branches of the military, they have indicated that they would be more pleased if I did not use their names. Other experts who can, and should, be thanked include Richard Garwin and Paul Bracken. Desmond Ball, with whom I ultimately did talk at great length, deserves my special gratitude, as does Kurt Gottfried, who originally called my attention to Ball's work.

The official channels of information about the strategic command and control system are, understandably, somewhat narrow. Nevertheless, within the limits of the prevailing security restrictions, officials at the Office of the Secretary of Defense, the Joint Chiefs of Staff, the Strategic Air Command, the North American Aerospace Command, the Defense Communications Agency, the General Accounting Office, and at the various military bases I visited provided key information on a wide range of topics.

As challenging as information gathering proved to be, assessing the implications of the facts was a task of a different order. If this book is more than a compendium of isolated details about strategic command and control, this results from the efforts of Henry Kendall and Frank von Hippel to help me look at the larger issues. The search for the right perspective was also aided by recent works on the history of U.S. nuclear policy, notably Lawrence Freedman's *The Evolution of Nuclear Strategy* and Fred Kaplan's *The Wizards of Armageddon*.

Finally, I am in debt, as usual, to the editorial staff at *The New Yorker* and at Simon and Schuster. William McKibbon, at the magazine, performed the first round of getting the manuscript into shape, and Alice Mayhew at S&S oversaw its growth into a book. Other friends, notably Steven Nadis, were helpful—that is to say, bluntly critical—when I asked for their views on what I was trying to say.

To Regina, Fred, and Jim

CONTENTS

Ulrich recalled a similar experience dating from his military period. The squadron rode in double file and "Passing on of orders" was practiced, an order spoken in a low voice being passed on from man to man. Now, if the order given in front was: "Sergeant-major move to the head of the column," what came out at the rear was: "Eight troopers to be shot immediately," or something of that sort. And it is in a similar manner that world history came about.

—Robert Musil,
The Man Without Qualities

Nothing caused the Germans more trouble . . . than communications. Belgians cut telephone and telegraph wires; the powerful Eiffel Tower wireless station jammed the air waves so that messages came through so garbled they had to be repeated three or four times before sense could be made of them. [The German Supreme Headquarters'] single receiving station became so clogged that messages took from eight to twelve hours to get through. This was one of the "frictions" the German General Staff, misled by the ease of communications in war games, had not planned for.

—Barbara Tuchman,
The Guns of August

FOREWORD

United States civilian and military leaders have stated in solemn and unqualified terms that they would never use the country's nuclear forces in an unprovoked offensive attack—a first strike—against the Soviet Union. In private, officials refer to this not as an inflexible principle but as merely the nation's "declaratory policy." They distinguish, that is, between formal reassurances made for political purposes and the Pentagon's real contingency plans for using nuclear weapons.

The American people strongly support a policy of retaliation—of counterstrikes after a Soviet attack on our homeland—as the only morally defensible posture. Public declarations against the use of U.S. nuclear weapons for offensive purposes are intended to reflect such scruples. The statements do not reflect what Pentagon planners regard as military reality.

The actual U.S. preparations for nuclear war attach secondary importance to retaliation. The primary emergency plan—the one that is more likely to be executed if a nuclear showdown appeared inevitable—involves a massive first strike on key military targets in the Soviet Union. One of its principal aims would be to kill Soviet leaders and thereby immediately paralyze the highly centralized Soviet war machine.

The Soviets are undeceived about the existence of Pentagon first-strike plans—which are, almost certainly, a mirror image of the Soviet military's own thinking—although the American public has no knowledge of this radical departure from the announced national policy. While Americans are deeply suspicious of Soviet intentions, there has been no awakening to the danger that if there is a World War III, we might be the ones to start it. Our incentive to do so, of course, is nil—so long as we feel safe from attack. Should that danger materialize, however, or appear to, the Pentagon has a preferred course of action. Like the Kremlin, its outlook is imbued with the traditional military presumption that there will be a large advantage from getting in the first blow. Our military is also concerned that although the United States has a great deal of nuclear muscle, the nervous system that is supposed to make it flex—the communications network for delivering emergency orders—may not work very well, or at all, after a Soviet attack.

It is obvious that the Pentagon must make a wide variety of plans for using the vast array of nuclear weapons that it has at its disposal. That is the job of responsible military officers, one for which they will be held accountable should war come. There is a tendency in peacetime, as Winston Churchill noted, to regard someone engaged in war planning as "a plotting knave, or at best an overgrown child playing with toys, and dangerous toys at that." No such insinuation is intended here in calling attention to the first-strike option contained in U.S. war plans. There is no evidence whatever to suggest that the Pentagon has embraced any scheme for destroying the Soviet Union at the first opportunity, or that any branch within our military has abandoned the crucial objective of avoiding nuclear conflict.

It is not inconsistent for a peace-loving nation to have many fallback positions to deal with the gravest crises, such as a plan to go on the offensive if that is the only way to thwart or blunt the effects of an imminent enemy attack. This does not testify to a yearning for battle. Still, whatever the narrow military logic behind them, there is the danger that elaborate offensive preparations could have unintended consequences. U.S. leaders may fervently wish to avoid conflict, but the complex war plans and the nature of the weapons systems on which they depend could deprive them in certain circumstances of any real choice. U.S. missiles are primed to go, and the special set of arrangements that have been made for firing them could suddenly turn today's nuclear peace into tomorrow's nuclear conflict.

The extraordinary dangers associated with U.S. and Soviet first-strike plans do not manifest themselves in normal, peacetime conditions. The attack plans locked away in Pentagon safes and at secret Soviet command posts are like insurance policies written to cover some extremely remote eventuality. Few in the military expect these contingency plans to be used, since it is in the interests of both superpowers to avoid any confrontation that could grow into nuclear conflict. For obvious reasons, each nation has been and remains deterred from actions that could bring on a devastating nuclear rejoinder by the other.

Even if the alarm bells sounded—as a result, say, of a false alert from one of the computers or automatic sensors that are supposed to warn of an enemy attack—the need for restraint is so clear that the last thing officials would want to do would be to rush to launch their missiles. An impressive system of safeguards, on both sides, works very well to guard against such accidents.

There is nothing, however, to guarantee that the mutual deterrence that prevails in peacetime can survive the stress of a major crisis, or that the conflicting interests and ideological differences of the two nations will not lead to severe clashes in the future. Another affair like the Cuban Missile Crisis—replayed when both sides have far more missiles than the handful they possessed in 1962—always looms on the horizon. It is in such an unstable situation that the existence of first-strike plans, and the technical requirements for executing them, could quickly and irreversibly lead to the rapid abandonment of all restraint and, in effect, propel the two nations into a nuclear war that neither wanted.

For offensive nuclear war plans and offensive weapons systems totally change the chemistry of the two nations' decision-making processes when coexistence is replaced by face-to-face confrontation. As routine meetings gave way to emergency sessions, which everyone involved knew were potential councils of war, a dramatic transformation would take place. If the issue that brought about the confrontation were not resolved quickly, suspicions and tensions would mount. After a certain threshold is crossed—the point at which war begins to seem to the Pentagon or the Kremlin as not only theoretically possible, but likely—the circumspection the two nations have maintained in their accustomed peacetime standoff would dwindle and disappear. Given their mutual predisposition, if pushed hard enough, to strike first, their peacetime sense of security would be replaced by panic as each side calculated the risk that the other was about to make the first move.

The greater your suspicions of your opponent's offensive intent, of course, the greater the incentive to go on the offensive yourself. So much for mutual deterrence in a crisis. According to the script that each side has prepared for nuclear war, any previous hesitancy about attacking could give way to a rush to open the gun lockers and use the available ordnance, and the communications systems that send out the orders for firing it, before everything was destroyed by the other side. Ironically enough, the net effect of being prepared to strike first is to encourage the other side to make the preemptive attack itself. Deterrence, far from being assured, would thus quickly unravel when it is needed most, especially given the realization that your own worst designs on your enemy were likely to correspond precisely to his designs on you.

The U.S. nuclear war plan—which is known as the Single Integrated Operational Plan, or S.I.O.P.—is extraordinarily sensitive. Yet it is possible, with some effort, to learn a great deal about it. As in standard military analyses, it is unnecessary to get access to the planning documents themselves to gain an insight into how and when Pentagon plans call for U.S. leaders to push the button. Every military organization, by what it does, by the kinds of weapons and related apparatus it deploys, will inevitably provide many clues to its aims and to the selected responses it intends to make to various provocations. Form, as the biologists say, indicates function, and the technical characteristics of weapons can be used to divine their military roles. How individual weapons are all put together with other equipment will be further evidence of the general strategy that has been adopted.

In addition to assembling the circumstantial evidence, it is also possible, of course, to ask Pentagon strategists what they have in mind. Senior officials who have worked on the S.I.O.P., without compromising security restrictions, are able to provide remarkable details about the offensive strategy that now dominates U.S. nuclear war planning. The Pentagon's highest officials have admitted, moreover, at least to each other, that the major new weapons being added to the U.S. stra-

tegic nuclear arsenal—such as the MX intercontinental ballistic missile
and the Trident D-5 submarine-launched missile—are specifically intended to give the United States the means in a crisis to make preemptive attacks on the Soviet Union.

The Pentagon, for planning purposes, has been responsive to what
it accepts as the unimpeachable military logic of preserving the option
of getting in the first blow: destroying Soviet nuclear forces before
they can be used against us. The plan, moreover, seeks to capitalize
on the new technology that is available—in particular, the highly accurate guidance systems—that permits U.S. missiles to be used for
direct attacks on Soviet nuclear forces and central command posts.
Finally, the plan compensates for a profound U.S. national security
weakness that the Pentagon tacitly admits but has been loath to discuss
in public—that if the United States does not strike first in a crisis that
develops into a nuclear war, it may be unable to strike back at all in
any organized way.

This book, which examines the last problem in detail, was not
begun as a broad inquiry into overall U.S. nuclear strategy. Its original
purpose was to look at a much narrower technical question: how the
so-called button is supposed to work. These issues, concerning what
the military calls the command and control of nuclear forces, have
not received much attention outside official circles. Despite all the
public debate and discussion about nuclear weapons, the exceedingly
basic question of how—or whether—the United States could really use
its nuclear weapons if it were forced to do so has been overlooked.

It has been taken for granted that the President, by reaching into
his famous black briefcase (the so-called Football), can simply pull
out the secret passwords and order the launching of nuclear missiles
in response to Soviet attack. Just like King Arthur in the medieval
legend, proving himself leader of the Britons by miraculously pulling
the sword Excalibur from a stone, the President has been said to have
sole authority over the use of nuclear weapons. This standard account
of presidential control—and of the use of nuclear weapons only in
retaliation for Soviet attack—turns out to be a piece of contemporary
folklore.

There is, to be sure, a black bag that is carried by the President's
military aide. It does, in fact, contain authentication codes as well as
a notebook whose heavily laminated pages outline the various options

in the S.I.O.P. The current war plan, however, as described in Chapters 3 and 4 of this book, is divided into two main parts: it has a wide range of attack options, not just a set of attack-response plans. The military, moreover, which prepares the codes and accompanying documents with the assistance of the National Security Agency, does not provide them merely to the President. It keeps copies—several copies—for itself. This prevents control over the nation's strategic forces from being dangerously overcentralized.

Still, it is one thing for the President or designated officers to select a course of action; communicating their instructions to the forces is a separate problem. The Roman centurion who is quoted in the New Testament was able to boast of his direct authority over his soldiers— "I say to one 'Go,' and he goes; and I say to another 'Come,' and he comes; and to my servant, 'Do this,' and he does it." This book's analysis of the U.S. military's emergency communications systems—which is its main subject—suggests that no one with the overall authority to order a U.S. retaliatory strike can make such a confident claim.

The Pentagon and selected military headquarters do indeed have equipment that is supposed to broadcast orders to U.S. missile, submarine, and bomber crews. Many military communications specialists are nevertheless skeptical about the ability of the President or anyone else to issue emergency messages following a Soviet attack. The military's command-system machinery was installed in the 1950s and 1960s, and it has been left largely unchanged despite knowledge of its pronounced vulnerability to the kind of Soviet attack that would now be expected at the outset of a nuclear war.

Even in day-to-day operation the military's message-distribution system works quite poorly, and while the experts on military technology disagree on many issues, they tend to share a common view of the chronic communications problem. Key portions of the Pentagon's Worldwide Military Command and Control System, the main instrument for conveying orders to U.S. forces, are regarded as nonfunctional under normal conditions, and the military's communications systems are expected to work badly or not at all as emergencies arise.

No greater emergency can be imagined than a Soviet nuclear attack on the United States. Yet—again, according to the engineers who work in this field—most Pentagon communications gear, including some of the special systems relied upon to convey the order to retaliate, is able to operate only in a benign, peacetime environment. They say that a well-targeted Soviet strike—involving perhaps just a few dozen weapons—could promptly break the fragile communications hookups between senior commanders and the nation's far-flung nuclear forces.

Accordingly, despite the controversy in recent years over the adequacy of the U.S. nuclear deterrent—a debate focussed on topics such as the MX missile—the outstanding problem affecting U.S. retaliatory capability which is analyzed in this book has not been mentioned. The problem isn't the need for advanced new missiles, but the potential inability to communicate the necessary orders to fire the thousands of missiles we already have.

On the other hand, if the Pentagon felt compelled to strike first, the experts judge the existing command and control arrangements satisfactory. The communications system installed two decades ago to deliver orders to the forces can reliably convey the necessary targeting and timing instructions for a first strike, since just about any primitive communications method is good enough for this purpose. The formats for such orders have been deliberately designed, that is, so that a single short code, containing all the required information, can be delivered even over nonsecure public telephone lines.

Thus, the existing command and control system—once its technical features and limitations are analyzed—reveals the kind of options the U.S. nuclear war plan contains. A command system unready to deliver orders for retaliation but streamlined to convey commands for a first strike suggests the way the Pentagon thinks a nuclear war may have to be fought. The dubious ability to respond to a Soviet attack in accordance with the stated national policy of retaliation is therefore not obvious evidence of dereliction on the part of the military. It merely indicates the size of the gap between official rhetoric and Pentagon plans. Preparations for nuclear retaliation are naturally deemphasized if the military—according to the preferred Major Attack Option in the S.I.O.P.—intends, if it has to fight at all, to strike first.

There is a circularity in the thinking going into U.S. war planning. The lack of satisfactory methods for retaliating in a coordinated way reflects dependence on a first-strike plan. The inherent technical problems in retaliating then reinforce the idea that a first strike is, by default, the preferred military option in a real showdown with the Soviet Union. Given the difficulties in communicating the orders to retaliate, and the obvious temptation for the Soviets to exploit this weakness by attacking the communications system directly, U.S. leaders could thus be caught in a crisis in a technological box canyon. It would be responsible military officers who could find themselves forced to recommend a preemptive attack as the only viable way to counter an expected Soviet first strike.

This book, accordingly, moves beyond an examination of the technical details of how the "button" works—or, in some cases, may not work. It looks at the combination of military doctrine and technological circumstances that is leading the United States away from the defensive policy of retaliation to an offensive strategic posture that will inevitably lead us closer to nuclear war. Particular attention is given to the thirty to forty billion dollar Reagan Administration program to build a new command and control system to improve U.S. nuclear warfighting capability—a major initiative that has received scant public or Congressional attention—and the tremendous risk that in the attempt to close various gaps, other greater dangers to our national security are being created.

1

SET TRIGGER

Cheyenne Mountain is a granite edifice at the southern end of the front range of the Rocky Mountains, not far from Pikes Peak and the city of Colorado Springs. During the early 1960s, dynamite blasters working for the United States Department of Defense dug out a set of caves inside it to provide an underground headquarters for NORAD—the North American Aerospace Defense Command. The installation is jointly staffed by personnel of the United States and Royal Canadian Air Forces, and their central mission is to determine whether the Soviet Union has launched a missile or bomber attack against North America. The NORAD Cheyenne Mountain Complex is the front end, so to speak, of the entire strategic command and control system: the warning it provides triggers the back end of the system, which is set up to execute various preplanned retaliatory strikes.

The apex of the decision-making process at NORAD is its Commander in Chief, CINCNORAD as he is designated by the Pentagon. His place during an emergency would be in the main Command Post, the famous room with the wailing alarm Klaxons and giant (seventeen feet by seventeen feet) display screens that has been depicted in the classic nuclear-war movies. When I visited the Command Post, it was hushed, staffed by only a handful of officers on its lower level, its lighting dim and tinged by the greenish glow from the computer display screens. The battle station, on the balcony at the back of the Command Post overlooking the entire room, was unoccupied at the time, but during a missile alert, CINCNORAD—at present General James V. Hartinger—would go there to make his "attack assessment," the formal determination of whether the country is under attack.

There are five telephones next to the NORAD commander's battle-station desk—four on a console to the left of it and one on top of an adjacent computer display screen. Brigadier General Paul Wagoner, who is in charge of NORAD combat operations and the day-to-day management of the Cheyenne Mountain Complex, and who was show-ing me around, stood behind the desk and explained the function of each telephone. A black phone, labeled "Secure," provides a direct link between the NORAD Command Post and the National Military Command Center in the Pentagon, he said. Should CINCNORAD believe that a Soviet attack may be taking place, the Pentagon is sup-posed to set up a conference call on that line immediately. The parti-cipants in the discussion would include, among others, the Commander in Chief of the Strategic Air Command, the Chairman of the Joint Chiefs of Staff, the Secretary of Defense, and the President.

With the black conferencing phone to one ear, General Wagoner said, the NORAD commander would be holding a beige phone to his other ear so he could talk with the NORAD Missile Warning Center, which is in another of the buildings inside the mountain. General Wagoner added that if the commander had another hand, he'd prob-ably want to be holding a red phone that was also on the console. It is connected to a NORAD intelligence center that receives data from the reconnaissance satellites operated by the Central Intelligence Agency and the National Security Agency as well as information from other United States intelligence sources. A fourth phone was a hookup with the Joint Chiefs of Staff, and the fifth phone was there "in case his wife wants to tell him to bring home a loaf of bread."

A fact sheet that NORAD gives to reporters says, "When we pick up a telephone, we expect to talk to someone at the other end—right now." It occurred to me to ask General Wagoner to demonstrate this, starting with the special black phone that would be used to talk to the President. He picked up the phone briskly and punched the button next to it, which lit up right away. I looked at my watch and waited. He waited, too, the phone to his ear. About twenty seconds elapsed and nothing happened. The General, who seemed somewhat flustered, hung up, mumbled something about perhaps needing "a special operator," and started to talk about other features of the Command Post. I interrupted and pointed to another of the five telephones by the Commander in Chief's desk, the one General Wagoner had said was a direct line to the Joint Chiefs of Staff. He picked it up, a bit less confidently than before. Once again, nothing happened. A communications officer then said to the General that the second phone was a "one-way, receive-only" link. I looked at the other three phones, but General Wagoner decided to terminate his testing of the communications system.

NORAD replied to my subsequent written question about the trouble with the black phone to the National Military Command Center by saying that it was also "strictly for incoming NMCC calls." That is incorrect. I spoke with General Wagoner again and he explained what had gone wrong. "The black phone was an outgoing phone," he said. "I just flat screwed up." At the time, he had been in charge of NORAD combat operations for only a few months, he continued, and was not completely familiar with the communications procedures. He was embarrassed that he had given me a "dumb, dumb demonstration" of NORAD's communications capabilities. There is a high level of redundancy, he emphasized, with several alternate means of transmitting vital messages always available—radio, microwave, satellite, or other telephone hookups. When I pressed for information on the specific problem with the call he had placed to the Pentagon, he said, "I didn't know that I had to dial '0' to get the operator."

The installation of multiple communications systems at NORAD is undeniable. Still, there will be precious little time to search for a working backup once Soviet missiles have been launched. Moreover, according to several recent Pentagon studies, it may be very hard to find *any* working communications circuits once Soviet bombs have begun to fall on U.S. soil. This will be an especially severe problem if—as seems likely to the Pentagon—the key U.S. military command posts and message-relay stations are the highest priority targets of a major Soviet attack. In that case, the President will be put in the difficult position of having to make an extremely fast decision on whether the attack that appears on NORAD computer screens is real and, if he thinks it is, whether to order the launching of U.S. Minuteman missiles and other nuclear forces in retaliation. If he does not give the orders quickly, he may not be able to give them at all. For neither the White House nor the communications lines it depends on are likely to survive the initial phase of a shrewdly planned Soviet first strike.

Officials caution that the "horror stories" detailed in the Pentagon's studies of U.S. wartime communications capabilities are too sensitive to discuss in detail. "Documents on this subject that were labeled 'SECRET' two years ago are now 'TOP SECRET,' " a member of one of the government panels that have investigated the problem told me. Some of the reports have been put under a special security classification the code name of which is itself classified. It is possible, nevertheless, without encroaching upon protected information, to outline the basic problems with the methods that are supposed to trigger the launching of a U.S. retaliatory strike.

––––––––

A friend who is interested in guns invited me to lunch one weekend a while back and to join him and his wife afterward for pistol practice. We used a double-action Smith & Wesson .38-caliber revolver. It can be fired simply by pulling the trigger, which is rather stiff, or by cocking the hammer first and then gently squeezing the firing mechanism. It is easier to fire the gun when it is cocked, and a number of times as I took aim, it seemed to go off by itself. "That's a conventional trigger," I was told. "If you think that's something, you should see what a real hair trigger is like."

Daniel Cullity is one of the leading gunsmiths called on by small-arms enthusiasts and museums to restore antique weapons. He also does other special jobs, such as making dueling pistols with solid gold barrels. "I'll give you a little bit of a background on hair triggers," he told me during my visit to his shop, which is in East Sandwich, Massachusetts, on Cape Cod. "They do have a background, historically. A hair trigger has been in use for all ballistic weaponry that's ever been invented—for instance, like the crossbow or a matchlock or a wheel-lock. The whole idea is that you have a mechanical system under a good deal of tension, and it's your potential unleashing of it that is controlled by that very fine hair trigger." The same principle is used in an ordinary mousetrap, "a very unsophisticated and unreliable mechanism, but it gives an analogy to what is happening. You have a large, heavy spring which is caught and held back by a very, very small lever."

Cullity pointed to the Schuetzen rifle, first made in Germany during the 1870s, which "brought the hair trigger to its apogee." He handed me the firing mechanism taken from one of these rifles and said that like most hair triggers, it was known technically as a set trigger or double trigger. "There are two triggers, and you pull one to cock the mechanism, and then you just touch the front trigger and the thing goes off."

We pulled the enabling trigger several times and experimented with ways of setting off the hair trigger. It was exceedingly sensitive, with the slightest pressure or jiggling causing it to fire. I could not even get the sensation of touching it before it went off. A feather, conveniently available from Cullity's chicken coop, easily discharged it. Without our doing anything, the trigger went off by itself. After all, it was a lever under a great deal of stress, he explained, "resting on a metal ledge only about a thousandth of an inch wide."

Hair triggers are mainly used in target shooting by marksmen who want to reduce the movement required to pull a heavy trigger, which could disturb their sighting. "No commercial arm that I know of can be bought with a hair trigger on it," the gunsmith told me. "The reason is they're a complicated mechanism and they're subject to any kind of abuse or friction and may get out of kilter. In the hands of somebody who is inexperienced, they're very dangerous."

Nor do standard military weapons use them. "The military usually takes the opposite tack on triggers. They usually have what they call military take-up, where the trigger will move maybe a quarter of an inch before it's accomplishing any work at all, and then there'll be a pretty strong pull. The point of it is to make it a very, very conscious act to fire a military weapon, so that there are fewer accidents under the strain of battle."

––––––––

Extreme caution with the firing mechanism is clearly all the more necessary in the case of nuclear weapons. Given their immense destructive power, there must be foolproof methods for preventing accidental launching or detonation. Without such controls, nuclear firepower would be a danger, not an asset. In addition, if a punishing retaliatory strike is counted on by the United States to deter Soviet aggression, reliable provisions to follow through with such a threat have to be made. Launching a counterattack implies that one is able to detect an enemy attack in the first place, to assess its nature and extent, and to decide on an appropriate response. Officials must then be sure that they will not get a busy signal—or no answer—when they pick up the phone to give their orders. It is equally important that leaders be able to communicate at all times with their forces to make sure that nuclear weapons are *not* fired if the official decision is to try to ride out the attack. Without a command and control system to do all this, a nuclear arsenal would be no more useful than a fortune locked away in a safety deposit box to which one had lost the keys.

While some kind of firing mechanism is needed, plainly the last thing anyone would want would be for U.S. and Soviet nuclear weapons to be kept on anything resembling a hair trigger. It is popularly assumed that every technical precaution possible, as well as the most stringent procedural controls and impeccable personal restraint, would keep statesmen and military officers on both sides from any hasty decision to use nuclear weapons. The requisite degree of conservatism in such matters was displayed in the 1964 movie *Fail Safe*. U.S. bombers had received a miscue and had set out toward the USSR. Yet a sober and resolute President, played by Henry Fonda, cooperated with an equally sane and responsible Soviet Premier to head off all-out war.

In the 1980s, there is no longer a quaranteed grace period for hot-line consultations while opposing bombers, at subsonic speeds, approach each other's territory. The technology has changed—today's intercontinental ballistic missiles (ICBMs) fly at speeds in excess of fifteen thousand miles per hour—and this has prompted changes in the kinds of firing mechanisms relied upon to assure retaliation. It must now be recognized that in an actual U.S.-Soviet confrontation, the good sense of leaders on both sides could be overwhelmed by the brute fact that they might have little warning time or opportunity to deliberate, a situation made all the more acute by the vulnerability of the leaders themselves to each other's nuclear weapons. Common sense demands deliberation and restraint, but the arrangements now in place for assuring retaliation depend on the ability to take speedy action at the first sign—or apparent sign—of an enemy attack.

"We've got to realize the implication of what we have done," Dr. John Steinbruner, the Director of Foreign Policy Studies at the Brookings Institution, said. "I think that like many things, one doesn't want to overdo the set trigger analogy, but to a first approximation that is the way to think about the situation. We have rigged it so there is not *a* safety catch. There are many safety catches under normal circumstances. We've never taken them all off, and let's hope we never do, because the situation that would obtain would be so volatile I doubt if anybody could control it. It is primed to go—massively—and it would take very little to set it off. And the reason is that that's the only way it can operate, given the extreme vulnerability of the entire [command and control] mechanism to the preemptive moves of the opponent."

The Pentagon's view on this subject was explained to me by Air Force Lieutenant General Robert Herres, who is in charge of command, control, and communications systems for the Joint Chiefs of Staff. "There's a lot of malevolent genius involved in this business," he said, and "the whole system needs to be able to react very quickly" to assure that the Soviets could not execute "a decapitating attack"—one that killed U.S. leaders in Washington and destroyed the main U.S. command posts and message-relay stations before orders for a counterattack could be sent out. The United States has detailed contingency plans to preclude such an eventuality, he added.

Discussions, and caricatures, of the U.S. nuclear command and control system make reference to the so-called "button." There are manual firing mechanisms on the individual weapons, but there is no single button, switch, knob, lever, key, or electronic unit, no simple control device of any kind that the President or anyone else can push, turn, or wiggle to fire off the country's entire arsenal of nuclear missiles. The term is just a shorthand way of talking about the elaborate means of ordering a nuclear strike against an adversary. Military officials, for obvious reasons, are reluctant to talk about the details of these arrangements. Among other things, they prefer to keep the Soviet Union guessing about how the United States would respond to an attack. They are also hesitant about advertising the hair trigger arrangement, or the fact that the United States may not be able to strike back very well—or at all—under certain conditions.

The deficiencies in the existing command and control system have been the subject of urgent internal investigations carried out by the Joint Chiefs of Staff, the Defense Science Board, the Strategic Air Command, and other official bodies. In the new Pentagon buzzword, these reviews are referred to as "connectivity" studies. The word sounds "pretty awful," General Herres admitted. "I finally gave up and looked it up in the dictionary. It is in the dictionary. I didn't think I was going to find it. It's the state of being connected."

William Perry, the Under Secretary of Defense for Research and Engineering in the Carter Administration, offered a more detailed definition in a recent article: "Connectivity—the ability of the national command authorities to determine the status of, and transmit commands to, the various elements of strategic forces in the presence of a variety of disrupting factors, including nuclear detonations and countermeasures."

It was Dr. Perry, in late 1977, who asked the Defense Science Board to try to determine how well the existing military communications systems would be able to maintain the necessary connections between the President and the country's nuclear forces following a Soviet attack. For many years, this had been an operational detail left to the military to resolve, but it had not received much attention. (The services were far more interested in new weaponry and were preoccupied with other matters, such as the war in Vietnam.) Moreover, to the extent that the White House, civilian defense strategists, and the public at large had thought about nuclear weapons, they had focused on general policy issues—the size of the U.S. and Soviet arsenals, the merits of arms control, and other topics—and had overlooked what Perry felt to be a key aspect of U.S. defense preparedness. He recognized that it was one thing for the country to have nuclear muscle; it was another matter to have a central nervous system—a communications setup—that could make the muscle flex if it ever had to.

Perry's request for a study of the military's emergency communications capabilities prompted a flurry of activity in the Pentagon. "When the services found out the Defense Science Board was looking at it, they said they'd look at their own skirts to make sure they were clean," Rear Admiral Paul Tomb, an aide to the Joint Chiefs of Staff, told me. Connectivity studies were suddenly "in," and they focused on what a former Pentagon official referred to as "force execution in the crudest sense: Can we retaliate? Is our tiger paper or fur?" The reviews reached "very pessimistic conclusions," he said, and showed, as Dr. Perry reported to Congress in 1979, that the necessary communications channels were "perhaps the weakest link in our strategic forces today."

The situation was brought directly to President Carter's attention when he tried to practice what he would have to do to execute the U.S. war plan—the Single Integrated Operational Plan, or S.I.O.P. The drill in which the President participated has been recounted by Robert Rosenberg, who served on the National Security Council staff.

"I know of no other President who actually has conducted S.I.O.P. exercises," Rosenberg said. Carter "participated in a series of what we call CPXs, communications, command and control exercises, in which there is an end-to-end runthrough with different scenarios where the Commander in Chief is in communication with the [commanders] responsible for executing the S.I.O.P." What was "probably the most telling experience they all had was a scenario the Red planners (as opposed to the Blue planners) developed, in which the Soviets [aimed] at our critical command and control and intelligence nodes. . . . The exercise ground to a halt."

The connectivity studies done in 1978 and 1979 produced more than a hundred findings and recommendations on various deficiencies and how they should be corrected. President Carter himself issued Presidential Directives 53 (on telecommunications policy) and 59 (on strategic nuclear policy), which, among other things, ordered the Pentagon to correct the widespread vulnerabilities in the strategic command and control system that could deprive the President of a functioning communications network after the first few Soviet shots had been fired. The Reagan Administration has endorsed its predecessor's initiatives to fill in the gaps in the system, but results are not expected for many years. "It may be relatively simple and inexpensive to fill those gaps," Lieutenant General Hillman Dickinson, who has worked on the plans for doing so, said. "That's the good news. The bad news is that there are a lot of gaps, and it's not always easy to get someone to respond to fill a gap at an early time."

Improvements have been made in the past few years, such as streamlining the procedures for issuing orders, but the fundamental problem of getting those orders delivered to the forces remains. One member of the 1978 Defense Science Board panel that urged major changes in the command and control system told me that there has been "little follow-through" to effect the necessary changes in the communications apparatus. Another member of the group said that "the same report could be written with some minor modifications today."

Problems with the nation's most vital communications links were obvious long before the Carter Administration reviews. President John Kennedy, for example, personally discovered a large gap in the strategic command and control system. He announced to his science adviser, Dr. Jerome Wiesner, that he had looked around the Oval Office and could not find the "red telephone" that was supposed to inform him of a Soviet attack. Wiesner replied that President Eisenhower had kept the phone in a drawer in his desk, but when Kennedy and Wiesner pulled out all the drawers, they still could not find it. As it happened, the new President's wife was redecorating the White House and had found an elegant desk given to President Rutherford B. Hayes in 1880 by Queen Victoria. When this desk—made from the timbers of *H.M.S. Resolute*—was substituted for President Eisenhower's, the red telephone was disconnected and removed. "We did not have a command and control system then," Wiesner said. "And we don't have one now."

Another suggestion that there might be weaknesses in the command and control of nuclear forces came in a memorable scene from Stanley Kubrick's 1964 film, *Dr. Strangelove*. Captain Mandrake (Peter Sellers) was depicted trying to call Washington, D.C., from Burpelson Air Force Base in Britain. He wanted to relay the message that U.S. nuclear bombers were on their way to Russia and needed to be recalled. The panic-stricken officer, who had to use a pay phone, broke into a Coke machine to get a few coins. "I think we would all like to be reassured that the Defense Department does not rely on pay phones for its defense communications, or if it does, that it has change," Steven Weinberg, the Nobel laureate in physics, remarked at a February 1983 conference on crisis management at the University of Texas.

Actually, the movie's portrayal of the U.S. military communications system that existed in 1964—and still exists—is not that far from the truth. At that meeting in Texas in 1983, Lieutenant General William Hillsman, who was then the Director of the Defense Communications Agency, explained that the military communications system—including the part that carries the most urgent national security messages—depends almost totally on telephone lines leased by the government.

The warning system, for instance, "begins a bit on the perimeter of the United States where we have a gang of radars out there that are looking," Hillsman said. "Those radars today are tied into Cheyenne Mountain, the North American Aerospace Defense Command, by telephone lines. And I may blow your mind [but] we do not have defense communications systems that provide that. Everything we do here in the United States that ties us together in terms of warning and deterrence is provided to us by the common carrier system, the private sector, the AT&Ts and the GT&Es."

The National Military Command Center in the Pentagon—which Brigadier General Wagoner tried unsuccessfully to telephone—is the hub for both routine and emergency U.S. military communications. Operated by the Joint Chiefs of Staff, it is the principal message-distribution center through which the President would issue orders for a strike on the Soviet Union. It, too, uses leased telephone lines, Hillsman noted, when it sends emergency orders to U.S. strategic forces. At Strategic Air Command (SAC) Headquarters, which is located near Omaha, Nebraska, the Emergency Action Messages from the National Military Command Center would be relayed to U.S. missile and bomber forces over what is called the Primary Alerting System. This likewise consists of a telephone hookup. "Everything that General Davis does today, our SAC commander, from way down in the basement of Omaha to his Minuteman silos, rides AT&T and GT&E systems," Hillsman said.

Because of its dependence on the Bell System, the Department of Defense opposed the antitrust suit aimed at breaking up AT&T, and it took strong exception to the settlement agreement drawn up between the Department of Justice and the company. A brief in the case prepared in April 1982 by William H. Taft IV, the General Counsel of the Department of Defense, stated, "[As] the Federal Government's telecommunications needs in the United States have evolved, it has relied primarily upon the commercial carriers to satisfy its requirements. For example, in planning, engineering, operating and managing the long-haul, point-to-point domestic telecommunications requirements of the National Command Authorities, which includes the President, the DoD leases more than 85 percent of the DCS"—Defense Communications System—"from commercial carriers. . . . The Federal government today obtains more than 94 percent of its most critical domestic telecommunications circuits from commercial carriers."

When I visited the SAC underground command post, the officer who briefed me on the facility sat me down in the chair that General Bennie L. Davis, the present Commander in Chief, would occupy in an emergency. My attention was directed to the "gold phone" on the nearby desk—it looked yellow to me, but no matter—and it was explained that General Davis would be able to use it to consult with the President and senior military officials in the event of a nuclear attack. It seemed like a fairly ordinary telephone, and it was.

There are some radio and satellite backups to the miltary's telephone network, and some classified systems as well, but the connectivity studies have shown that the strain of nuclear war could quickly and thoroughly unhinge the entire communications system. With the main command posts, such as the Pentagon and SAC Headquarters, filled with dead officers and dead telephones, a coordinated counterattack might be impossible, although the Soviets would face retribution from individual U.S. submarines firing on their own initiative. The submarine counterattack would very likely consist of ragged, poorly synchronized and militarily pointless salvos ordered by commanders isolated both from the civilian hierarchy and from each other. It might be much delayed and blindly aimed at the USSR.

Rear Admiral Tomb, who has been a member of the Joint Connectivity Staff, an advisory group set up in 1980 to help plan improvements in strategic command and control, maintains that the vulnerability of the existing system had been overemphasized: "If somebody says there's a weakness, immediately they say it's going to fail. My statement is, 'I can't assure you it will work after it's exposed to something.' " He said there were "worst-case scenarios" that showed that the United States "couldn't react" after certain kinds of Soviet attack, but their probability was low. "With the improvements that have been recommended, that we have made—and we're getting very good support in Congress, for budget, and in the services—I'd say that there's no chance that we could lose connectivity. At all. I'm talking in terms of days and weeks."

"I am not a pessimist," Tomb continued. "You know, after we hit Hiroshima—I guess it was Nagasaki—hit them in the afternoon and the next morning the trolley cars are running. The electrical system's working." After a Soviet attack on the United States, he said, "I think something's going to work. We've got a lot of beautiful systems here that work all the time, day and night, and I defy you to stop it under normal conditions. So in stress, I think that you'll have links that exist. You know, a twister hits Arkansas, and ten minutes later you've got a TV van in there showing the whole picture, and everybody in the United States [via] satellite can see what's going on. Floods. Fires. The whole nine yards. So we have very good communications. Modern communications."

The Admiral's recounting of Nagasaki was inaccurate. The bomb went off at 11:02 A.M., not in the afternoon. More significantly, the photographs taken there in the days after the blast do not show commuters on the public transit system on their way to work. They show seven square kilometers of the city reduced to rubble. Most analysts also draw more of a distinction between the effects of "twisters" and the damage that can be done by nuclear weapons. The present command system "works," William Perry explained, in the sense that if the United States were struck by Soviet missiles, the system would be "useful for alerting the National Command Authorities [the President and the Secretary of Defense] to a surprise attack." However, the equipment in place is "of questionable reliability," he said, in terms of its ability to convey Presidential orders for the firing of U.S. missiles. That was the conclusion of the Pentagon's major connectivity studies, and one shared by other leading experts who have studied the problem.

A member of the Defense Science Board panel told me that "no one would argue" that connectivity would last "more than hours." The SAC Commander in Chief, General Davis, said it would last for "five hours down to thirty minutes." In 1957, General Omar Bradley forecast that the nuclear arms race would lead to an "electronic house of cards" that would "inevitably" collapse. A number of experts who have studied the present U.S. strategic communications system believe that that point has been reached, and that the command and control system would fall apart in the opening moments of any major attack by the Soviet Union.

Dr. Desmond Ball, the Head of the Australian National University's Strategic and Defense Studies Centre, has written the most definitive assessment of the command and control problem that is available in the open literature. "The way the warning systems work, there's redundancy there," he said. "There's synergism there. You can't knock out one warning system without in fact giving warning to another warning system that the attack's under way. So you will always get your warning. You will always, with one exception, be able to get a message back to the forces to respond." He noted that the response might be quite "messy"—not aimed at any particularly well-chosen set of targets—and that the "one exception" that might prevent retaliation was an attack aimed directly at the President and the national military leadership.

Thus, to protect against a sudden Soviet attack that could kill key officials, the firing mechanism for U.S. missiles has been honed to permit an extremely rapid response—one that can be executed in the few minutes before Soviet missiles fired from submarines off U.S. coasts hit targets such as Washington, D.C., and before the telephone system collapses. The set trigger for U.S. nuclear forces consists not of springs and levers but of people and electronic equipment programmed to fire all of the country's strategic nuclear missiles on a few minutes' notice. There are many impressive things done to prevent unauthorized or accidental launching—all of which are supposed to be spontaneously undone when a decision to fire is made. Whether this can be carried out in time to permit a coordinated retaliatory strike remains in doubt.

U.S. leaders, William Perry noted, may not have sufficient confidence in the warning systems and, fearing that the alert may be false, may not give the orders quickly enough. "Theoretically, we can do a Minuteman launch under attack," the head of one of the connectivity studies told me. In practice, though, it would be "extremely difficult," since the whole process of assessing an apparent attack, analyzing and selecting options, and issuing orders could take more time than was available. "If I were a Soviet planner, I could design a strategy that would preclude Minuteman launch."

A large number of procedural checks and verifications have to be completed before U.S. missiles can be fired. Vice Admiral Gerald Miller, the former Deputy Director of the Joint Strategic Target Planning Staff, which prepares the U.S. nuclear war plan, told Congress that the United States might "actually be unable to release and launch a nuclear weapon or weapons if it decided to do so, even with the civilian hierarchy intact, in full control of their faculties, and all communications systems in full working order." Another former member of the Joint Strategic Target Planning Staff told me, "If there were a bolt out of the blue, we would be unlikely to be able to launch our Minuteman missiles in any coherent way."

The real time constraint, Desmond Ball explained, is not the delay in getting warning data to the President and orders back to the forces.

The hardware in place—if it works according to specifications—will do that in minutes. The major problem is in the decision-making process, the time it would take the President and his advisers to grasp what was happening and to select an appropriate course of action. A senior military officer who has worked on the U.S. strategic war plan, or S.I.O.P., explained some of the problems to me.

"I used to be the editor of 'the black book' before it was approved and went to the President," he said. "The President's basic problem in decision-making under attack is the extraordinarily difficult problem of deciding which of the many and the complicated S.I.O.P. options to execute. The black book lays out the options and an estimate of their consequences. Do you hit Lower Slobovia or not? That kind of thing. The complexity is not the result of obfuscation but of the multitude of factors. It is very complex even to implement a more or less knee-jerk retaliatory strike."

The S.I.O.P. is usually described as consisting of a relatively small number of major preplanned attacks. But as this senior officer noted, "Although the number of options may not exceed the number of my fingers and toes, it is still very complex." Part of the difficulty is that down-to-the-minute scheduling is required to execute various kinds of retaliatory strikes. Otherwise, the weapons dropped onto the Soviet Union by U.S. missiles or bombers might interfere with each other, causing U.S. forces to blow themselves up rather than their nominal targets. These issues are resolved by elaborate computerized timing programs. If, for various technical reasons, the preset strike plans could not be executed, this official noted, "you can't just combine part of one option with part of another." That is, you cannot randomly substitute, say, submarine missiles for Minuteman missiles, given the differences in range, warhead size, accuracy, preprogrammed targets loaded into their guidance systems, and other factors. The S.I.O.P. may contain a relatively small menu of attack possibilities, but it is not possible to scan it quickly and order a la carte.

"The personality issue more than anything else matters," a senior NORAD officer commented. "Would the President of the United States make the decision?" Henry Kissinger, describing the decision-making process he observed in the White House, noted, "Nobody who knows anything about how our government operates will believe that it is possible for our presidents to get the Secretary of State, Secretary of

Defense, [etc.] to a conference call in the fifteen minutes that may be available to make a decision, much less to issue an order that then travels down the line of command in fifteen minutes. So the only way you can implement that strategy is by delegating the authority down to some field commander who must be given discretion so that when he thinks a nuclear war has started, he can retaliate."

That is, since the President may not be fast enough on the trigger, the solution is to build more triggers—ones placed in the hands of the military, all the public pronouncements about "Presidential control of nuclear weapons" notwithstanding. At the beginning of the nuclear age, President Harry Truman strongly asserted his Constitutional authority, as Commander in Chief, to specify how and when any atomic bombs would be employed. He told Secretary of Defense James Forrestal that he did not want "to have some dashing lieutenant colonel decide when would be the proper time to drop one." Yet according to contingency plans that have been developed and periodically modified over the years, strict Presidential control has quietly given way to a different arrangement. Any retaliation following a major Soviet attack would probably have to be organized by the military. Since the officers in charge would suffer from severe communications problems, they would be under pressure to react quickly, and massively, before incoming Soviet missiles deprived them of all means of issuing orders to their forces.

———

The emphasis on speed is a relatively recent development in the evolution of the U.S. nuclear command and control system, and it reflects changes in weapons technology, like the increasing importance of missiles over manned bombers, as well as the shift in the strategic balance over the past three decades. When nuclear weapons were first introduced, the last thing anybody wanted was knee-jerk decisions about using them. Since the Soviets had no nuclear weapons until 1949, and had few bombers during the 1950s capable of reaching the continental United States, there was little likelihood that a U.S. President would have to make a quick decision about whether to order nuclear retaliation. Nor did the military regard such a contingency as likely. The Strategic Air Command, during most of this period, kept its bombers in a low state of readiness—it would have required at least several hours to prepare them for flight—since there was no feeling that the

United States would have to make an instantaneous response to any
Soviet initiatives.

Even when the Soviets began to deploy long-range missiles in
1960–61, there was little threat of a lightning attack that could force
the President to make a snap judgment on whether to launch U.S. retaliatory forces. The so-called "missile gap" that figured prominently
in the 1960 Presidential campaign of John Kennedy was entirely spurious, as Eisenhower Administration officials had maintained and as
their successors, once in office, had to admit. The United States actually
had many more missiles in the early 1960s, and the few the Soviets
possessed at the time were so unreliable that they may have been about
as likely to blow up on the launching pads as they were to land in
North America. Soviet Premier Nikita Khrushchev delayed deployment of large numbers of missiles until more advanced and reliable ones
could be developed.

A U.S. advantage in the number of nuclear missiles continued
throughout the 1960s. When the Strategic Air Command's Minuteman
missiles became operational in 1962–67, one of their features—as the
name itself was supposed to suggest—was that they could be fired very
quickly. It is true that they could be, but the United States was under
little pressure to rig the overall command and control system in this
direction. The country still enjoyed tremendous superiority over the
Soviet Union, which remained far behind in missile production. Since
there was no possibility of the Soviets' wiping out the much larger U.S.
nuclear arsenal, there was no pressure, as the Air Force saying goes,
to "launch or lose" those forces. Accordingly, there was no need to
have the President's—or the SAC commander's—finger poised above
any button.

By the 1970s, the strategic situation had begun to change. The
comfortable U.S. lead in the number and quality of missiles was sharply
eroded as the Soviets engaged in a buildup that gave them an arsenal
of comparable size. The Soviets still have disadvantages in some categories of strategic weaponry—far fewer submarine-launched warheads
and long-range bombers, for example—but they have surged ahead in
the building of very large land-based missiles. The most notable ones,
which are referred to by the Pentagon as the SS-18s, carry about five
hundred times as much firepower as the bomb dropped on Hiroshima.
The SS-18s with multiple warheads are accurate enough, in theory, to

destroy the underground silos that protect the one thousand U.S. Minuteman missiles, which are located in six missile bases stretching from Missouri to Montana. These are the Soviet missiles that create the so-called window of vulnerability—the possibility that the Minuteman force could be destroyed, like so many sitting ducks, in a Soviet first strike.

A capability to launch some or all of the Minuteman missiles very quickly—right after warning systems have detected a Soviet attack upon them—is a possible way to eliminate any Soviet temptation to attack them. If that maneuver were executed, the Minuteman force could hardly be considered sitting ducks. The U.S. missiles would already be in flight by the time the SS-18 warheads landed, and the Soviets would end up merely destroying the empty silos they had left behind. The Soviets would also have disarmed themselves unilaterally in the process, expending their SS-18 force in a pointless attack, and they would have brought about massive destruction of the Soviet homeland.

Thus, a rapid-response capability, according to the physicist Richard Garwin of IBM, is a straightforward way to redress the potential vulnerability of the Minuteman force to a Soviet first strike. Having a reliable means to launch the missiles quickly is "important so people will sleep better at night," he said. Garwin, who played a major role in the invention of the hydrogen bomb and has served as a Presidential science adviser and Pentagon consultant, adds several caveats to his proposal. (These qualifications have been overlooked by a number of those who have responded critically to his scheme for Minuteman launch.)

Garwin cautions that the need to launch the Minuteman missiles quickly applies only when the general U.S. nuclear deterrent, not just the Minuteman force, is vulnerable. "No way I would want to launch my missiles, which are under attack, unless the strategic force were overall vulnerable. It's just too dangerous." U.S. nuclear submarines on patrol are invulnerable to Soviet attack—they are hidden in the ocean depths where the Soviets cannot find them—although this conclusion, which the Pentagon does not dispute, is not a factor that weighs heavily in Air Force thinking about the window of vulnerability. (To acknowledge dependence on submarines would be to cede primacy in strategic deterrence to the Navy.) A further condition attached to his

plan for quick Minuteman launch, Garwin noted, is that it would require a far more reliable warning system than the one NORAD maintains today.

U.S. military officials have been extremely reluctant to discuss in
public whether they have in fact moved to such a quick-response policy,
which has two common versions: "launch on warning" (right after
U.S. early warning satellites and radars have detected incoming Soviet
missiles) and "launch under attack" (after Soviet warheads have already begun to detonate). The standard official answer to this question
uses the ambiguous wording, "Nothing prevents the United States from
launching its missiles immediately if it chooses to do so." In April 1983,
however, an Air Force Lieutenant Colonel, whom the Pentagon re-
buked for "speaking out of school," told a Chamber of Commerce
luncheon group in Wyoming that the United States was moving toward
a policy of launch on warning. Fred C. Iklé, the Under Secretary of
Defense for Policy, in a formal statement issued in response to this
disclosure, said: "It is our policy not to explain in detail how we would
respond to a missile attack, to increase the uncertainties in the minds
of Soviet planners. However, the United States does not rely on its
capability for launch on warning or launch under attack to ensure the
credibility of its deterrent."

Mr. Iklé's precisely worded statement is entirely correct, as far as
it goes. The United States does not, as a matter of publicly declared
"policy," depend on a strategy of launch on warning or launch under
attack. That says nothing about the actual provisions in the war plan.
According to those familiar with the S.I.O.P., launch under attack has
always been included as a specific option—since the very first S.I.O.P.,
which was adopted in 1960. The reluctance to talk about it hardly de-
rives from any hesitancy about letting the Soviets know that this possibility exists. It is an advantage to let them know that they may face
prompt reprisal if they attack.

Instead, it may be the American public's reaction to the way the
nuclear firing mechanism has been set that concerns the Pentagon. The
freeze movement, after all, received some of its impetus in the fall of
1981 when President Reagan—walking across the White House lawn
as he answered a reporter's question—said that he thought nuclear
weapons could be used to fight a limited nuclear war. The continuing
public anxieties stirred up by that statement could be worsened by

discussion of the launch-under-attack option in the black book that is never far from the President's reach. People might conclude, as Under Secretary of Defense Iklé himself did, "It would be a hair-triggered, dangerous situation if we were to depend . . . on such a posture."

The possible vulnerability of the Minuteman force, however, is only part of the reason for the priority placed on quick action in U.S. war plans. For one thing, the accuracy of Soviet missiles, and the probability of their hitting all or a large portion of the one thousand Minuteman silos, are subject to some uncertainty. Soviet experts, like our own, clearly understand that how well Soviet missiles perform in test flights is no sure indicator of how well they will perform in an actual attack. Subtle factors—such as programming errors in the missiles' guidance systems—could make enough difference in the flight paths of Soviet warheads to deprive them of the accuracy needed to destroy their targets. (The warheads must come within about three hundred to seven hundred feet to destroy the underground Minuteman silos, which are said to be able to withstand a blast pressure up to about two thousand pounds per square inch.) When I stood on top of a Minuteman silo at Whiteman Air Force Base in Missouri, one of the SAC Minuteman bases, the Air Force sergeant who was going to take me down inside it did not seem overly concerned about the window of vulnerability. He commented, "If you're throwing a javelin six hundred miles trying to hit an orange slice on a pavement, it's kind of rough. It's just a long way [for the Soviets] to throw a bomb and have it hit that close."

More important, even if the SS-18s had perfect accuracy, the Minuteman force would still be carrying only about a fifth of all U.S. strategic nuclear bombs. The Soviet Union could be the Machiavellian "evil empire" described by President Reagan, but in any scheme for destroying the United States its leaders would have to recognize that there was no point in simply hitting the relatively small fraction of U.S. weaponry carried by land-based missiles—and, at the same time, creating radioactive fallout that could kill tens of millions of people downwind of the Minuteman bases. This kind of attack would leave highly provoked U.S. leaders with thousands of other nuclear weapons that could still be fired against the USSR by submarine-launched missiles and bombers. Presumably, as cold-blooded schemers, the Soviets would abide by the master-plotter's advice about the danger of making nonfatal attacks on your opponents. "They will revenge themselves for small injuries, but cannot do so for great ones," Machiavelli wrote in *The Prince.* "The injury therefore that we do to a man must be such that we need not fear his vengeance." No plausible scenario for a Soviet attack strictly limited to U.S. Minuteman forces meets this guideline.

The *main* reason for having a launch-under-attack option in the U.S. war plan has little to do with the vulnerability of our nuclear forces. Indeed, this provision was made long before the SS-18 missiles were ever deployed. The emphasis on quick response is a by-product of the Pentagon's increasing concern that its communications apparatus— unlike the missiles housed in blast-resistant underground silos or the submarines hidden at sea—is so fragile and exposed that it may not be able to function for very long after a nuclear war starts. This would especially be the case if an enemy attack were aimed at the components of the command network—such as the Pentagon and various critical nodes in the communications system that transmit orders to U.S. strategic forces. The command system was built in the 1950s and '60s, during the era of U.S. nuclear superiority, and as a representative of the Strategic Air Command told me, "Not many people gave much thought to system survivability." Nor has the original system been upgraded over the years to improve its survivability. Instead of taking account of the exigencies of nuclear warfare, and taking advantage of the new communications technologies that have become available, the Pentagon has what retired Admiral Bobby Inman termed "a command and control structure developed in the immediate post–World War II period and designed to fight another World War II."

A detailed account of the vulnerability of the command and control system to Soviet attack has emerged from the Pentagon connectivity studies of the past six years. The problems are also discussed in an important paper by Desmond Ball—"Can Nuclear War Be Controlled?"—that was published in 1981 by the International Institute for Strategic Studies in London. Using unclassified data, Ball has catalogued and assessed the frailties that exist throughout the control system, doing so at a level of detail that has dismayed some members of the defense establishment. A number of Air Force officers said to Ball, he recalled, "Why go into such detail? Why not just say that the command and control system is vulnerable?" Ball replied that he'd been saying that for years, and nobody had listened. The Soviets, in any event, are surely able to comb the extant technical literature on the subject and obtain the same information.

The main deficiencies, Ball suggests, arise from planning gaffes (such as the failure to build adequate backup facilities to duplicate key installations) as well as from the inherent susceptibility of all fixed installations and conventional communications equipment to the direct and indirect effects of nuclear detonations. In the field of strategic studies, an academic discipline in which the scholarship often involves the turgid rehashing of a small set of old arguments, Ball has made a refreshing contribution. Officials are reluctant to comment on the record about his findings, but the Pentagon's leading experts say privately that it is "a very good piece of work."

According to Desmond Ball's analysis and the Pentagon's own estimates, it would take fewer than fifty Soviet weapons to disable the entire U.S. command and control system. In addition to the White House and the Pentagon, the targets of such an attack would include: the Alternate National Military Command Center, an underground facility at Fort Ritchie, Maryland, which is about seventy-five miles from Washington; Strategic Air Command Headquarters near Omaha, Nebraska; the alternate SAC Headquarters at Barksdale Air Force Base in Louisiana and March Air Force Base in California; the headquarters for the Atlantic Fleet in Norfolk, Virginia, and for the Pacific Fleet, in Hawaii; the key AT&T switching centers—such as the ones in Lyons, Nebraska; Fairview, Kansas; Hillsboro, Missouri; and Lamar, Colorado —that handle certain critical military communications; the ground stations for key U.S. defense satellites; the very low frequency (VLF) radio transmitters in Cutler, Maine, and Jim Creek, Washington, and on the Northwest Cape in Australia (which broadcast orders to U.S. submarines); and a handful of other targets, some of which are in classified locations. To increase the element of surprise and confusion, the thirteen early warning sites used to detect incoming Soviet missiles would also be obvious targets.

"These and other key facilities present Soviet planners with a relatively small number of targets, especially when compared to the thousands of nuclear weapons the Soviet Union deploys," one government study noted. The Soviets need not limit themselves to fifty weapons against these command centers and message-relay points. Western analysts believe that some four hundred Soviet warheads are targeted on them in current Soviet war plans. As a result of strikes aimed at this short list of command-system components, connectivity between the President and U.S. nuclear forces may abruptly end almost as soon as an attack begins. Hence the perceived need for a quick finger on the trigger to assure that U.S. missiles can be fired with some kind of overall control before the command system collapses.

The lack of precise control over the retaliatory salvos may not really matter, in the sense that even hit-or-miss strikes against the Soviet Union by U.S. submarines can be counted on to wreak massive damage. Each of the thirty-one U.S. Poseidon submarines, for example, carries sixteen missiles. Each missile has at least ten warheads. Each warhead is equal to three Hiroshima-size nuclear bombs. The minimum of one hundred and sixty bombs from such a submarine could be used for simultaneous attacks on a wide range of targets in the USSR. The newer and larger Trident submarines, as well as the Poseidon subs that have been retrofitted with Trident I missiles (which have fewer warheads, but ones with higher explosive power), could bring about even greater destruction. The U.S. submarine fleet, which one Reagan Administration adviser referred to as "the revenge force," carries a total destructive power roughly equivalent to twenty-three thousand Hiroshimas.

Thus, whatever the Soviets might do to destroy the U.S. central command system, it would not give them any realistic hope of escaping massive retaliation. Frank von Hippel, the Princeton University physicist, makes the important point: "Lack of centralized control is not the same as lack of nuclear deterrence. What do Soviet leaders think U.S. nuclear submarine crews are going to do if they learn that the United States has been destroyed? Go to Tahiti and retire?"

The U.S. submarines on patrol have various means of receiving orders, "familygrams," and other messages. In normal circumstances, they monitor very low frequencies (VLF) over which the Navy continuously broadcasts a coded "We're happy" message. This informs the fleet that the United States and the Soviet Union are at peace. If a crisis developed, the code would be changed to an alert message that indicated the severity of the situation. The submarines have underwater receiving antennas to get these important status reports on which stage of the DEFCON, or "defense condition," prevails. If a war with the Soviet Union begins, the submarines will be told that a DEFCON 1— code-named "Cocked Pistol"—has been declared. They will then prepare to receive orders to launch their missiles.

Should a submarine fail to receive its reassuring peacetime message through normal channels, or if an alert message is interrupted, the crew has orders to switch to other frequencies—for example, to use different antennas, or, if there is still no message, to come up close to the surface and deploy antennas that can communicate with Navy satellites or get radio messages broadcast over the Navy's high frequency (HF) channels.

The Soviets can, of course, destroy the Navy's small number of central broadcasting stations and all of the elements in its message-relay system. Needless to say, that would stop the transmission of the "We're happy" message and all other traffic and serve as a de facto alert to the submarines. No surviving Navy headquarters would then be required to order the launching of the submarine missiles. The Soviet attack on the command system would get that message across.

However, none of these elementary considerations about the submarine force and the Navy's "fail-deadly" communications system affect the brand of deterrence to which the Strategic Air Command, or recent Administrations, subscribe. SAC and the Pentagon bureaucracy, which have a great deal at stake in trying to justify continued reliance on land-based missiles and manned bombers, are not inclined to call attention to the potency of the nuclear submarine fleet—which actually carries almost five thousand warheads, more than twice as many as the SAC Minuteman force. Nor is the Reagan Administration, which cites Soviet SS-18s as the primary justification for its program to expand the U.S. strategic arsenal, eager to emphasize the fact that the existing U.S. submarine fleet can already negate any Soviet temptation to fire these missiles.

In a bureaucratic context, it is not difficult to see how the slighting of the submarine force has come about. The sole mission of SAC is strategic deterrence, and it is very aggressive in promoting its programs for new missiles and bombers (the MX and the B-1) and its policies, such as launch under attack, to protect its Minuteman force. The Navy, on the other hand, has a much broader mission—it is mostly involved with conventional defense—as well as long-standing traditions. The Navy has always focused on surface ships, and even in the nuclear age, it still does. The Navy grudgingly operates nuclear-missile submarines, but it would much rather devote its resources to aircraft carriers and battleships. (In the 1950s, when nuclear submarines were under development, there was an intense internal struggle within the Navy, which has a disdain of submarines, nuclear or otherwise; even today, a former Pentagon official noted, "submariners are an embattled clique" within the Navy.)

Moreover, since the submarines are hidden at sea, the Navy has no fear that they are subject to direct attack like the Minuteman missiles in fixed, known locations. The Navy therefore has no "launch or lose" mentality. It doesn't really matter to them whether the submarines retaliate ten minutes or ten days after a Soviet attack—the devastation would be the same and the prospect of it is still enough to deter the Soviets from starting a nuclear war. The Navy, accordingly, thinks there is very little risk of a Soviet nuclear attack and would prefer not to waste money on command and control equipment intended solely for use in such an unlikely situation. It takes a much more relaxed attitude toward nuclear war planning than SAC, and thinks its submarines already have all the command and control apparatus they need.

The U.S. war plan itself is supposed to be developed by the Joint Strategic Target Planning Staff (JSTPS) under guidelines from the Joint Chiefs of Staff. The JSTPS is a "joint" operation, of which the Director is the Commander in Chief of SAC and the Deputy Director is a naval officer. The Navy, however, thinks very little of the whole planning process, and it is more than symbolic that the work of the joint planning staff—without protest from the Navy—takes place at SAC headquarters in Omaha. Strategic war planning is a pointless, pro forma activity, as far as the Navy is concerned, and the Navy representatives who participate in the process defer to the Air Force on how the firing mechanism for the Minuteman force should be set. The war plan is thus imbued with the SAC "use it or lose it" attitude despite the invulnerability of the submarines. Thus, it is not the technical requirements of maintaining deterrence but a deep-seated institutional bias that is responsible for keeping the country's Minuteman missiles set at all times for immediate launch.

No one is more familiar with the arrangements for firing the Minuteman missiles than the SAC commander, General Davis, the principal military officer in charge of both preparing and executing U.S. war plans. "I'm very familiar with the popular terms 'launch on warning' or 'launch under attack,' " he told me. The kind of retaliation the United States would respond with "depends on the magnitude of the attack, and our tactical warning and assessment system is very good. It can give you the size of that attack and about where that attack is coming, and then based on the information, the President and his advisers—and I'm one of those advisers—are able to talk to the President, and the President makes the decision. And the idea is an immediate response."

The Soviets have a very different command system, one that has been extensively hardened to operate after a U.S. first strike. It is much less sophisticated in many ways, but has other features—such as a large network of underground facilities to protect Soviet leadership, and highly redundant communications systems—that make it far less vulnerable to disruption. Moreover, while the United States has kept its forces on a high state of alert, the Soviets have traditionally maintained a much lower state of readiness. Unlike the Minuteman missiles introduced in the 1960s, which can be fired more or less at the turn of a few keys after properly authenticated orders are received, the long-range missiles built by the Soviets in that era had no quick-response capability.

In part, the low state of readiness of Soviet forces resulted from technological backwardness. One problem has been their reliance on liquid fuels. The Soviet chemical industry has had difficulty mass-producing solid propellants similar to those used in Minuteman missiles. Liquid fuels of the kind developed for their early missiles could not be stored in the missiles because they were highly corrosive. The missiles on hand had to be unfueled, and it would have taken hours to prepare them for launching. Another obstacle to the quick launch of Soviet missiles was their guidance systems. The gyroscopes used to stabilize the missiles in flight depended on metal ball bearings that would fail from stress after several hours of use, thereby preventing the missiles from being kept on continuous alert.

The new SS-18s, however, and other improved Soviet missiles, have advanced guidance systems and a storable type of liquid fuel that can permit them to be launched within an estimated four to eight minutes. The mobile SS-20s, a recent addition to the Soviet arsenal, have solid fuel.

A strategic consideration that permitted the Soviets to maintain a low state of readiness was the kind of threat posed by U.S. forces. While U.S. missiles have had the capability to obliterate Soviet cities and industry many times over, only a fraction of them have the accuracy needed to destroy hardened underground targets, such as Soviet missile silos and command posts. The Soviets have also put some of their SS-18s in southern parts of the USSR where they are out of the normal range of many U.S. Minuteman missiles. Therefore, there has been little danger of a complete knockout blow by the United States that could wipe out all Soviet nuclear forces—and thus no need for a launch-under-attack policy.

However, as the United States continues with the deployment of advanced new missiles—such as the MX, the Pershing II, and the Trident D-5—the situation facing the Soviet Union will change. The new, high-accuracy U.S. missiles have what the Pentagon calls "prompt hard target kill capability"—this is the official euphemism for weapons with inherent first-strike potential—and will be able to threaten previously well-protected Soviet military assets. The USSR will soon find itself pressured to adopt a quick-draw mechanism of its own to protect itself from a potential U.S. surprise attack.

According to Donald Latham, the Assistant Secretary of Defense who oversees the Reagan Administration's command-system programs, the Soviets have made "very scary statements" that they may adopt a policy of launch on warning. A number of Western analysts believe that they may already have done so. Barry Blechman of the Institute for Strategic Studies at Georgetown University referred to U.S. and Soviet launch-under-attack capabilities as "a fact of life in the nuclear age."

Neither side has yet turned over the launching of its missiles to computers. Automated systems do provide the warning data, but they do not fire the missiles. "It's not as though the computer were making a decision," General Davis said. "The computer certainly isn't." Yet as more first-strike weapons are deployed by both sides, the need for quick decisions, and the physical vulnerability of the decision-makers, could force them to alter the passive assignment now given to computers. Instead of being supporting actors, computers may become the star performers in the command and control systems of the future.

———

Mutual reliance on vulnerable command systems—whether they are ultimately managed by civilians, military officers, or supercomputers—dramatically undermines the goal of achieving a stable balance of power. To fulfill this objective, the United States and the Soviet Union have each endeavored to build an invulnerable "second-strike" capability. This means being able to absorb a full-scale attack and still being capable of responding with a devastating counterattack. Sobered by the prospect of *inevitable* retribution, neither country would ever have any incentive to launch a first strike. Nor would there be any need for their nation, should war begin—or appear on some radar screen to have begun—to return fire instantaneously. With secure second-strike capability, there would be an opportunity to think first.

This has been the conventional theory of deterrence. Without survivable command and control systems, it is a theory that in the minds of U.S. war planners no longer works. "No one in his senses would look at the present command system and conclude that you could ride it out," a former Air Force officer who participated in one of the most recent connectivity studies commented. General Bennie Davis, in May 1983 testimony before Congress, said in response to questions by Senator Sam Nunn that "of course" it would be desirable if the United States could "ride out an attack rather than retaliating while under attack." He qualified this with the further statement, "As a practical matter we have been unable to attain that [capability]" and must therefore make "a prompt response."

Frank von Hippel and other experts note that the United States could in principle plan to ride out Soviet attacks without compromising deterrence—that is, without creating a temptation for them to attack. U.S. submarines, in his words, would guarantee "retaliation from the grave" no matter what the Soviets did to the command and control system or to the Minuteman force. The Air Force continues to discount the role of the submarine, however, with General Davis, at the May 1983 Senate hearing, asserting that most U.S. submarines could be destroyed in a Soviet surprise attack.

It is obvious that the one-third or so of the submarine fleet normally in port could be destroyed, but the majority are at sea and are therefore invulnerable. Under questioning by Senator Nunn, General Davis explained that he reached his conclusion by assuming that the additional submarines in the fleet, shuttling back and forth from their patrol areas, would also be targeted and destroyed. He was apparently unaware that they traveled underwater. When asked about this by Senator Nunn, General Davis replied, "Are they proceeding to station underwater?" Senator Nunn said, "Well, I ask you. You are the expert." This interchange with the senior military officer in charge of the preparation of the U.S. war plan created considerable astonishment in the hearing room.

———

Whatever their favored theory of deterrence and opinions on the importance of submarines, none of the experts who have analyzed the U.S. command and control system believes that the Soviets are likely to try to exploit its weaknesses by launching a "bolt-out-of-the-blue" surprise attack. That threat is dismissed out of hand. The problem is subtler. Like an automobile with badly designed emergency brakes, the United States can have a defective strategic command and control system and go along for many years with no apparent harm. It is only in a crisis that the repercussions will be graphically displayed. For in a major confrontation, the latent weaknesses in the command apparatus could decisively influence both Soviet and U.S. thinking.

If the Soviets, for example, began to fear a U.S. attack—and the vast defensive preparations they have made suggest the degree to which they harbor such concerns—the vulnerability of our command system would give them another option besides waiting to be destroyed: a first strike that would have some chance of crippling a major part of the U.S. nuclear war machine. This kind of move, which would be too risky to contemplate under normal circumstances, could surface as the prime Soviet military option in a desperate situation. "Unfortunately, a preemptive attack on the U.S. command structure is a rational defensive act for the Soviets once they have judged that nuclear war can no longer be avoided," John Steinbruner noted. "Although it would preclude a bargained end of war, it offers two important advantages: First, by eliminating central coordination it sharply reduces the military effectiveness of opposing strategic forces; second, it offers some small chance that complete decapitation will occur and no retaliation will follow. The latter possibility, however slight, is probably the only imaginable route to decisive victory in nuclear war."

The behavior of the United States itself in a major confrontation will be markedly influenced by the Pentagon's own realization that its strategic command and control system is likely to fail when it is needed most. U.S. military leaders will be acutely aware of the Soviet temptation to exploit U.S. vulnerabilities in a first strike. Worried about their ability to fire second, Pentagon officials and Presidential advisers could well conclude that the United States had no choice but to fire first. "One of the most destabilizing things that we and the other side will have to live with is the case where one side knows the other side's command and control and communications system, or weapon system, is vulnerable," General Richard Ellis, the former Commander in Chief of the Strategic Air Command, said. "That is an incentive for the side living with that vulnerability to go first."

In point of fact, the "case" cited by General Ellis in which a vulnerable command system leads to consideration of possible first strikes is not just a hypothetical one. As the former chief U.S. war planner, he was not speaking of abstract military principles. He was hinting at something that is never explicitly discussed by U.S. military leaders: that the S.I.O.P., by necessity, contains a first-strike option. The first-strike plan—as Chapters 3 and 4 will explain—exists not solely because of the command-system problem. A major factor in its inclusion in the S.I.O.P. is the Air Force's desire for quick, decisive offensive action that tries to destroy at the outset of a nuclear war as much of the Soviet strategic arsenal as possible. Still, as Ellis notes, the plan is maintained as a matter not just of general preference but of perceived military necessity. It reflects the U.S. war planners' awareness that if our leaders think they are being forced into war and cannot retaliate because of command vulnerability (or whatever reason), a first strike is their only other military option.

Thus, the vulnerable command systems now in place—as well as the kind of offensive thinking favored by the Air Force—may sway responsible leaders on both sides and could force them to use nuclear weapons whether they liked it or not. Military logic will shape each side's behavior in a crisis, and it has its own dynamic, as Bismarck observed, that can shatter a nation's political objectives. The most pernicious manifestation of this will occur when one side is compelled, by ordinary prudence, to take what it regards as purely defensive measures—but which the opposing side, with impeccable logic of its own, interprets as offensive preparations.

Thus, among the contingency plans that have been prepared, General Herres noted, is one to increase the alert level of U.S. bombers during a crisis. That is, in order to prevent the Soviets from destroying them on the ground, more bombers would be taken out of hangars, manned, and readied for quick takeoff. No Presidential order is required for this, the authority to execute certain protective-reaction steps having already been given to the Strategic Air Command. "Right now we have about thirty percent of all the airplanes on alert," Herres said. "That can be advanced to, say, sixty percent. And there's a plan for how that's done. And there are time schedules for when the next airplane comes up on alert, and when the next one comes after that. Everybody responds automatically when his [order] is to implement Plan X. Everybody knows exactly what he's supposed to do and what's expected."

As Soviet reconnaissance monitored the increase in activity at U.S. bomber bases, what seemed like a sensible precaution to the Strategic Air Command could be interpreted in Moscow as the sign of an imminent attack on the USSR. The Soviets will be prompted to take measures of their own to reduce their vulnerability to U.S. attack—for example, sending their nuclear submarine fleet, which is mostly kept in port, to sea. Many other steps are sure to be taken as the Soviets go on alert—such as evacuating the leadership from Moscow. U.S. leaders will have difficulty distinguishing defensive actions from the readying of the system for an attack on the United States.

The United States has never witnessed a full-scale Soviet alert, and this will add greatly to the confusion in assessing what the Soviets may be doing in a crisis. Presumably, as with the U.S. DEFCON (or defense condition) there are various alert levels and specified actions that accompany them, running the gamut from simple steps, such as cancelling routine maintenance on missiles, to final preparations for war, such as shutting off all the peacetime safeguards so that missiles will be ready for immediate launching. As each side's war machine is shifted from its peacetime mode to its "fully generated" state—that is, its war-ready configuration—the other side, to the extent that it can monitor the transformation, will quite naturally respond with the most profound apprehension. The conclusion that all of the safety catches are being removed from your opponent's nuclear forces will be a signal to launch your own while you still can.

Once one side makes even a tentative assessment, moreover, that the other side was preparing to strike or that war had become inevitable, that perception may prove difficult to alter—may prove, indeed, a self-fulfilling prophecy. For the jolt of fear that such a conclusion would create may irreversibly affect the crisis by coloring all subsequent judgments about what the other side was doing and stimulating the potential victim to take steps to preempt its would-be attacker. Once in the grip of a full-scale crisis, the adrenalin in the pounding hearts of opposing military and civilian decision-makers could make cornered animals out of them very quickly.

The recent work of two psychologists, Amos Tversky of Stanford University and Daniel Kahneman of the University of British Columbia, focuses on how people weigh risks, and it raises intriguing questions about how the superpowers might behave in a crisis. People in general were found to have a deep-seated tendency to avoid risks, even when the rewards might be large. That certainly conforms with the behavior of the two superpowers in peacetime of forgoing various military opportunities, even ones from which they might gain a great deal, if there is a chance that these will lead to a major confrontation.

On the other hand, the two psychologists found that people will often accept substantial risks in order to avoid losses. The willingness to take risks, moreover, was out of proportion to the amount of loss involved—many people were stubbornly willing to expose themselves to substantial penalties to avoid giving up something they already had. It's not so uncommon, for instance, for someone to fight an armed attacker to save the small amount of money in his wallet. The possibility of a corresponding tendency on the part of the leaders of the superpowers to take major risks in a crisis to prevent even small defeats, or to take inordinate risks to forestall major losses, would be worrisome if a real showdown ever occurs.

Paul Bracken and John Steinbruner are two national security analysts who have called attention to the terrifying pressures that are likely to build if both sides ever go on high alert. So complicated are the wheels within wheels in each of the respective military machines, they note, and so great is the perceived requirement to take steps to offset what the other side is doing, that there is the grave possibility that a "two-sided" strategic alert would itself be tantamount to a mutual declaration of war.

Furthermore, there is the possibility in a tense confrontation that opposing military machines would nudge each other in ways that could produce what Steinbruner terms "unintended crisis interactions"—steps that one side may not even know it was taking but which were highly provocative to the other. To illustrate how this could happen, he points to a little-known event that occurred during the Cuban Missile Crisis. Despite all efforts by President Kennedy and his advisers to maintain the strictest control over U.S. military activities, the Navy—unbeknownst to the White House—was engaged in wartime pursuit of Soviet submarines in the North Atlantic. In the course of this, the Navy pinpointed the nuclear submarines that provided what was, at the time, the Soviet's only effective means of retaliating promptly against the United States. The Navy positioned itself to destroy those subs, to strip the Soviets of their main nuclear force.

"That's the strongest thing militarily we did in the course of the entire crisis," Steinbruner said. "And the President was not aware that this was going on." The Navy, which was following standing orders, was not doing anything unauthorized or unreasonable, he added, nor were the President and his advisers being cavalier in supervising the Navy. It is simply not possible to provide absolute central control over the multitude of actions that a complex military machine is programmed to carry out once it is put into action. The lesson of all of this is that once a crisis turns into a strategic alert, once the safety catches that are on in peacetime begin to be taken off, a confrontation can become so volatile that its outcome may be out of the control of leaders on either side.

Negotiations to try to end a crisis can take place, but the diplomats are likely to find their efforts nullified by preprogrammed behavior on the part of the opposing military organizations. Like the peacemakers who tried to head off World War I, the negotiators could be undermined, in Winston Churchill's words, by "a deep tide of calculated military purpose." "As the ill-fated nations approached the verge," he wrote, "the sinister machines of war began to develop their own momentum and eventually to control themselves."

Indeed, as General Herres described the precise time schedules that have been worked out in the S.I.O.P. in the last two decades, he could just as well have been describing the famous Schlieffen plan. This was the meticulously crafted war plan that the German General Staff began to develop in 1893 and finally saw implemented at the outset of World War I. The Schlieffen plan was exceedingly rigid and mechanical, as were the plans of the other opposing powers on the Continent. Once one side started a given set of preparations, the other parties automatically initiated preplanned countermoves. All it took was a catalyst —the assassination of a member of the Austrian nobility in Sarajevo— to set the plans in motion. The various war machines began to work, and they stimulated each other in ways that no one could control. The Austrian novelist Robert Musil captured the spirit of the process: "The machine was there; and because it was there, it had to work, and once it was running, it began to accelerate."

The present S.I.O.P. is such a machine, and once an alert began it could quickly proceed toward what retired Lieutenant General Brent Scowcroft referred to as "the automatic phase of the war. That is the time at which the quick response systems are discharged against predetermined targets and so on, and the battle plan unfolds more or less automatically."

I talked with General Herres about the Schlieffen plan, and also about the communications failure that occurred on August 3, 1914, the climactic night described by Barbara Tuchman in *The Guns of August*. German troops stood poised on the Luxembourg border, ready for the opening offensive of the war. Kaiser Wilhelm II and his advisers were awaiting a response to the ultimatum that had been given to Britain and France. "It was now minutes before seven o'clock, the hour when the 16th Division was scheduled to move into Luxembourg," Tuchman wrote. "Bethmann [the German Chancellor] excitedly insisted that Luxembourg must not be entered under any circumstances while waiting for the British answer. Instantly the Kaiser, without asking Moltke [the Chief of the General Staff], ordered his aide-de-camp to telephone and telegraph 16th Division Headquarters at Trier to cancel the movement."

The order that would have halted the opening move of World War I did not reach the troops in time. It was not until 7:30 P.M.—thirty minutes too late, and after the objective, a railway station and telegraph office, had been seized—that messengers arrived by automobile with the Kaiser's revised instructions. The bearers of this belated directive told the troops that "a mistake has been made." Four years of murderous fighting followed. "There's never any safety catch in this part," Daniel Cullity told me as he pointed to the Schuetzen rifle's double trigger. He noted that once the hair trigger is set, it is difficult to unset it—except by firing it, or by waiting for it to go off by itself.

General Herres said that he had not read *The Guns of August*. I wanted to ask him, nevertheless, as the military's highest authority on the U.S. command system, whether he thought the United States and the Soviet Union could find themselves, like the European powers in August 1914, with forces on alert and no one able to halt the rapid execution of their mobilization plans. "What you're really talking about is the so-called hair trigger argument," he replied. "Well," he continued after a pause, "the only way I can respond to that is, I think, by saying simply that no one likes the so-called hair trigger posture. I doubt that the Russians like it any better than we do. But unfortunately, we didn't make the situation in which we find ourselves. . . . The technology put us in this posture. We don't like it at all."

The attribution of our predicament to the bogeyman "technology" suggests that nuclear weapons floated in on a tide that swept "us," mere bystanders, away. Yet what is at issue is not just mechanical systems but national policies that "we" have put in place. True, the technical features of existing weapons systems do restrict us in certain ways. Like a pilot in mid-air, we face constraints on what we can safely do. If the pilot permits the plane's air speed to fall too low, it will stall and start to plummet from the sky; likewise, if the air speed gets too high, the stress may tear the craft apart. As the engineers say, there is an "envelope" within which a plane of particular design must operate (and no plane can be easily redesigned and rebuilt in the air). Still, none of this means that the pilot, seeing a storm ahead, cannot try to change course. It may even be possible to land, to permit the passengers to get out, and to let them proceed in another way.

Thus, the Pentagon could, if it chose, without any new technology, without waiting for any Soviet actions, and without ceding any ground to them, back off from the hair trigger posture maintained today. To accomplish this would not break any laws of nature, although it would demand something perhaps more difficult: changes in military thinking.

It would require U.S. strategists to rethink the emphasis in their contingency plans on preemptive attacks on the Soviet Union—a strategy that would only provoke Soviets, in a crisis, to make the lunge against the United States. It would require the Strategic Air Command to acknowledge that the day of fixed land-based missiles had passed and that U.S. nuclear submarines—which carry most of our nuclear warheads anyway—were at present and for the foreseeable future the real basis of the deterrent against Soviet attack. It would also be necessary for the Pentagon to admit, at least to itself, that whatever we might say to the Soviets about our capability for prompt action, it would probably be better in all circumstances to wait and see what was really happening than to respond impetuously to what we suspected they were doing.

These are difficult premises for the Strategic Air Command and the Pentagon to accept. What really traps us, accordingly, is not the impersonal force of technology but the attitudes of large bureaucracies already committed to certain weapons systems and ways of thinking. The Air Force is in the ICBM and bomber business and is strongly committed to an offensive nuclear strategy. It does not want the nation to retire its pilots and depend on the Navy or on a nuclear deterrent based solely on retaliation. This kind of bias, which is common in human affairs, not just in the military, is seldom overcome through analysis, argumentation, or arbitration. The difficulty of shifting people's basic ideas was described by the Nobel laureate Max Planck, who observed how the older school of physicists resisted revolutionary new ideas, such as the theory of quantum mechanics he had introduced. They never did come around to the new way of thinking, he said, but just gradually died off. It seems correspondingly unlikely, until a new generation of military leaders assumes responsibility for nuclear weapons policy, that the outlook that has led to the first-strike option in the S.I.O.P., and to the present hair trigger arrangement for launching U.S. missiles, will change.

2

H HOUR

H Hour is the time at which a military operation begins. It is the instant at which the attacker schedules troops or planes or ships to make their first move. It is the occasion that puts the grand designs of offensive and defensive strategists to the test.

H Hour may be the start of an engagement that moves to a swift conclusion or the beginning of mayhem that no one is able to stop. It may be the opening phase of a predictable maneuver by an adversary or the inaugural display of unaccountably terrifying new tactics or weaponry.

H Hour may signal a skirmish that will end with the taking of a few worthless acres. It may be the curtain rise for a tragedy that will not conclude until civilization lies in ruins.

One thing is certain about H Hour, especially in the nuclear age: should some unforeseen event or berserk instinct weaken the well-founded reluctance of the superpowers to risk a nuclear showdown, any confrontation that ensues will involve a severe test of their warning and intelligence systems. Numberless battles have shown the mix of ingredients that make for military success or failure. No unique recipe for victory exists, but the historians who study the grim records of military encounters mention, among the frequent causes of defeat, a commander's lack of timely intelligence and reliable means of communications. Those who plan a nuclear attack will not overlook this, and those who seek to deter must be just as mindful of it.

War, after all, is a game for opportunists. Those who win have recognized, and grasped, the unfolding possibilities. Without timely warning, a commander will be unable to avoid the traps into which his forces may be about to fall. Without the means to relay orders to the troops, a commander will be unable to seize the transient advantages that arise. The impotence of battlefield officers who do not know the whereabouts of forces—the enemy's and their own—and who lack the ability to transmit directives speedily, is one of the abiding lessons of military science. "Signal Corps officers like to remind us," General Omar Bradley said, "that 'although Congress can make a general, it takes communications to make him a commander.'"

Historian Bruce Catton, in his account of the last year of the American Civil War, eloquently describes the frustration of the commander who lacks adequate information. Of one "titanic wrestle in the darkening woods" of Virginia, Catton wrote:

> The whole thing was invisible. It was smothered down out of sight in five miles of smoking wilderness, and even men who were in the storm center of it saw no more than fragmentary pictures—little groups of men moving in and out of a spooky, reddish luminous haze, with rifles flashing indistinctly in the gloom, the everlasting trees and brush always in the way, the weight of the smoke tamping down everything except the evil flames that sprang up wherever men fought . . . for this was the battle no man saw . . . all cramped and close and ugly, like a duel fought with knives in a cellar far under ground.

Such was the "complete pandemonium," he continued, that

> [t]he commanders behind the lines—[General Ulysses] Grant, smoking and whittling and noting all the dispatches . . . had no conception of what was really going on up in front. . . . In effect, the army was fighting blindfolded and most of the generals knew little more than the men in the ranks knew.

Military technology has come a long way since galloping messengers were relied upon to bring information to commanders and deliver orders to the troops. Still, as the wars of our own century demonstrate, the lack of warning of impending attack remains a nightmare for all military leaders. The major debacle at the outset of World War II showed the tragic consequences when urgent messages do not get through.

As the Japanese armada approached Hawaii, the United States was equipped with a warning system that was nominally far superior to any commander's in history. U.S. intelligence had the capability to intercept and decode the secret communiqués which were sent to Tokyo by Japanese diplomats in Washington, and which discussed the upcoming surprise attack. Some important indicators of an impending action were lost, however, among voluminous other reports in Washington, and the warnings that were transmitted to U.S. commanders in Hawaii were ignored—a fact that went unappreciated in Washington. In the days preceding the "day of infamy" at Pearl Harbor, there had been so many messages from Washington to Hawaii about a possible Japanese attack that key War Department officials thought the fleet had already been put out to sea to avoid the risk of destruction in port.

At the end of World War II, the failure of U.S. commanders to protect the fleet was investigated by a special Congressional panel. It determined that the main preoccupation of the two principal U.S. military leaders in Hawaii at the time, Admiral Kimmel and General Short, had not been the Japanese threat but a contentious interservice dispute. It was less significant, on its face, than the recent disputes between the Air Force and the Navy over nuclear strategy, but it remains typical of the bickering that has long preoccupied the turf-conscious military services. At issue was which of them would be in charge of Wake and Midway islands when the Marines there were replaced by soldiers. There was no "unity of command" in Hawaii, the 1946 Congressional report stated. Instead, there was "jealous adherence to departmental prerogatives and unwillingness to make concessions in the interest of both the Army and the Navy." The official analysis of America's worst military setback concluded: "It is proper to suggest that, had both commanding officers in Hawaii been less concerned between November 27 and December 7 about preserving their individual prerogatives with respect to Wake and Midway and more concerned about working together to defend the Hawaiian Coastal Frontier in the light of warnings they had received, the defensive situation confronting the Japanese on the morning of December 7 might well have been entirely different."

Also involved, as is the case today with each service's steadfast commitment to particular weapons systems, was a psychological factor: in this case, the Navy's inability to conceive that a new weapon, the aircraft-carrier-launched fighter plane, could threaten traditional battleships. Admiral Noel Gayler, the former Commander in Chief of U.S. forces in the Pacific, notes that the dismissive term the Navy used at the time to describe the airplane threat—an air "raid"—suggested not a potential assault of major military consequence but an annoying possibility akin to an insect bite. Warnings of the approaching aircraft carriers, given this mind-set, were automatically downplayed.

Even when unambiguous warnings were available to the War Department, complications with the communications system—including disturbances in the upper atmosphere on December 7 which interfered with radio signals—stymied efforts to alert U.S. forces in Hawaii. The final warning message, sent by Army Chief of Staff George C. Marshall several hours before the attack, had to go out over commercial telegraph and radio. Delivered by a Western Union bicycle messenger, it got to Fort Shafter in Honolulu two hours after the attack had begun. The U.S. fleet, which could have been safely dispersed at sea if a timely alert had been received and acted upon, smoldered in the tight confines of its home port.

––––––

The imperative of avoiding an atomic Pearl Harbor prompted the Pentagon in the 1950s and early '60s to spend billions of dollars on a vastly improved early warning network that feeds information into the NORAD Cheyenne Mountain Complex in Colorado. NORAD has little margin for error in executing its assignment. An inability to detect a sneak attack could tempt an adversary, in a crisis, to try one. Even a few minutes' delay in recognizing incoming missiles—or confusion in interpreting precisely what was happening—could have dire consequences. If the United States were caught unaware, the White House, the Pentagon, and other key command posts might be destroyed before retaliatory orders could be given. U.S. B-52 and FB-111 bombers could be caught on the ground unless they got into the air quickly. Support aircraft, such as the aerial tankers that can refuel the bombers in flight, could also be the victims of a no-warning attack.

A NORAD false alert, on the other hand, an alarm cry that mistakenly announced incoming Soviet missiles or bombers, could lead to a panicky decision to launch U.S. retaliatory forces—a blunder that would invite the Soviets to respond in kind. Other mistakes, such as an inaccurate depiction of the scale of an attack—declaring that a large-scale strike was in progress when a more limited one was taking place —could prompt a U.S. response completely out of proportion to the real threat and lead to the uncontrolled escalation of a lesser conflict into all-out war.

There are fifteen steel buildings in the cold, gloomy tunnels of NORAD's netherworld installation, and they are connected to a world-wide set of sensors—early warning satellites in outer space and ground-based radars. The data from these detectors, and other intelligence information, are relayed to the Cheyenne Mountain Complex by various means, processed by eighty-seven computers, and evaluated by dozens of technical experts. "Lifelines fo the facility—links with the outside— are the communications circuits," NORAD officials state. The channels that handle critical data traffic, they add, "must be fast and reliable." No one could disagree, and the central question on my mind as I talked with personnel at Cheyenne Mountain, the Pentagon, Strategic Air Command Headquarters, and other U.S. military installations was how well the message links into and out of NORAD fulfilled these require-ments. I wondered exactly what NORAD would know, and how quickly, if there was a nuclear attack against the United States.

Nuclear war, like any form of combat, can be choreographed in many different ways. The superpowers have a large assortment of forces —land-based missiles, submarine-launched missiles, cruise missiles, medium- and long-range bombers—that can be used separately or in various combinations. The strikes can be quick or slow, from different launch sites or a single one, and aimed at a broad range of targets or just a few. NORAD planners must do the best they can to anticipate the likeliest scenarios—which can include several forms of flank attacks as well as frontal assaults—and design the warning system accordingly. There will always be the nagging concern, expressed by one command-system designer, that "poverty of imagination" could leave the United States vulnerable to devastating modes of attack that had been over-looked.

"If the enemy attacks us, what will it look like?" an Air Force consultant said to me. "Imagine the Israelis, only a little more brutal." The stunning surprise attack against the Egyptian Air Force at the outset of the 1967 war displayed the kind of unconventional tactics that some analysts think the Soviets might wish to emulate at the outset of a nuclear conflict. Hitting the Egyptian airfields from the east at dawn would have been advantageous to the Israeli pilots, since the bright sun just above the horizon and behind the strike force would blind the defenders. Israeli commanders suspected that the Egyptians would surely understand this and be on the outlook. On the other hand, if no attack came at dawn, the Israelis reasoned, their opponents would stand down from alert and resume their normal routine, thinking the period of maximum danger over for that day. That was exactly what happened. When the Israelis attacked—in mid-morning—they came in low, to evade radar detection, and wiped out the Egyptian planes parked on the tarmac.

NORAD capabilities to detect Soviet attacks were shown to me by Air Force personnel who operate the room in the Cheyenne Mountain Complex called the Missile Warning Center. It receives data from all the early warning sensors, analyzes it, and passes its findings to NORAD's main Command Post. The Missile Warning Center has a normal staff of two officers and four enlisted personnel, and the small room they occupy, with its rows of computer terminals, looks a bit like the office of a modest-size brokerage company. Its video screens are programmed by computer to indicate the trajectories of incoming Soviet missiles. The staff is not required to sit and stare at the scopes; an alarm from the computer tells them when to look. When I saw the screens, they were blank. One wall of the room has a long display panel that resembles an old-fashioned baseball stadium scoreboard: there were box windows to indicate how many missiles (or possible ones) had been picked up by the various early warning radars. This monitor also showed that nothing was happening. The two nations were at peace.

As a hypothetical question, as a means of evaluating U.S. readiness to retaliate, one can ask, "What if a Soviet attack suddenly took place?" What data would NORAD have received if the Soviets had set H Hour for 11:00 A.M. Rocky Mountain Time on Monday morning, October 24, 1983, just as I walked into the Missile Warning Center? Auditors sometimes show up unannounced at a bank and ask to look at the books. My visit to NORAD on that day had been scheduled in advance, and I was limited by security restrictions in what I could see. My purpose, nonetheless, was similar to the bank examiners'. I wanted to try to make a spot check of NORAD's readiness and to determine, as precisely as I could, what NORAD could realistically expect to know if the Soviets attacked at some randomly selected time. War itself, as the historians say, is the great auditor of institutions, but there are less costly ways of judging how well an organization such as NORAD can perform its mission.

———

Some twenty-two thousand miles above the Indian Ocean, there is a U.S. early warning satellite that constantly monitors the Eastern Hemisphere. This electronic sentinel looks down on the Eurasian landmass and takes all of the twenty-six Soviet missile bases into its purview. A Code 647 Defense Support Program satellite—known at NORAD as "DSP East"—it is approximately twenty feet long and nine feet wide and weighs more than a ton. The main piece of equipment on board is a twelve-foot-long Schmidt infrared telescope outfitted with thousands of tiny lead sulfide detectors designed to pick up the hot flame produced by large rocket engines. The sensors at the focus of the telescope do not detect missiles at the instant they emerge from their silos, but about thirty seconds later, during the boost phase of their flight, as they come up out of the lower part of the atmosphere. Flight time of the Soviet warheads to the continental United States: approximately twenty-five to thirty minutes.

The first experimental early warning satellites were launched in the late 1960s, and since the early 1970s at least one Code 647 satellite has been operating in an orbit that assures comprehensive surveillance of the Soviet missile fields. (The missile bases stretch across the entire USSR, roughly following the track of the Trans-Siberian Railway.) The satellite keeps to an orbit more or less above the equator, giving it a vantage point from which it can maintain good coverage all the way up into the northern latitudes of the Soviet Union. The satellite spins constantly, and this permits the telescope to scan quickly over all areas of interest.

"These satellites have only been around for about ten years and are really 'first generation' satellites," one government official noted. "They're really not all that sophisticated. They basically just give you an early indication that something is probably happening. Part of the problem is the time requirement. If you could collect data from all the systems and sit down for a couple of days to analyze it, you could probably do a very good job. There really is a saturation problem." A general who has worked at NORAD concurred and explained that the precise number of Soviet missiles that had been fired might be hard to determine. "An infrared system can only count so many [rocket] plumes," he said. He emphasized that the satellite's limitations may not matter too much, though, because "by the time the system gets flooded it will probably have done its job, as long as it can guarantee that the leading edge of the attack is identified."

In addition to indicating that Soviet missiles have been fired, data from DSP East will reveal something else of great importance to the U.S. military: the kind of missiles they are and the approximate launch sites they come from. The classification of the missiles is determined partly by comparing the infrared glow from the rocket plumes with observations made during Soviet test flights, which the satellite also monitors. The hot gases streaming out of the rockets, that is, leave a distinctive "signature." In addition, over the last two decades U.S. "close look" reconnaissance satellites—which fly in much lower orbits than DSP East—have taken large numbers of photographs of the loading of Soviet missile silos. Thus, data from DSP East about which launch sites have been used will provide a further clue to the identity of the Soviet missiles. The DSP satellites have not had the ability to pinpoint the exact silos from which the missiles come, but future U.S. early warning satellites are expected to have that capability.

It would make a great deal of difference, for example, whether Soviet SS-18s (which would come from six launch areas in south central Siberia) or SS-11s (which would come from the western part of the country, the Urals, or from three areas near the Mongolian border) were fired. Unlike the SS-18s, the SS-11s do not have the destructive power and theoretical accuracy to knock out Minuteman missiles and would be indicative of a different kind of Soviet strike plan—one that might be aimed at softer targets such as bomber bases, or U.S. cities.

The Soviets have no known means, at the moment, for destroying the early warning satellite that is kept in high orbit over the Eastern Hemisphere (although they have tested, with mixed results, anti-satellite weapons designed to knock out satellites in very low orbits). There is still the possibility that they could attempt to jam DSP East— to flood it with so much energy that it could not detect the heat produced by missile launches. (DSP East's sensors were accidentally over-loaded in December 1975 when they picked up the heat from a massive fire caused by an explosion in a natural gas field in Siberia.) Other forms of interference with the early warning satellite are also possible.

Thus, if the Soviets knew the coded signals used to tell the DSP satellite what to do, they could possibly try to turn it off or spoof it in some way that prevented the detection of ICBM launches. As a former Air Force official explained, "A hostile nation with the capability to send spoofing or suicide-inducing commands to highly important satellites at the outbreak of hostilities or in time to conceal war preparations would have a distinct advantage. With these spurious commands, properly coded and appropriately timed, it is conceivable that the enemy could alter a satellite's position; . . . deny it power by disorienting sun-pointing antennas; fire thrusters causing orbital decay; trigger and receive stored radio transmissions . . . ; falsely cause nuclear power sources to self-destruct; render electronic countermeasures equipment inoperative; or render inactive defensive maneuver gear or defensive weapons."

The early warning satellites are supposed to be designed to detect and counter efforts to disable them, but categorical statements about their ability to do so are hard to make. "Anything that receives—a communications receiver, sensor receiver—all receivers can be interfered with, and it is a high state of art that tries to cope with that," Lieutenant General Herres explained. "And there are things one can do, and we spend a lot of time and money—and that's one of the reasons why command and control systems are expensive—because it takes special kinds of genius to figure out ways to cope with that. And every time you think you've got one threat whipped, then somebody thinks up another one. It's a never-ending cycle. I rail at the guys that think one of these days we'll have all the money spent we need to spend on this and everything will be all right. It'll never be all right."

Tampering with an early warning satellite would run the risk of alerting the United States to an imminent missile launch. On the other hand, there might be a military advantage in attempting to disable the orbiting early warning station, even if it had to be done in a crude and obvious way. If the satellite were out of business, the United States would not know which Soviet missiles had been fired and which Soviet missile fields still contained loaded silos. It would then be difficult to try to launch a counterattack to knock out the Soviet missiles held in reserve. No one would know where to aim.

If a mechanical or electrical problem or some other kind of fault occurs with DSP East, Air Force ground controllers can try to diagnose and fix it by remote control. In addition, spare satellites are usually available. New early warning satellites are sent up every three years or so, but the older ones are left in orbit. One of the retired satellites could be turned back on by the ground controllers, and other satellites might also be pressed into service if something happened to one that was supposed to be watching over Soviet missile bases. The United States has a number of multipurpose satellites, and some of the other ones, whose principal mission may be communications or electronic eavesdropping, have sensors tacked on that could help detect missile launches. They might not be within range, however, if a sudden Soviet attack took place. Thus, turning on or repositioning additional satellites could take some time, which is why one NORAD official likened nuclear war to a "come-as-you-are party." "Whatever we have in orbit is what you will go to war with," he said.

———

A further reason for not counting on the ability to increase surveillance capability quickly at the outbreak of nuclear war is the vulnerability of the Air Force's main satellite ground control center, which one expert described as "within bazooka range of a highway." It would be one of the likely targets for Soviet attack, or sabotage, in the opening phase of a nuclear war. Unclassified Pentagon testimony before Congress in March 1983 mentioned the exact site of that ground station when it referred to U.S. strategic connectivity as "dependent on the single satellite control facility (SCF) located at Sunnyvale, California." (The facility is euphemistically designated the "Satellite Test Center.") If that installation—the hub of a worldwide defense-satellite control network—were attacked, not only would that hinder the repositioning of additional satellites, but the continued operation of all U.S. defense satellites would also come into question.

There are several dozen U.S. defense satellites now in orbit—providing communications, photoreconnaissance, electronic intelligence, navigational, meteorological, and other data—and they require contact with the Sunnyvale ground control station and its seven substations around the globe in order to remain functional. A great deal of fine-tuning, for example, is needed to steer the satellites in precise orbits and to keep their sensors and antennas aimed properly. The importance of the Sunnyvale facility was noted in a report by the General Accounting Office, which said that "the existing [Satellite Control Facility] is located within 18 miles of three major earthquake faults and has no comparable backup. The buildings associated with the facility do not meet today's construction standards and are expected to suffer significant damage if there is a major earthquake. A catastrophic loss of this control center would result in a major disruption of communications, tracking, and control of its space systems. Consequently, there would be a critically adverse impact on national security. Also, SCF is located on a crowded 20-acre site surrounded by major highways and industrial parks. This provides a highly vulnerable target to possible saboteurs."

Precisely what would happen if Sunnyvale were knocked out would depend on a number of factors, such as the type of satellite, when it had last received instructions from the ground, what it was doing at the time the SCF was destroyed, and how much autonomy it had to perform the adjustments necessary to keep itself functional and in the proper orbit. The Sunnyvale facility makes some ninety thousand contacts per year with its satellites, or about five contacts per satellite per day. Admiral Tomb said, "The satellites don't fall down because Sunnyvale gets hit." Instead, the satellites would have "a degraded capability over a period of time."

Other officials are less optimistic. "We lose the SCF and the satellites basically go haywire," a Pentagon expert who has studied this subject told me. "The communications satellites drift off to Pluto." Certain intelligence-gathering satellites in low-earth orbit would be in especially bad shape, he said, since the Sunnyvale facility has to "feed them" with instructions every time they complete an orbit. "You should see them scrambling when one of these satellites comes within range." Desmond Ball estimated that the typical U.S. defense satellite might be able to remain in operation for three to four days without the Sunnyvale SCF; the most critical satellites, such as DSP East, which require a great deal of caretaking attention from the ground, could go out of service within hours.

In some cases, a high level of redundancy is built into the strategic command system, with a large number of backup facilities and alternate means for carrying out critical tasks. In other cases, the system is dangerously thin. The Sunnyvale facility is one of the obvious weak links.

According to the information I saw at NORAD on October 24, 1983, the early warning satellite known as DSP East was reported to be functioning normally. (In the Missile Warning Center, officials refused to discuss the status of the satellite; in the Command Post, however, I observed the green light indicating that DSP East was in service.) Assuming that it could not be jammed or otherwise incapacitated, this sensor would be able to gather data about the launching of Soviet ICBMs at the time I have designated as H Hour. This information would then have to be transmitted back to NORAD—which is something that DSP East cannot do directly. Cheyenne Mountain is on the other side of the globe, and an extended set of communications links must be used to retrieve its warning signals.

A key part of the communications setup between NORAD and its principal early warning satellite is a ground station in Australia that functions as the "downlink" for the satellite. It receives raw data from DSP East, processes it immediately using dual IBM 360-75J computers, and relays the results back to NORAD. The Australian station, code-named "Casino," is located at Nurrungar, South Australia, about three hundred miles northwest of Adelaide, and it has been for many years the only "readout station" for our most important early warning satellite. The station has various means—radio, satellite, and undersea cable—for getting urgent data back to the United States.

Dependence on a single downlink for DSP East, like the reliance on the unique installation at Sunnyvale, has been a major cause for concern, especially since the eight-acre Australian station consists of a highly exposed set of antennas, transmitters, and computational facilities that present extremely "soft" targets to any enemy. The station can be directly attacked by a Soviet submarine-launched missile. It can also be readily disabled by means far less dramatic than nuclear bombardment. Its two forty-foot satellite antennas (housed inside plastic domes) or its power supplies or its communications lines could be rendered inoperable by what the military refers to as "sappers"—a small team of technically adept saboteurs—armed only with conventional weapons and explosives.

"Since relatively few fixed installations are involved, sabotage must also be considered a significant threat in a sudden nuclear attack," a special report to Congress concluded in 1981. "A coordinated series of sabotage incidents could be particularly disruptive in such a time-sensitive scenario as a nuclear attack. Obviously, poorly executed sabotage efforts could serve to increase warning time. Nonetheless, if acts of sabotage confounded clear evaluation for only a few tens of minutes, command-post aircraft, bombers, and tanker aircraft might be destroyed on the ground."

"It is inconceivable to me that if the Russians were going to start a war, they'd not start by knocking out the early warning sites," one of the Pentagon's leading experts on command-system design told me. "If I were going to do it, that's how I'd do it," a NORAD general said. The danger of attacks against the sensor sites was also emphasized by the Pentagon connectivity studies of the last few years, which noted the particularly acute vulnerability of NORAD's Australian link. An official familiar with the specific deficiencies said they were very good examples of the "small, trivial, silly, sad problems" that were found. It turned out that it would not even be necessary to attack the Nurrungar ground station itself, since other, subtler means were available for breaking its connection back to Cheyenne Mountain. Thus, government investigators discovered to their amazement the ease with which saboteurs could simply cut the undersea cable from Australia at the point where it came ashore in California. The target for such an attack: an unprotected AT&T building in San Francisco.

"A lot of things were overlooked as we built those systems," General Richard Ellis conceded. "Anyone could just walk in the door to a switching center [in San Francisco] with the name of the originating terminal on a sign. In other words, it identified the overseas station, and you knew right away that this was the United States terminal for that information, highly vulnerable to anything anybody wanted to do to it."

Another official, General Robert Marsh, the head of the Air Force Systems Command, acknowledged, "We have highly visible, highly vulnerable switching nodes throughout our communications environment. We put up big signs on our coastline, 'Submarine cable, do not dredge here,' and so on, and some of those are our only lifeline to important sensor stations." The routing of military and commercial submarine cables across the Pacific is such that in addition to (or instead of) severing the main cable connection in Northern California, saboteurs could just as well try to cut it at its Australian end (in

Sydney) or at other points along its long route (such as Wellington, New Zealand, or Hawaii).

NORAD informed me that the "situation" with the AT&T building in San Francisco "has been corrected." It did not say how. One government expert said that about all you could do was put in "rudimentary security arrangements"—some fences, guards, and locked doors. One could also take down the sign identifying the cable. Such improvements would do little to protect against determined attacks. The futility of such measures was suggested by another step NORAD has taken to conceal the vulnerability of its Australian connection. In the information packet it hands out to reporters, there is a map showing the "support organizations" connected to NORAD. The name of the Australian ground station is now covered over by a strip of white correcting tape, the kind that typists use. The name is plainly visible when the document is held up to the light.

The radio and satellite links that are available to the Nurrungar station to transmit data to NORAD suffer from problems comparable to those affecting the undersea cable. Officials might try to use high frequency (HF) radio links to relay a message, say, to Clark Air Force Base in the Philippines, which could retransmit it to NORAD. Or they could use the Defense Satellite Communications System (DSCS). (Nurrungar is equipped with an AN/MSC-46 satellite antenna which, according to information on file with the International Telecommunications Union in Geneva, is assigned a transmission frequency of 8040.526 MHz.) The Soviets could readily interfere with these communications links, especially by means of jamming, since neither the radio nor DSCS satellite hookups are well-protected at present from this form of electronic warfare.

In addition, there is the problem that the one defense communications satellite available to the Australian ground station—it is known as DSCS WESTPAC and it hovers over the western Pacific—cannot send messages directly to NORAD. It is out of range. Messages thus have to be sent up to the satellite from Australia and then relayed down to other ground stations before they get to NORAD. The DSCS WESTPAC satellite merely hands the warning message to the U.S. Pacific Command's switching station in Wahiawa, near Honolulu. From there, the message has to be rebroadcast over the defense communications satellite orbiting over the eastern Pacific (DSCS EASTPAC).

However, even this satellite is still out of range of NORAD. The warning message has to be passed to ground stations in California—either at Sunnyvale or Camp Roberts—for relay to NORAD. All of these intermediary ground stations are obvious weak points in the Nurrungar-to-NORAD link. Officials at the Australian station could also attempt to use commercial satellite links, but there would still be no guarantee of getting a message back to NORAD. To tie into the commercial satellite system, Nurrungar would have to use vulnerable landlines to hook up with an Intelsat broadcasting station at Moree, several hundred miles to the east. Those lines, and the satellite transmitter there, could be sabotaged with ease. As Major General J. C. Pfautz of the U.S. Pacific Command said in a 1982 speech, the command and control system in the Pacific is "vulnerable to the most rudimentary form of enemy attack."

NORAD would probably know immediately if its tie-in with DSP East suddenly failed. This would not necessarily trigger anything more than a routine inquiry, since in any complex system various components are subject to temporary outages. Depending on the type of sabotage or jamming, officials at the Cheyenne Mountain Complex might not be able to get through to Australia quickly, or vice versa, to discuss what was happening. Even if they did make contact, the situation could easily appear to be ambiguous. A "fire of unknown origin," say, might be the apparent cause of the station's difficulties. There might be no immediate evidence that the disruption was deliberate—that it had been timed to knock out the ground station just as DSP East was about to transmit data indicating that Soviet ICBMs were on the initial leg of their rapid journey to targets in the United States.

———

A Soviet nuclear attack does not have to start with a precisely timed attack on Nurrungar followed by an ICBM launch. The list of attack options is much longer. A strike could begin, instead, with submarine-launched ballistic missiles (SLBMs). The Soviets have a fleet of sixty-five missile-launching submarines, although for reasons Western analysts do not fully understand, they keep only about six or eight of them on routine patrol. (The United States has at least half of its ballistic missile submarines at sea at all times.) The three common explanations for the large number of Soviet subs kept in port are: the unreliability of their nuclear reactors, Moscow's difficulty in communicating with the subs on patrol, and the Kremlin's possible distrust of the crews and fear of defections.

The withholding of Soviet subs from routine patrols does not mean that their missiles cannot be used. Some of the missiles can travel several thousand miles, and those known to Western observers as the SS-N-8 and SS-N-18 can hit targets in the United States without their subs' having to leave their home ports of Petropavlovsk (on the Kamchatka Peninsula) and Severomorsk (on the Barents Sea). They can be fired right from dockside. In a crisis, moreover, the subs could be put to sea —weather permitting (since the ports are icebound from November to April)—where they would be free to roam broad stretches of the oceans and remain within range of their assigned targets. The Soviets could also station dozens of submarines right off the Atlantic, Pacific, and Gulf coasts of the United States. Missiles fired from such close-in positions would have some important military advantages over ICBMs coming from missile fields in the Soviet homeland. Instead of the thirty minutes or so it would take an SS-18 to hit U.S. bomber bases in the Midwest, NORAD Headquarters in Colorado, or the Strategic Air Command Headquarters in Omaha, submarine-launched missiles could hit those targets in half that time. Targets near the coasts—such as Sunnyvale, California, or the Pentagon in Washington—could be destroyed even more quickly.

Because of the threat posed by Soviet submarine-launched missiles, the United States has deployed two early warning satellites that continuously watch the Atlantic and Pacific oceans. Like their sister satellite, perched over the Indian Ocean, the satellites that scan the waters of the Western Hemisphere—the pair known at NORAD as "DSP West"—hover about twenty-two thousand miles above the equator. All three early warning satellites fly close to what are called geosynchronous orbits: they keep up with the rotation of the earth and therefore hold to a more or less fixed position above the equator.

These two additional DSP satellites must relay data to NORAD through a ground station. In their case, since they are within line of sight of the continental United States, the communications link is more direct. It still has its potential weaknesses, since the large ground station to which they report needs receiving antennas that are, of necessity, above ground and therefore vulnerable to elementary forms of conventional attack or sabotage.

The downlink for DSP West is located at Buckley Air National Guard Base in Colorado, which is about sixty miles from NORAD. It passes data to NORAD by means of a set of microwave towers. (The microwave hookup goes to Peterson Air Force Base in Colorado Springs, and from there up to the Cheyenne Mountain Complex.) Thus, as with the undersea cable from Australia, the flow of warning information can be interrupted, without attacking the ground station at Buckley directly, by cutting the electronic umbilical cord that ties it to NORAD—a microwave tower being something that can be disabled in nothing flat by a knowledgeable saboteur.

To date, the Air Force has made two main responses to the vulnerability of the large ground stations for the early warning satellites. First, it attempted to build a new kind of ground station, a mobile one that could be quickly deployed in undisclosed locations. The plans called for it to be transported in an Air Force C-5A or C-141 cargo plane. Known as the Simplified Processing Station, or SPS, it was not designed to do all of the sophisticated data processing that is done at the primary stations. The scaled-down ground station still turned out to be so large—with two thirty-eight-foot satellite dishes, for example—that it would take weeks to relocate it and was not, in any practical sense, mobile. The SPS became operational in December 1978 at the Cornhusker Army Ammunition Plant in Nebraska, but an official noted that it "had a serious amount of technical problems and required a lot of debugging work." There were "major deficiencies which would prevent the SPS from becoming operationally effective," a Pentagon report said. These included excessive "computer-generated" message errors that could cause warnings of missile attacks to get "lost." When it was finally put in working order, the SPS still had communications lines with the same susceptibility to sabotage and direct attack as the setup at Buckley. The Nebraska installation has now been closed down and the equipment relocated overseas. Plans to produce a second SPS were canceled.

The other principal attempt to strengthen the fragile connection between DSP West and NORAD is the addition of new communications equipment: a satellite communications link to supplement the microwave hookup. With a satellite transmitter, the ground station at Buckley, for example, will be able to relay information to the gargantuan satellite receiver that sits next to the Officers' Club at Peterson

Air Force Base in Colorado Springs. From there, the warning message can be relayed to Cheyenne Mountain a few miles away—provided, that is, that a delivery truck bringing supplies to the dining room just before H Hour is not full of high explosives.

The attempt to back up the vulnerable ground station in Colorado with another equally exposed one in Nebraska, and the decision to add another interruptible communications link to the one that has been used, have not greatly increased NORAD's capability to retrieve data from DSP West. Nor does the building of another ground station for DSP East compensate for the vulnerability of Nurrungar. (The new readout station for DSP East, using the equipment of the old Nebraska SPS, has been located at a classified site in Europe, although one expert called the siting decision very peculiar, for when DSP East is in range of this new ground station it is out of range of certain major Soviet missile bases!) None of the actions to date solves the problem of over-dependence on an exceedingly small number of critical ground stations.

Nor does the new technology that will be added to the early warning satellites appear to resolve the difficulties. The equipment will provide what is referred to as a "cross-linking" capability. DSP East, that is, instead of going through a ground station in Australia, could transmit information to another satellite—such as the Pacific DSP West—which would relay it to the ground station at Buckley. From there it could go to NORAD. The Air Force and the Pentagon decline to say when the capability to cross-link the satellites will be available. When it is provided, though, it will make little overall difference in the critical lack of redundancy in the satellite early warning system. Cross-linking may reduce dependence on the Australian or other Eastern Hemisphere ground station, but it simply increases dependence on the one at Buckley. The number of Achilles tendons that will need to be cut to cripple the NORAD satellite early warning system will remain remarkably small.

———

The three DSP satellites are the most important but not the only assets in the U.S. early warning system. They are the first bell-ringers that alert NORAD to an actual missile launch, and the only sensors that directly monitor launch sites in the USSR. But NORAD insists on what it calls "dual phenomenology" to prove that a missile warning is real. The presence of incoming missiles must be independently confirmed, that is, by at least two warning systems, the principal complement to the satellites being the radars that are deployed in strategic locations.

Thus, about ten minutes after a Soviet ICBM leaves its silo en route, over the northern polar regions, to the United States, it is supposed to be picked up by a radar at Thule, Greenland. Equipment for this outpost, which is about seven hundred miles from the North Pole, was designed in the late 1950s and became operational in December 1960. The radar has a range of about three thousands miles, but until a modernization program is completed, it will remain quite antiquated by today's technological standards. The computers and ancillary equipment there, which are of the same vintage, have also had severe limitations. A substantial maintenance effort is required to keep this aging apparatus in working condition.

Farther from the Arctic Circle, two other companion radar installations were built, using essentially the same equipment installed at Thule, as part of what was called the Ballistic Missile Early Warning System. They are in Fylingdales Moor, England, and Clear, Alaska. Their range is the same (three thousand miles), and their coverage partly overlaps that of Thule: the radar in Great Britain naturally extends its sweep farther over the eastern part of the USSR, and the Alaskan radar is capable of looking at approach paths to the United States from all of Siberia.

Thule, Fylingdales Moor, and Clear would be obvious targets if the Soviets wanted to increase the element of surprise in an ICBM attack. These radars could be destroyed by direct nuclear or non-nuclear attack and their communications lines back to NORAD could also be severed. Low-flying bombers or cruise missiles or submarine-launched missiles could hit and destroy them before they detected any ICBMs. In addition, one of the connectivity studies showed that these radars are "so easily tricked and fooled" that they could also be jammed.

Radars emit microwave beams that bounce off objects in their path; these reflected rays show up on the radar scopes. Jamming—which is analogous to what hecklers try to do in shouting down a speaker—involves directing so much electronic noise at a radar (or other receiver) that the signal coming back from the missile or other source will be lost or obscured. Success in jamming depends on many things, including the attacker's knowledge of the radar's technical characteristics. The relevant information is not difficult to obtain: just send a suitably equipped reconnaissance plane into the radar beam, and it will promptly determine the nature of the emissions. Every radar station gives away this information about itself whenever it is turned on— which for the early warning radars is supposed to be as close to one hundred percent of the time as possible. It is considered highly likely that the jamming of these radars is well within the capability of the USSR, which has devoted considerable effort to the perfection of this form of electronic warfare.

"The early warning radars are supposed to detect the incoming reentry vehicles as they're coming over the pole," Richard Garwin said. "You could jam them fairly readily by sending along with these reentry vehicles battery-operated jammers, that is, radio transmitters with an antenna which is focused down on the radars. It just requires providing them more signal than they are able to handle, even though they're trying to look away. You can have the analogue of the optical dazzle— that there's so much electrical energy around that no matter where they look they see targets. So that kind of jamming is feasible. You can also drop jammers close to the radar, so they're just sitting there talking to the radar a few feet away."

Radar operators, if their equipment is properly designed, Garwin added, should know when jamming—which in itself is a signal that something is up—is taking place. Means of countering jamming are available, but it is hard to predict who will be the winner in the combat between jamming and anti-jamming techniques. There is always, he said, "a big battle between electronic countermeasures, ECM, and counter-countermeasures, ECCM, and ECCCM, counter-counter-countermeasures, and so on. The answer is that if you do your job you're going to know that you're being jammed. So I'm quite sure we would know we were being jammed. Of course, those radars are very vulnerable, too. They could be destroyed with no difficulty."

At the hypothetical H Hour on October 24, 1983, it turns out, a Soviet effort to destroy or interfere with the U.S. radars at Thule, Fylingdales Moor, and Clear would not have been entirely necessary. The NORAD Missile Warning Center showed a yellow light on its main display panel, indicating that the Thule radar was reduced to partial capacity. There was a red light indicating that the Fylingdales Moor radar was not operating at all. A green light showed that only the radar at Clear was operating normally.

I asked NORAD why this set of handicaps had occurred, and in a written statement I was told that both Thule and Fylingdales were undergoing testing of new computers. It also said that the radars could be switched back over to their older computers immediately, were that necessary. This contradicted what officials in the warning center had told me. They said that while a yellow light indicated that the system could be restored to full operation quickly, a red light meant that this could not be counted on. (Brigadier General Wagoner confirmed that officers in the warning center had given me the correct interpretation of what the monitor lights were supposed to indicate.) One government expert commented that the situation I had observed was "not atypical." A display panel "mostly yellow and no go" happens, a NORAD official also said, since the Ballistic Missile Early Warning System "is twenty-five years old, operates on vacuum tube technology, and should have been replaced ten years ago."

Dependability aside, a further question about the three radars is the quality of the information they gather when they do work. "In general, the system is not designed to provide very good attack assessment," one official explained. The early warning radars, he continued, were essentially "tripwires to alert the military to defend itself—for example to get the bombers into the air. They won't give you a very detailed attack assessment." A former Pentagon official compared the radars to household smoke detectors—relatively primitive devices that indicate that a fire has started without providing technical information on the kind of blaze.

The three radars, other experts agree, have little capability to provide an accurate count of the number of incoming missiles or warheads. They were built in an era when a major missile attack was defined as twenty missiles or more, and before missiles had multiple warheads that could throw thousands of small objects into the radar's beam.

A senior Pentagon adviser said that the major deficiency of the older radars had to do with their large "resolution boxes," the region in space within which multiple objects cannot be separately identified and appear to be a single object. "Hundreds of missiles coming in from one direction would be seen as one missile," he noted. The radar reports would be all the more confused since modern ICBMs can carry not only live warheads, but also large numbers of decoys as well as reflective "chaff" intended to confuse the early warning radars. U.S. missile experts estimate that the actual warheads could thus be hidden in among one or two hundred thousand other small objects thrown out into space by current Soviet missiles.

More modern radars have been added to the early warning system in the past few years. They are COBRA DANE at Shemya Island, Alaska, PAVE PAWS West at Beale Air Force Base, California, and PAVE PAWS East at Otis Air Force Station on Cape Cod, Massachusetts. These AN/FPS-115 radars were all designed and built by Raytheon in the late 1970s and use the same technology. The beam they emit scans rapidly from one part of the sky to another—out to more than three thousand miles—but these radars have no moving parts. Their beams are controlled entirely by phased electronic signals. (PAWS is the acronym for Phased Array Warning System.) As sophisticated as these new radars are, they still have serious limitations in providing detailed attack assessments. "At low rates of fire, they do a good job, but there is a problem of saturation," one NORAD specialist told me. "They can't track everything at once. It is extremely difficult to arrive at any decent count of warheads."

COBRA DANE's main function is to monitor Soviet ICBM tests, although it is also part of the early warning system. The PAVE PAWS sites on the two coasts are primarily intended to look for submarine-launched missiles, but they also track objects in space and are a backup to Thule, Fylingdales Moor, and Clear for detecting ICBM warheads. The PAVE PAWS radars also have the capability to detect long-range Soviet submarine-launched missiles that might come from areas not monitored on a continuous basis by the early warning satellites. (Satellites in geosynchronous orbit cannot see all the way to the North and South Poles; they can detect launches well up into the Arctic and Antarctic Circles, but not much beyond about eighty degrees north and south latitude.)

When I visited PAVE PAWS East I was impressed with the advances that have been made in radar technology, but reminded as well of the persistent danger of sabotage at all the early warning stations. The site on Cape Cod consists of a few acres atop a hill on the old Otis Air Force Base. Except for the area immediately adjacent to the radar building and its power station, which are inside a security fence, the several square miles around the installation are referred to by the

Air Force as a "semi-secure" military reservation. This means that there are signs forbidding access, but no routine security patrols or physical means of keeping out intruders—a situation well known to local motorcycle enthusiasts who make free use of the trails running through the base.

Saboteurs planning an attack on PAVE PAWS East would be aided by the fact that very little about the equipment installed there is classified, since radar technology is so widely used commercially. Even cursory study of the facility reveals that the diesel generator building, which is its vital on-site power supply, and the water tower, which provides necessary cooling for the thousands of transmitter/receiver boxes connected to its stationary antennas, are obvious, highly exposed targets. The attackers would face no more than a small number of guards and would not need to get within the security perimeter to launch the few mortar shells that could disable the key components of the station.

Still, at "H Hour" on October 24, 1983, it would have been unnecessary for the Soviets to have gone to any trouble to knock out PAVE PAWS East. The red light at the NORAD Missile Warning Center reported that it was not operating. No one need have done anything, either, to destroy or disable COBRA DANE in Alaska. Another red light. Of the three phased-array radars, only PAVE PAWS West was reported to be operating normally. Air Force officials at Otis declined to say why PAVE PAWS East was not operating, but NORAD later said that it was out of service for scheduled radar maintenance. COBRA DANE was down for scheduled maintenance on its computers.

The Soviets can readily monitor the radars by various means, such as reconnaissance aircraft or floating electronic intelligence-gathering stations that masquerade as fishing vessels. Accordingly, in executing a surprise attack, they would be able to take advantage of any holes in the early warning fence that were created by nonfunctioning radars. On the other hand, if a major U.S.-Soviet crisis had already occurred, one that threatened a possible nuclear confrontation, maintenance could be delayed and other steps taken to try to close any gaps in the warning system. "A lot of problems go away when the system is on alert," a former Pentagon official said. Another official cautioned, however, that there was also the strong chance that other deficiencies, not now apparent, could surface when the apparatus reporting to

NORAD was put under major stress. After all, there will never be any comprehensive testing of the warning system's strengths and weaknesses until the first Soviet missile salvos are launched against the United States.

————

What, if any, data were received from what, if any, early warning sensors were functioning at H Hour are supposed to be processed and evaluated quickly. "All that information comes in to NORAD," General Richard Ellis explained. "It's ground up in their computer programs and presented to them in a matter of minutes, in some cases seconds, as fused information, which indicates to the commander out there that such and such is happening. All one can do is hope that the software"—the complex operating instructions that tell computers what to do—"isn't faulty, or the hardware isn't spooky, or the person is not making a hasty judgment. Things can go wrong."

The type of computer problem that can arise was illustrated in the early morning hours of June 3, 1980, when a component in the complex NORAD computer system suddenly malfunctioned and sent a message to Strategic Air Command Headquarters. The emergency message indicated that two Soviet submarine-launched missiles had been fired at the United States. Eighteen seconds later, the NORAD system declared that further submarine-launched missiles were on their way. SAC B-52 bomber crews went racing to their alert aircraft, started the engines, and prepared to take off. The warning message, however, vanished from the SAC display screen as quickly as it had appeared. SAC Headquarters called NORAD, which reported that none of the early warning satellites or radars had detected any missiles. The bomber crews shut down their engines, but remained in their aircraft.

Then, right after getting the NORAD all-clear, SAC was alerted once again by the errant system at NORAD that a massive Soviet ICBM attack had been initiated. To complicate matters further, NORAD sent the Pentagon a different message: that submarine-launched missiles had just been fired against the country. Unlike television stations, which take the precaution of having monitors to show what they are broadcasting, NORAD had no display that let officials in the Cheyenne Mountain Complex see the messages they were sending out. This contributed to the confusion in assessing what was happening.

NORAD subsequently attributed the false alert to a defective forty-six-cent computer chip that was manufactured in Taiwan and installed in 1975 in a communications multiplexer, a device that transmits messages from NORAD's main computers to the rest of the defense establishment. "The chip was on a communications board that essentially talks to AT&T," an expert on the NORAD computer system explained. "You could practically go down to Radio Shack and buy one. It was not some exotic chip." The chip itself was not at fault, NORAD stated, but "the trouble was isolated to the grounding circuitry." The circuit board, which was designed by Ford Aerospace, the "civilian integration contractor" for the NORAD computer system, "was checked on a periodic basis by the 47th Communications Group in the Cheyenne Mountain Complex," officials added. NORAD did not explain why the defective design had not been detected during the design review process, or why the testing of the equipment had not revealed the fault.

Computer experts regard NORAD's explanation of the false alert with suspicion. "Computer technology is sufficient that [component] failures can either be identified by the computer itself or identified and compensated for so that operations continue," a government computer specialist said. One official involved in the investigation of the June 1980 mishap said that the chip merely "surfaced" a deeper problem in the NORAD computer system. This was the fundamental blunder in the design of the communications computer, which lacked an adequate error-checking capability. For the same reason that publishers have proofreaders, the communications computer was supposed to have a routine method to make sure that the messages it broadcast were consistent with the data it had received. The checking methods were very superficial, the official said. "It was a sophomoric mistake," another computer expert commented, emphasizing that the required procedures for error detection were well known and widely used in commercial computer systems. Lieutenant General Hillsman, the former head of the Defense Communications Agency, commented on the false alert, "Everybody would have told you it was technically impossible."

Major General Winston Powers, the current Director of the Defense Communications Agency, came to his post from NORAD, where he had been assigned the job of trying to improve its computer system. At a 1981 symposium, another expert asked him whether NORAD had "ever done an exercise on how a Soviet agent in your organization could louse up the warning system." General Powers said no but added that "there's times I thought we've had about forty or fifty of those guys in the mountain."

For several years before the June 1980 incident—one of a number of false alerts that have occurred—the flaws in the NORAD computers had been extensively documented in in-house studies and in reviews by outside contractors. NORAD consultants, such as the MITRE Corporation, had described the "intolerable situation" created by the frequency and duration of NORAD computer failures. They had pointed to problems ranging from the computers' inability to keep an accurate count of incoming warheads to their potential inability to operate at all due to the lack of a dependable power supply. The Cheyenne Mountain Complex depended on commercial electric power, the reports noted, and while it did have backup diesel generators, it lacked adequate means to protect its computers from the kind of brief power outages that can raise havoc with computer performance. One report by the Congressional General Accounting Office noted that power failures lasting less than half a second could lead to "catastrophic damage to data files vital to NORAD's mission performance. . . . Minor fluctuations in the power supply could disconnect computer-related equipment from the central processing unit with a corresponding loss or alteration of data and information. Some of this data cannot be reconstructed because it is the original data received from [early warning] sensors."

A 1978 study by a blue-ribbon panel found that NORAD "suffers frequent power interruptions due to electrical storm activity in Colorado." It is ironic, a GAO auditor told me, that the utility company supplying NORAD with electricity kept its own accounts-receivable file in a computer that had an independent power source. If lightning— or a saboteur—struck a power line in the region, NORAD's computers might fail but the company's customers would still get their bills. A 1982 report by the Committee on Government Operations of the House of Representatives noted that NORAD had ignored the repeated warnings about the undependability of its power supplies. The Air Force Finance Center, the Congressional panel observed, had an "uninterruptible power supply" but NORAD still did not. "The Air Force would seem to have its priorities reversed when it ensures continued operations of its payroll system, but not the critical attack warning system at NORAD," the Congressmen observed. NORAD is working to correct its power supply problem, a GAO auditor said, but "whether they'll be successful is another question."

Even with uninterruptible power, NORAD would still have fundamental computer problems. These derive from the decision in 1970 to install—over NORAD's protest—the Honeywell 6000 series computer, a machine that NORAD believed to be ill suited to its particular data-processing requirements. The Department of Defense had decided to make a bulk purchase of thirty-five Honeywell computers and to use them as the basic equipment for the Worldwide Military Command and Control System; the Pentagon dismissed the protest from NORAD's Commander in Chief at the time, General Seth McKee, that it was the wrong equipment for his organization's purposes. It also dismissed a report from the General Accounting Office that the computers were being purchased and installed with little advance planning for how they would meet any of the military's data-processing needs. Congressman Jack Brooks of Texas, who has criticized the Pentagon's management of computer systems, called "the combination of NORAD and WWMCCS" a "shotgun marriage ordered by the Joint Chiefs of Staff." One senior Pentagon consultant said that the purchase of the Honeywell equipment was "one of the stupidest decisions DOD ever made."

The problem is not that the Honeywell machine is an inherently bad computer; it is the mismatching of its features with NORAD's data-processing requirements. The basic technical characteristic of the Honeywell system is that it is a "batch processor" that takes information and handles it in a predetermined, step-by-step sequence. NORAD, in contrast, needs to operate in what it calls a "real-time environment"— to get immediate access to key data and to keep up with rapidly changing events. If one imagines a plodding student whose only idea of how to look up a word in the dictionary is to begin on page one and keep on searching, then the problems with sequential processing will be apparent.

"If the student had a dictionary with tabs on it, and could go to tab such and such, then that would speed things up," a government computer expert explained. "He could 'batch process' from there. The

tabbed approach, and the 'direct accessing' philosophy, is the way the
modern computer system should work." Unfortunately, he explained,
the manufacturers of large computers in the 1960s were mostly oriented
toward batch processing—the IBM 360 computers installed at the
Nurrungar ground station are also of this type—although there were
companies, including Honeywell, that offered machines with direct
access. However, as one GAO report noted, the Pentagon, without
systematically evaluating the needs of its computer users or the advantages of the various technologies that were available, "fell into the trap"
of batch processing "with horrendous results." In 1974, the Pentagon
responded to the problems NORAD was having with its new Honeywell 6000 computer by giving it another Honeywell 6000 computer.

To overcome the kind of "traffic jams" that can occur inside its
computers when they are given large assignments—such as tracking
thousands of warheads coming at the United States—NORAD developed elaborate operating procedures to make the machines perform
more nimbly. It was like trying to turn a bus into a sports car, and the
success was only partial. NORAD also tried to patch together supple-
mentary computers and data-handling machines to alleviate the Honeywell computer's limitations. The Air Force Inspector General concluded
in a 1980 report that the new system, which was years late and two
hundred to three hundred percent over budget, had only "marginal
performance" and must be considered "an unsuccessful acquisition,"
adding, "In the final analysis, the overriding criterion for determining
the success of a program is whether the final product meets the needs
of the user."

The net result of NORAD's computer development effort has been
to create for the 1980s a clumsy computer system that, when it works,
just about matches the capabilities of the 1960s equipment that was
supposed to be replaced. According to a series of reports prepared over
the last decade by the General Accounting Office, the new equipment
is slow, unreliable, and essentially incapable of performing the NORAD
mission. The Congressional auditing agency has recommended the
"abrupt replacement" of the current computers, but that will not happen
anytime soon.

The Department of Defense has for years steadfastly resisted the
GAO recommendations on the WWMCCS computer system. Assistant
Secretary of Defense Gerald Dinneen said in a November 1979 letter

to the Congressional auditing agency that the Honeywell computer system "is viewed by the operational community as a major success." A few months later, however, the Department of Defense's own survey of system users concluded that these automatic data-processing machines were "not viewed as adequate or responsive to user needs" and that the "information retrieval capabilities of the Honeywell-based system are clearly not up to the state of the art, nor is system reliability viewed as satisfactory." Dr. Dinneen, who is now a vice president of Honeywell, said in a subsequent interview that he thought the computers had been given "a bum rap."

GAO officials maintain that despite some "tweaking" and "minor upgrades" of the Honeywell computer system, NORAD's ability to assess a major missile crisis in the brief time allotted remains doubtful. "The computers couldn't keep up with a mass attack," an exasperated GAO official told me. "No way. They would be overloaded. A variety of things can happen. Most likely, you'd just lose data. If they were trying to track a dozen warheads, they might only get data on three or four. They cannot predict the impact points very accurately. Was Chicago being attacked? They couldn't say."

Even with faster computers, NORAD would have very little ability to determine where incoming warheads will land: the data needed to make such estimations would not be available. The early warning satellites, for example, are incapable of providing useful information about warhead trajectories. Once the brief powered portion of a missile's flight is over—and this takes only three to four minutes—there are no longer strong infrared signals for the satellites to use to track the warhead trajectories. There will be an eerie intermission at NORAD in the six or seven minutes between the apparent detection of ICBM launches and the time the warheads are supposed to be picked up by the early warning radars. The radars, and NORAD itself, have computers that are programmed to try to calculate the likely targets, but they cannot do this with any precision in the short time available—and they can't do it at all, of course, if the radar sites are destroyed or the equipment happens to be down for maintenance when the attack takes place.

Assuming the radars were operating, one expert said, "we would have reasonable confidence in knowing—plus or minus seventy-five percent—how many weapons were launched. We'd know we were the country under attack. We'd know who launched the attack. We'd have moderate confidence which third of the U.S. was being attacked." Other experts think the error band may be much less than seventy-five percent, although they all say that how accurate a count of incoming warheads can be made is extremely "scenario-dependent"—that is, it has much to do with the assumptions made about the precise nature of the attack, the reliability of the sensors, and the extent and effectiveness of Soviet measures to confuse, jam, or silence the radars.

There is one additional radar that, in principle, could provide NORAD with more detailed data about the number of incoming warheads and the parts of the United States that were at risk, although it is not one of the forward-based radars installed as part of the early warning system. This radar is a leftover piece of equipment from the anti-ballistic missile installation that was built in the late 1960s at Concrete, North Dakota. (The rest of the facility, intended to shoot incoming warheads out of the sky, was shut down in 1974, after the Pentagon finally conceded that this was not technically feasible with the equipment available at the time.) Known as the Enhanced Perimeter Acquisition Radar Characterization System (EPARCS), it has a range of twenty-five hundred miles. It will therefore not see Soviet warheads and start to determine their precise trajectories until the final leg of their intercontinental flight. It can pick them up about twenty minutes after launch—ten minutes before impact.

The EPARCS radar was operating at "H Hour," according to a green light in the Missile Warning Center. However, it would not be very likely to see any Soviet ICBM warheads. As part of an attack on key sensor stations, the Soviets would be likely to knock out EPARCS with missiles launched from submarines off the coast. They could hit Concrete, North Dakota, about fifteen minutes after H Hour—which would be just before the ICBM warheads came into range of the radar there. Since EPARCS can be destroyed in such an attack, the experts do not expect it can be counted on to provide much help to NORAD in coming up with a detailed attack assessment.

Although it is heavily dependent on computers, NORAD wants a large element of human involvement in its decision-making process. Thus, within a minute of sending a missile alert to Cheyenne Mountain, the duty officer at the sensor site transmitting this information is required to provide a follow-up "confidence assessment" report. Radar operators, that is, would check with maintenance personnel to determine whether any equipment malfunctions might be responsible for the alert. The technicians, in sixty seconds, cannot make a thorough check of the equipment; they must consult computers that monitor the status of the system and are supposed to report any faults. Hence, although some degree of judgment and cross-checking may be involved, the humans in the process may be unable to do anything more than relay assurances from various computers that other computers and machines are working properly.

The radar operators' exercise of independent judgment would be further constrained by the fact that none had ever witnessed a large-scale missile launch—and the first person to do so cannot spend very much time pondering what may be on the scope. "What you've got out there is some young fellow with a couple of years of training who is looking at a phenomenon he may never have seen before and making his judgment on what it is," General Ellis said. "At that end it's an iffy business." The spurious missile alerts that have occurred—such as the time the Thule radar, shortly after going into operation, mistook the rising of the moon for a large missile attack—reinforce that impression.

Back at NORAD, officials in the Missile Warning Center will be consulting with the rest of the NORAD staff to determine if something other than a missile launch could account for the alert. They will talk, for example, to the staff in the neighboring room, the Space Surveillance Center, who keep track of all the objects orbiting the earth— which, at "H Hour," included some five thousand and twenty-six items. These ranged from operating U.S. and Soviet satellites to various pieces of "space junk," such as old rocket boosters and defunct satellites that had not yet fallen back to earth or burned up in the upper atmosphere. A key reason for keeping tabs on these objects is that one of them returning to earth could otherwise be picked up by the early warning sensors and mistaken for Soviet missiles—which happened, for example, on October 3, 1979. The computers in the Space Surveillance Center are not tied in to the computers in the Missile Warning Center; the cross-checking between the two staffs has to be done verbally. Indeed, despite the dozens of computers at NORAD, an actual missile alert involves a lot of people talking to each other on the telephone and running around with messages. One wall of the Missile Warning Center has a large map of the United States covered in plastic.

"The map is up there in case it all breaks and we have to use a grease pencil," Major Robert Walden, a member of the staff, commented.

Whatever data and analyses NORAD computers and personnel produce would go promptly to the main Command Post, where the NORAD Commander in Chief would make his assessment of whether a Soviet attack was taking place. A framed cartoon next to the staircase leading up to the battle station shows General Hartinger with both thumbs pointing down, the caption reading "A no, is a no, is a no." A secondary caption reads, "And . . . a yes, is a yes, is a yes." General Hartinger recently told the *New York Times*, "I have confidence in the integrity of our sensor systems, our computers, our people, our operational procedures, and consequently am 100 percent confident in my assessments."

The principal basis for CINCNORAD's judgment would be the reports received from the early warning system. The small number of sensors, their susceptibility to sabotage, direct attack, or jamming, and the vulnerability of the communications lines back to NORAD make it improbable that NORAD would have a very complete picture of an attack in progress. Just as a surgeon makes sure to have a preparatory anesthetic given to the patient, Soviet strategists would obviously wish to cut or dull the nerve endings that feed information back to the brain center inside Cheyenne Mountain. Any such Soviet precautions would have been aided by the fact that only two of the six principal radars that warn of ICBM attacks were operating normally at "H Hour."

Hollywood dramatizations typically show the NORAD operations center inundated with data after a Soviet missile attack. The screens light up with data. Maps are all aglow. Missile trajectories are plotted showing how deeply the strike will penetrate into U.S. territory. Instead of information overload, though, CINCNORAD's actual problem may be information deprivation. Even if NORAD's computers work reliably and correctly evaluate the data they receive—an assumption that may be overgenerous—these machines cannot perform magic. The computers have no way to compensate for critical satellite or radar data that are simply missing. Nor can any mathematical tricks convert highly uncertain information—such as reports from the older radars that may be unable to distinguish one missile from a hundred—into an unambiguous picture of an attack in progress.

CINCNORAD might conclude from the partial information available to him, and from such factors as the sudden loss or apparent jamming of certain sensors, that something was up. Still, like General Grant whittling by his tent and listening to vague and contradictory reports from the front, he would be hard pressed to say what was really happening. The NORAD commander might have no definitive evidence of whether an all-out attack or a more limited strike was taking place. Any shrewd aggressor would wish to create as much confusion as possible. Striking all the early warning sites at once—which may be infeasible anyway—would be too obvious a tipoff that a major assault was planned. Instead, the aggressor might make a selective attack on certain sensors and a limited missile launch as a first move. Having disabled certain parts of the command system and key U.S. military installations with this attack, the enemy could then quickly follow up with a broader offensive.

A submarine-missile attack against Washington, for example, might be timed to coincide with sabotage against only a few sensor sites, such as PAVE PAWS East and the ground connections for DSP West. If this happened, most of the sensors—DSP East and the other early warning radars—would be telling NORAD that all was calm. This reassuring information might prompt officials, at least initially, to regard malfunctions at Buckley and at the Otis radar installation as routine trouble rather than as signs of an assault in progress. If NORAD maintained this illusion for as little as five minutes, the Pentagon and the White House would be destroyed before retaliatory orders could be given.

"Even in an ordinary war, you learn to discount the first report, only give partial credence to the second report, and only believe it when you hear it the third time," a senior U.S. commander told me. "The chances for misappreciation of information, for communications foulups, for human errors are enormous. Even in tactical exercises—with people not under emotional stress—in hot washups after the exercise, that is, in sessions immediately after the exercise while things are fresh in people's minds, when you analyze what happened, I've never seen a commander who was not surprised by what had actually happened versus what he thought had happened."

"[P]eople have not yet learned how to deal with the possible fragility and ambiguities of these systems when they are under stress or attack," Charles Zraket of the MITRE Corporation told his colleagues at a 1983 symposium on command-system problems. As an example of the kind of information-system breakdown that can occur, he cited the command and control failures during the Three Mile Island accident.

During this March 1979 episode, the worst in the history of the commercial nuclear power industry, confusion about what was happening affected everyone from the operators in the plant's control room to the federal nuclear-safety officials in Washington who were trying to decide whether to evacuate the Harrisburg, Pennsylvania, area. Sensors and important communications lines failed repeatedly—and unexpectedly. The operators in the control room were unaware for hours that a critical valve had stuck open and was draining the vital cooling water out of the reactor. (A special red light that was supposed to warn them of this situation, it was discovered later, was not directly connected to the valve.) Federal officials sent to the plant found themselves, owing to a lack of telephones, unable to report their findings to Washington.

On March 31, 1979, when Joseph Hendrie, the Chairman of the Nuclear Regulatory Commission, was preparing to speak to Richard Thornburg, the Governor of Pennsylvania, about evacuating the area, he remarked to fellow officials, "His information is ambiguous, mine is nonexistent and—I don't know, it's like a couple of blind men staggering around making decisions." A few minutes after H Hour, facing a similarly bewildering lack of information, CINCNORAD could well have a correspondingly candid conversation with the President of the United States—assuming, that is, that NORAD had a working communications hookup with the White House or wherever the President happened to be.

———

How well the NORAD staff and the civilian decision-makers are prepared to respond to the confusion and appalling uncertainty that may accompany an actual or apparent attack is difficult to determine. "Our people don't shock very easy because they are so trained and disciplined on the crews that they have certain steps that they must perform, and they don't sit around and think about how many babies are going to die if they do something wrong," Brigadier General Wagoner said.

"They may do that on a coffee break, but when they're back sitting at the consoles and an event happens, it is just like an orchestra when the conductor says go, and they all have their individual acts to perform."

Others take a less optimistic view of how smoothly the attack assessment and decision-making process will go. The NORAD staff has been trained to handle a range of contingencies, but there is no guarantee that all eventualities have been covered in their drills and rehearsals. CINCNORAD, as their conductor, may say go, but if a gust of unexpected developments blows their scores away, who can predict what will happen?

Moreover, as Richard DeLauer, the Under Secretary of Defense for Research and Engineering, has noted, the civilian officials' preparation for their roles is less than impressive. "One of the things we have discussed over the years is the difficulty of getting the President even to sit down to practice," he said. "I guess President Carter was the first President ever to visit the National Command Post and sit down where he was supposed to sit and at least be briefed on what it all means. President Nixon never did, Johnson never did, and some of the security advisers, like Kissinger, never went down there." One of the reasons for the difficulties experienced in various military communications exercises, a retired Air Force officer told me, has been the participants' unfamiliarity both with their roles and with each other. He said, "Think of a basketball team made up of people who'd never played together before."

The President and his advisers are likely to be quite confused about the various courses of action available to them after a Soviet attack—a problem that is worsened, not mitigated, by the briefing book supposedly prepared to assist in this situation. Officials familiar with it say that the seventy-five pages in "the black book" present the President with an extremely complex, and virtually incomprehensible, set of choices. A senior officer who has worked on the option book said, "No one who had not done an enormously thorough study of it and refreshed himself periodically could possibly understand what he was doing." Bill Gulley, the former Director of the White House Military Office, which safeguards "the Football," noted that there is "a kind of mythology" that suggests that it is an "ever-ready Answer Box" that tells the President what to do. "The truth is that it raises as many questions as it answers.

"No new President in my time ever had more than one briefing on the contents of the Football, and that was before each one took office, when it was one briefing among dozens," Gulley noted. "Not one President, to my knowledge, and I know because it was in my care, ever got an update on the contents of the Football, although material in it is changed constantly. Not one President could open the Football —only the warrant officers, the military aides, and the director of the Military Office have the combination."

The President's potential difficulties in overseeing the execution of the U.S. war plan were candidly discussed at a 1981 conference at the Bedford, Massachusetts, headquarters of the MITRE Corporation. One of the speakers was retired Lieutenant General Brent Scowcroft, the former White House National Security Adviser who headed President Reagan's Commission on Strategic Forces. Some of his observations were "too hot" to be included in the published transcript of the MITRE conference, one of the attendees said, but his talk, as it happened, was also recorded on videotape. In remarks omitted from the official minutes of the get-together, General Scowcroft commented, "The President is a very powerful, in some sense, but a very lonely man. He is, perhaps, more isolated than any other senior official in Washington. He doesn't have, with the exception of his relatively small NSC [National Security Council] staff, he does not have at his beck and call, at his physical beck and call, the expertise to deal with the problems he would have to deal with in a strategic nuclear conflict."

Scowcroft continued, "Presidents normally, and I hope this one will be an exception, are reluctant to face up to this part of their responsibilities in the sense of being willing to participate in exercises, in discussions, and so on, about how the [nuclear command and control] system would work. It's been my experience that the first couple of days there's a kind of a feeling of stark terror when, all of a sudden, they realize, you know, this is all theirs and they're the ones that have to make the decision. But then, as they get into it, it's inherently distasteful to look at, to think about, it's always something that can be done tomorrow rather than today. And their staffs are always saying, 'Look, you know, if you start exercising these things, if you start having helicopters come in, and you start doing all these things, you're going to panic the people. They're gonna think a war will start, and let's just not do it.' So there's a great deal of inertia to overcome for the President to get involved in [such] a way that you can uncover possible glitches in the system which don't appear to be there."

One of the constraints on the President's understanding of the S.I.O.P., a former White House official said, "stems from the earlier days when the military perceived the attack option as their responsibility, and they weren't interested in anybody else becoming an expert." The President's only role if an attack came was "to say yes or no" to what the military proposed to do in response. This has changed considerably in recent years, although the last few Presidents have differed in the extent of their efforts to understand, and specify, the contents of the U.S. war plan. A former Pentagon official said that Richard Nixon was "the great neglector" of this subject while Jimmy Carter "had an almost morbid" interest in it and spent considerable time trying to master the intricacies of the S.I.O.P. Carter volunteered to sit down with his successor to discuss the subject, but his offer was rebuffed by President Reagan. The White House declined to say how often President Reagan has been briefed on the S.I.O.P. or what other steps have been taken to make sure that he understands the options it contains.

"War games" are one way to familiarize civilian officials with the decisions they might have to make in a crisis. These exercises, which can involve scores of people and go on for days, pit a "U.S. team" against a "Soviet team" and allow officials to vie against each other to see who can gain maximum advantage in a hypothetical confrontation. Elaborate war games have been held in recent years, Pentagon officials say, and very high-level Administration officials have participated. Each exercise focuses on a set of postulated events—for example, that there is an uprising in Czechoslovakia, a dispute on the German border, and a war between NATO and the Warsaw Pact which leads to the question of whether to use nuclear weapons. Other scenarios have also been explored in which U.S. leaders had to face such questions as whether to launch Minuteman missiles in response to a direct Soviet attack.

In most of the recent exercises, someone else has stood in for President Reagan, but Mr. Reagan has also participated himself. He did not, however, according to Pentagon evaluation reports, appear to grasp the complexities that were involved. "I was disappointed in the simple credulity he showed, his willingness to play it at the most superficial level," a Pentagon aide told me. "Carter was more careful. He'd make a decision, but not tell anyone what it was, except perhaps Harold

Brown [the Secretary of Defense]. He'd just say, 'I've made my decision.' He didn't want the whole system to be anticipating the President. On the other hand, Reagan has spent very little time at it. He acted like an automaton, like part of the set instead of the main actor. Reagan was saying things like, 'What do I do now? Do I push this button?' He was not very probing. Some fresh-faced Colonel says something—'Mr. President, you have to do such and such in seven minutes'—but there were no questions from Reagan."

The other senior officials with whom the President would be most likely to consult in a crisis are probably no better able to ask the right questions than he is. The Secretary of State, for example, probably knows less about the S.I.O.P. options than the President does, a senior official said, adding that Secretary of Defense Caspar Weinberger was also unlikely to be of much assistance in sorting through the complexities of the black book. "Weinberger looks at his job like a college president. He doesn't see himself as running the intellectual side of the Pentagon. His job is raising money. He's unlike Harold Brown, a physicist, a technician. Weinberger and Reagan together—there's no knowledge to share."

While the White House has refused to comment on the steps that have been taken to try to acquaint the President with what he may have to do to manage a potential nuclear confrontation, the President's statements on some of the most elementary aspects of strategic affairs are not indicative of any detailed familiarity with the subject. Thus, although a Reagan campaign theme in the 1980 elections was the "window of vulnerability," there was an embarrassed moment in an October 1981 press conference when the President was called upon to define what this term meant. He was unable to do so. Two more years in office did not appear to have remedied this uneasiness with the general subject. The *New York Times* reported in October 1983 that "the President told a group of Congressmen that he had not realized until recently that most of the Soviet Union's nuclear defenses were concentrated in its system of heavy land-based missiles." The President acknowledged, the article said, that he now understood why his demands that the Soviets dismantle these missiles may have been seen by them as unfair without correspondingly large concessions by the United States. The report continued, "Several listeners said afterward that . . .

they were flabbergasted at his comment and wondered whether Mr. Reagan was being sufficiently briefed on critical issues."

I spoke with a senior adviser to President Reagan who was intimately familiar with the circumstances leading to his statement on Soviet land-based missiles. He agreed that the President was not being adequately briefed but explained, "Look, this President, unlike Jimmy Carter, who in a sense was too interested in details, is not interested in details. He's not really much interested in this whole [nuclear weapons] business, and so he tends not to retain it, tends not to be very accessible for details."

In a developing crisis, this White House adviser continued, there would be time to acquaint the President with the necessary information, although the tutorial process would obviously work less well in a surprise attack. One can only hope that before catastrophic blunders are made, someone will remember to correct such potentially critical misunderstandings as the President's erroneous impression—according to a statement of his in May 1982—that missiles carried by nuclear submarines were "a conventional type of weapon" that "can be recalled."

The time constraints on decision-makers following an actual or apparent Soviet attack will be particularly severe. For one thing, U.S. officials must take into account the problem known as pindown. Soviet submarine-launched missiles off the U.S. coasts can lob warheads high into the sky above U.S. ICBM bases. All nuclear detonations produce, among other effects, massive bursts of X-rays. Possible "exoatmospheric" explosions high above the missile bases would therefore force the U.S. either to fire the Minuteman missiles quickly—in the fifteen minutes or so before submarine-launched warheads arrived over the Minuteman bases in the Midwest—or to keep the missiles inside their protective silos. Otherwise, the heat from the X-rays could destroy the exposed missiles as they headed off toward their targets.

Richard Garwin explained the basic problem of X-ray pindown in his study of the complications of launching under attack: "Multiple high-altitude nuclear explosions produce repeated bursts of X-rays (the thermal radiation from the exploding nuclear weapon at some 10 million degrees temperature), which can reliably damage not only the electronics of the ICBMs during boost phase but also the structure.

The latter comes about because the X-rays suddenly heat and vaporize the surface . . . of the booster, sending a high-pressure shock wave into the interior . . . leading to buckling and structural failure." Relatively small numbers of Soviet submarine-launched missiles could effectively suppress the launching of the Minuteman force, according to Garwin's calculations, if the Minuteman missiles were not fired quickly.

Moreover, if the missiles were left in their silos, they could be destroyed by incoming Soviet SS-18s. Thus, there may be only a very narrow "window of opportunity" during which the missiles can be launched after a Soviet attack is detected. There may be no more than five minutes between the confirmation of the attack by the early warning radars and the deadline for firing the missiles. (If the radars are down for maintenance, jammed, or destroyed, only the satellite early warning data will be available, assuming that those sensors and their communications links are working.) The resolution of all confusions and uncertainties about what is happening, the answering of all requests for reconfirmations of data, the presentation and analysis of all options, the issuing of orders to the forces—everything that needs to be done to execute a Minuteman launch must take place in a period of minutes.

Another major time constraint is that the Cheyenne Mountain Complex itself has a life expectancy in a major nuclear war that is no longer than the short flight time of a Soviet SS-18 missile to Colorado Springs. The facility is some twelve hundred to fourteen hundred feet below the peak of the eight-thousand-foot-high mountain, not underneath the entire mountain and shielded by its vast bulk. Although protected from sabotage—the principal reason for putting it in the side of the mountain—NORAD Headquarters is not hardened against the type of high-powered explosives that can now be deposited on top of it by Soviet missiles. The complex is not a safe haven that Air Force generals can use while they carry out extended deliberations on how best to orchestrate the nation's response to a major nuclear attack. CINCNORAD has a few minutes after H Hour to make an assessment and to tell the President and senior U.S. military leaders whatever he knows. After that, the Cheyenne Mountain Complex will no longer be his command post, but his grave. Those on the conference line with him, occupants of similarly vulnerable command posts, will share his predicament.

3

AD HOC-ERY

Before visiting NORAD, I attended a conference at the MITRE Corporation in Bedford, Massachusetts, and noticed an informal exhibit in a hallway. It was a handmade poster depicting the elements of the early warning system. The main caption said: "It hiccups but it works." Glued on below that was a grapefruit-size representation of the Western Hemisphere, made of Styrofoam. Fan-shaped wires were stuck in to indicate the areas covered by the various radars that report to NORAD. Onto this homely model someone had hung a sign: "Out of Order." As I saw at NORAD, this was not a joke. The director of one of the connectivity studies told me, "The early warning system is so primitive, so stupid, it is almost beyond belief."

Flaws in the present command and control system are not confined to the portion responsible for detecting incoming missiles. The apparatus relied upon to carry retaliatory orders has its own problems. The weaknesses at the back end of the command system are illustrated by the Navy's TACAMO aircraft. The acronym stands for "Take Charge and Move Out," and the aircraft in question are radio relay planes equipped with very low frequency (VLF) antennas that are supposed to convey orders from the President to the U.S. submarines on patrol.

95

The large land-based VLF antennas that normally broadcast orders to the submarine fleet are soft targets that could be destroyed at the outset of a nuclear attack. An airborne system was therefore established to provide "post-attack" communications.

The TACAMO planes are retrofitted C-130 transports stuffed with communications equipment. The planes, which were never designed as airborne radio stations, are grossly overweight, and several modifications have had to be made to permit them to carry all the heavy communications gear they need and still get into the air. "They thought they'd need pygmies to fly them," a Pentagon official said, explaining that the planes are barely able to lumber out to their patrol areas when, after an hour or so, they have to turn back to be refueled. He noted that the weight reductions made to get them aloft included taking off their bathroom doors, which caused problems when women crew members were on board, and although a curtain solved that difficulty, others remained. "On-station time is terrible, and dozens of planes have to be provided to keep a single one in the air at all times."

As a message-relay station, a TACAMO plane suffers from further limitations that compromise its basic mission. One problem has been that the plane has depended on a single antenna for both receiving and broadcasting messages. The lack of a "duplex antenna" has meant that the plane could jam itself—cut off incoming messages while it was broadcasting. The plane's worst limitation as a post-attack message-distribution center results from the fact that the single TACAMO plane over the Atlantic and its sister plane over the Pacific are rarely in an area where they can give a comprehensive order to all of the submarines on patrol. "It's never there when it's wanted, basically," Desmond Ball told me. Other experts confirmed this fact, and an Admiral commented, "The continuity of command from the President or Vice President to the transmitting stations for the submarines is not at all assured." The communications link with the submarines was as weak as what you would get if you put "a watch chain in connection with a battleship anchor cable."

The jury-rigged TACAMO communications planes, like the patched-together computer facility at NORAD, are evidence of the low priority assigned to strategic command and control programs needed to assure retaliation. The Pentagon belatedly acknowledges this, with Air Force General Robert Marsh referring to the evolution of the present command and control setup as a matter of "ad hoc-ery." The command and control network for the nation's nuclear deterrent evolved as a hodgepodge of command posts, early warning sensors, and communications hardware that was put together with little detailed thought about how the parts were supposed to form a coherent whole. As different technologies were invented, or as specific problems occurred, bits and pieces of equipment were simply grafted on to what in only a very loose sense can be referred to as a command and control "system."

"It was amazing," Rear Admiral Tomb said, describing his reaction when he went to SAC Headquarters and began to study how the command and control apparatus was organized. "There really wasn't a house plan to build the house. When I got to Nebraska in 1980, I couldn't find the plan." Major General Winston Powers had the same experience when he went to NORAD to investigate the computer problems leading to its false alerts. He said to the technical experts attending the 1981 MITRE Corporation conference on command and control, "I'll give you a dollar for every accurate interface control drawing you can find on the Ballistic Missile Early Warning System that goes back to 1960 and makes sense." Government auditors likewise discovered, when they tried to analyze the NORAD computer system, that the main contractor, Ford Aerospace, had never put together a systems manual on how the complex equipment all fit together. (This worked out to the company's advantage, the auditors noted, since it was impossible to give the maintenance contract for the system to anyone else since they wouldn't know where to begin.) One of the auditors told me that the "sad situation" with the computers at NORAD reflected the Air Force's tendency "to demand big new systems immediately, to overlook the need for front-end planning, and then to spend years trying to get themselves out of the mess they got themselves into."

He could just as well have been speaking of many other defense programs, or of various other human enterprises. The loose planning and informality in many undertakings is illustrated by a story that was told in 1966 when Jerome Wiesner was appointed Provost at the Massachusetts Institute of Technology. Some of his colleagues who were unfamiliar with this position asked, "What does a Provost do?" The answer was, "We don't know, but we decided to appoint Jerry and find out." The buildup of a large nuclear weapons arsenal in the United States, and the acquisition of a control system for it, have been carried out in a similar spirit. To understand the problems with strategic command and control, accordingly, it is helpful to look at a few of the larger technical, bureaucratic, and political influences on the overall U.S. nuclear weapons program.

———

Nuclear weapons, in a sense, just happened. They were not part of a preexisting military master plan. The scientists handed the new super-bombs to the Pentagon. The armed services had not asked for them and were actually somewhat confounded when they were invented. Indeed, the military's first reaction was one of fear—not so much dismay at the awesome power of "The Bomb," but concern that such extremely destructive weaponry could put them out of business: it might do away with the need for large conventional forces. General Curtis LeMay, who would later become head of the Strategic Air Command, referred to the atomic bomb in September 1945 as "the worst thing that ever happened to the Army Air Force."

The military quickly overcame its diffidence. It soon embraced the notion, advocated by Senator Edwin Johnson of Colorado, that with "vision and guts and plenty of A-bombs" the United States could "compel mankind to adopt the policy of peace . . . or be burned to a crisp." This was just rhetoric, though, not a precise plan that stipulated the kind of nuclear force that ought to be developed or the particular command and control system that would be needed for it. The military had barely begun to think about all the parctical questions when further technological developments overtook efforts at policy formulation. In 1952, the hydrogen bomb came along, which meant that bombs could be vastly more powerful than the original A-bombs. Nuclear submarines were then introduced in 1955, a novelty followed in 1957 by intercontinental ballistic missiles that could deliver H-bombs to the other side of the globe in under thirty minutes.

Thus, within little more than a decade after World War II, military thinking was required to shift from a framework in which hand-to-hand combat still mattered to one in which hostilities could be over and done with before soldiers on either side had time to fix bayonets. Moreover, after August 1949, when the Soviets tested their own atomic bomb, the U.S. military had to face a further anomaly: the prospect that no matter what it did, it would no longer be able to guarantee defense of the country against a nuclear-armed opponent. Inherited military tradition and experience would become obsolete in an era of nuclear stalemate, although this is not a situation that the military itself has been quick to recognize.

A major factor in the headlong expansion of the U.S. nuclear arsenal was the favorable economics of the new weapons. An initial investment of a few billion dollars was required to develop the designs for them and to build the production facilities that made the special raw material, enriched uranium and plutonium, that they used. Once this was done, bombs of immense destructive power could be mass-produced at essentially bargain prices. Compared with the cost of conventional weapons, and with the expense of maintaining a large standing army, they were decidedly cheap. Both the fiscally conservative Eisenhower Administration and U.S. allies in Europe, whose industrial plant had been badly damaged in World War II, were extremely gratified by the prospect of being able to offset the main Soviet military advantage— a large army—by relying on inexpensive nuclear weapons that could be deployed on the Continent by the thousands.

Had the manufacture of the new weapons involved a major burden for U.S. taxpayers, there might have been more restraint in the accumulation of a large nuclear arsenal. As it was, the United States found itself in somewhat the same situation as the British in the nineteenth century when, for nominal costs, that industrial power was able to churn out the weaponry that facilitated its domination of one colony after another. Historians have jested that the inexpensiveness of its colonial ventures permitted England to acquire an empire "in a fit of absence of mind."

"Absence of mind" may seem like too strong a phrase to characterize the U.S. acquisition and deployment of nuclear weapons, but there is a great deal of evidence in declassified material from the early 1950s and from other sources that suggests something less than careful planning. "I went overseas to England with the first tactical nuclear weapons unit deployed to Europe," General Richard Ellis recalled. "We had our weapons, we had our training, we knew how to deliver. We had state-of-the-art technology in delivery systems. We were ready —but we had no war plans. NATO didn't know what to do with the weapons when we got there." Since the United States enjoyed a tremendous lead over the Soviet Union in the 1950s and 1960s in the number of nuclear weapons, the Pentagon had the luxury of being able to defer thinking about some of the harder questions that would arise when the Soviets achieved a nuclear arsenal of comparable size.

With the rapid growth of the U.S. arsenal and the avalanche of continuing technological changes, it took the U.S. military and political leadership several years to appreciate the planning vacuum in which they were operating. U.S. nuclear weapons policies did develop, slowly and uncertainly, often shifting dramatically from one Administration to the next. Given the zigzag course of official thinking about nuclear strategy, it is little wonder that the acquisition of ancillary apparatus—such as a strategic command and control system—was a correspondingly disorderly process. The command and control system presumably ought to fit the prevailing nuclear weapons employment policy, but this was difficult to arrange when successive Administrations espoused very different policies on how U.S. nuclear weapons would be used if the country were forced to.

———

The announced U.S. nuclear weapons policies included: *(a)* Secretary of State John Foster Dulles's 1954 threat that the United States would use "massive retaliation" in response to Soviet aggression; *(b)* the concept of "flexible response" and "no-cities, counterforce" strikes, enunciated in 1962 by Secretary of Defense Robert McNamara, which meant that less than all-out nuclear rejoinders would be made to less than all-out Soviet attacks, and that the primary targets would be military forces and installations, not cities; *(c)* "mutual assured destruction," a revised McNamara policy, promulgated in 1965, that deemphasized strikes against military targets and said the United States would henceforth dissuade Soviet attacks with the threat that an "unacceptable" level of damage to Soviet cities and industry would result; *(d)* the policy of "limited nuclear options" adopted by the Nixon Administration, a return to the earlier McNamara counterforce doctrine of 1962; *(e)* the nuclear war-fighting strategy, embraced by the Carter and Reagan Administrations, based on the premise that it is possible to control escalation and use nuclear weapons to fight and "prevail" in a "protracted" nuclear war.

The markedly different official policies on the use of nuclear weapons reflected shifts in what the military refers to as "strategic doctrine" —a term whose religious connotations suggest the dominance of faith over reason in this branch of national policy-making. The current strategy of controlled escalation was adopted, to be sure, after innumerable studies by the last four Administrations. It is the end product of a debate over "limited nuclear war" that has been going on since the 1950s—an intellectual exercise that has sometimes had more resemblance to a debate over "how many angels can dance on the head of a pin" than to modern technical analysis. The much-ridiculed thirteenth-century Scholastic philosophers did not actually discuss this (it is a caricature of their work by later philosophers), but the churchmen came pretty close: they did argue about how many teeth horses had, without actually going out and counting them. The advocates of a limited nuclear war strategy have likewise shown little proclivity for going out and checking about mundane details—such as how the authorities on both sides are supposed to keep control of their nuclear forces in a conflict in which the control system itself could be one of the primary targets.

The civilian strategists who have championed the strategy of limited nuclear war—led by Henry Kissinger, Thomas Schelling, James Schlesinger, and the late Herman Kahn, among others—have been primarily concerned with the abstract issue of how to make threats to use nuclear weapons "credible" to the other side. Any major use of nuclear weapons invites nuclear retaliation on a comparable scale by the other side, making the actual large-scale use of nuclear weapons suicidal. The threat of full-scale retaliation may therefore not be believed. The small-scale use of nuclear weapons, in contrast, would not necessarily lead to total self-destruction—assuming that the other side also played by limited-war rules—and so the threat to apply U.S. nuclear forces in a gradual and controlled way was proposed as a more effective means to deter the Soviets from attacking U.S. vital interests around the globe. War could still be preserved as an instrument of U.S. policy, therefore, even in a confrontation with a nuclear-armed opponent. There are many subtleties in the arguments that have gone on about these points, so many that it has been said that "in the thermonuclear age military strategy begins to look like a game of chess without a chess board, that its mental construction and strategic anticipations are made in a world in which Kafka meets Lewis Carroll."

While the academicians and theoreticians who have developed the limited nuclear war doctrine may know their Clausewitz and their nineteenth-century history, they have not necessarily understood—and have sometimes arrogantly dismissed—what they categorize as the "technical details" of nuclear war-fighting. Paul Bracken, a Yale University political scientist with a background in engineering, is a former member of Herman Kahn's Hudson Institute, a leading think-tank which has worked for the Department of Defense and the defense industry. He is also the author of an important study, *The Command and Control of Nuclear Forces.* Bracken notes that "the extent to which the leading strategists are uninformed technically is shocking." One manifestation of this, he said, is the tendency of strategic planners to set goals with little attention to feasibility. The gap between the strategy of controlled escalation and the command and control system's present capability "is as far as from here to the planet Uranus," he said.

The military itself has little respect for the controlled-escalation notions of its would-be civilian mentors. A Pentagon technical expert who worked on the Reagan Administration's Nuclear Weapons Employment and Acquisition Master Plan said that professional military officers were universally skeptical of the "fancy" nuclear war-fighting ideas of the professors and consultants who have tried to impose their views on the Pentagon. In preparing the Master Plan, he said, the task force with which he worked attempted to implement a strategy outlined by Deputy Under Secretary of Defense Thomas K. Jones. He specified that the Pentagon should plan, among other things, to keep the command and control system running for six months after the start of a nuclear war. "We'd all sit in these windowless rooms, up the kazoo with classified information, just laughing at how crazy and hopeless it all was," this Pentagon analyst said. Problems such as keeping the intelligence system going for months after Soviet attack had to be solved, but it was clear that there was no technically feasible way to accomplish this. "I used to say that our surviving intelligence system amounted to Richard Pipes"—a former Harvard professor who served on the staff of the National Security Council—"out in a Toyota Corolla on the Blue Ridge Highway with a high frequency radio."

Even if the command and control apparatus were not targeted in the first Soviet salvos—if all sensors, computers, and communications lines remained functioning—there would still be insuperable technical problems in trying to implement a strategy of controlled escalation. As a participant in one of the connectivity studies observed, "The [civilian] strategy makers talk about flexible response and leave you with the impression that we have good attack characterization, but that's not really the case." If NORAD cannot be counted on to provide a reliable portrayal of the size of an incoming raid, he said, how can anyone possibly determine what a proportionate response would involve?

The Soviets, moreover, do not believe in controlled escalation. Their writings on nuclear strategy, according to most Western analysts who have studied them, emphasize massive attacks at the outset of nuclear war. This long-standing Soviet attitude is not the only impediment to keeping escalation under control. One technical problem is that they would have great difficulty distinguishing a "limited" U.S. strike against military targets in the USSR, such as their ICBM silos, from an all-out attack against their cities. Whereas the U.S. Minuteman bases in the Midwest, all of which are west of the Mississippi, are relatively far away from the nation's major cities, Soviet ICBM fields are located close to heavily populated areas, including Moscow. Unless the Soviets had very advanced computer capabilities—and this is an area in which they are notably behind the West—they would not know whether incoming U.S. warheads were heading toward their missile bases or their cities. Hence, if the United States wants to encourage the Soviets to stick to limited exchanges against military targets, does it have to donate new supercomputers to them to make sure they keep to the rules?

A further consequence of the siting of Soviet missile bases so close to their cities is that the radioactive fallout from an attack on these military targets would kill the nearby populations anyway. From a practical point of view, there may be no real distinction between a "counterforce" and a "countercity" attack on the USSR. This is true of the United States also, although advocates of the limited nuclear war strategy have tried to downplay the extent of the civilian casualties. Secretary of Defense James Schlesinger told Congress in 1974, for example, that only fifteen to twenty-five thousand people would die as a result of a Soviet attack on U.S. Minuteman bases. However, as the Pentagon subsequently had to admit, our missile bases may be farther away from major cities, but the prevailing winds would spread the lethal radioactive fallout for several hundred miles, far enough to cover many urban areas in the eastern half of the country even if the nominal targets were ICBM silos on the other side of the Mississippi. Tens of millions of people could be killed as a result of such a "limited" attack.

———

The physicist Richard Garwin, perhaps the nation's leading expert on the technical problems of nuclear war-fighting, explained that he thought that there was such a thing as limited nuclear war in a very minimal sense. One or both sides, that is, might make demonstration shots to send the "message" that they were seriously perturbed. The Soviets could destroy some military target—Pease Air Force Base in New Hampshire, say—and the United States could punish them for this by aiming a missile or two at some Soviet military installations or at something of major economic value, such as the giant Kama River truck factory near Naberezhnye Chelnyi. This is not a very good way of communicating, Garwin observed, and once the two nations got beyond such picayune and militarily pointless scrimmaging, the prospects for being able to fine-tune a real war were not very good.

"After there have been many, many nuclear explosions in the United States, it is, in my opinion, fantasy—even a greater fantasy than before war starts—to imagine that you're going to have a capability for conduct of limited nuclear war, of flexible response, or sizing up what has happened and using your weapons efficiently," Garwin said. "How can we have a good old protracted nuclear war if we can't get the information as to what's happening and can't command the forces, and so on?"

The most famous treatise on the subject of limited nuclear war, Herman Kahn's 1965 book, *On Escalation*, does not answer these questions. A theoretical physicist by training, Kahn provided no practical specifications for the kind of command-system apparatus needed to keep nuclear war under control. Instead, he simply denied that there were serious implications that could arise from poor communications. Kahn wrote that "there has been a systematic overestimation of the importance of the so-called 'fog of war'—the inevitable uncertainties, misinformation, disorganization, or even breakdown of organized units —that must be expected to influence central war operations." A command-system breakdown was possible, he conceded, but didn't really matter since "it may be possible to establish a certain capability to 'run a war' for the first day or so with little dependence on gathering and evaluating information. One of the greatest misconceptions current in discussions of command and control is a failure to understand how well a central war might be run, at least initially, by 'dead reckoning.' " Garwin comments that either side can start firing nuclear missiles without an elaborate command and control system, but how does it then "run" the ensuing war or, more important, end it?

With the civilian strategists' neglect of command-system requirements, and with the frequent changes in strategic doctrine that have occurred, the reasons for the chaos in the development of the present command system begin to emerge. Even when policy was relatively fixed, the high level of ambiguity caused serious problems in designing a command system capable of executing it. No one in the Eisenhower Administration specified, for example, what "massive" retaliation meant. A few months after his January 1954 speech, Dulles muddied the waters considerably in an article in *Foreign Affairs*. He suggested that he was actually prescribing a policy of "flexible retaliation" that included "massive retaliation" as one possibility. "It should not be stated in advance precisely what would be the scope of military action if new aggression occurred," he wrote. "That is a matter as to which the aggressor had best remain ignorant. But he can know and does know, in the light of present policies, that the choice in this respect is ours and not his."

Later civilian strategists, many of whom were economists, refined their favored nuclear weapons policies by using "game theory" and mathematical analyses of how rational individuals would optimize their gain or minimize their losses in a bargaining situation. "Mere prattle without practice is all his soldiership," Iago says in *Othello*, and that is pretty much how the military has regarded the refined notions of the academicians, Pentagon consultants, and Secretaries of Defense who have tried to shape official strategy on the use of nuclear weapons. The military takes a "this too shall pass" attitude toward these outsiders, and such patience has, by and large, been rewarded. People like Robert McNamara and James Schlesinger have come and gone; the Strategic Air Command and the Navy, with their outlooks unchanged, remain.

The military looks not to modern economic theory, civilian Pentagon officials, or academic experts for guidance but follows primitive traditions on what to do with whatever club or cannon or instrument of warfare technology makes available. It views nuclear weapons as blunt instruments that will be used for blunt purposes. Despite all the ephemeral policies advocated by self-appointed nuclear weapons strategists, the services have always had their own unabashedly crude operational doctrines on how nuclear weapons are to be used—although, as usual, given the rivalry between them, there is no single "military" point of view on this subject. Instead, each service advocates a nuclear weapons policy that is designed to justify the kind of weapons systems it has.

The basic Air Force attitude toward nuclear weapons was put forward in a 1955 policy statement of the Air Force Association, a lobbying group composed of former Air Force officers, which stated, "Massive retaliation, as a deterrent to war, as a hope for survival, is steadily becoming obsolete. There can be no practical retaliation after an all-out surprise attack with thermonuclear weapons, which destroys military bases simultaneously with centers of industry and population."

Instead, the Air Force position, as expressed by General Curtis LeMay in a top-secret briefing in 1954, was that "if the U.S. is pushed in the corner far enough we would not hesitate to strike first." When a member of a blue-ribbon Presidential panel pointed out to LeMay that preemptive attack was not official national policy, LeMay replied, "I don't care. It's my policy. That's what I'm going to do." In a 1968 book, LeMay insisted that military leaders like himself were "not prone to start wars." But politicians, he felt, were—he cited the "political miscalculations" growing out of Sarajevo—and the military had to be prepared, if a general nuclear war is initiated, to win it in the shortest possible time. "When I led the Strategic Air Command I operated on the premise that we should have some warning of enemy preparations to attack us," he wrote. "Toward this end we spent a great deal of our energies learning what the opposition was doing day to day. Believing I could foresee an attack, I was prepared to beat him to the draw and attack all of his bomber and missile bases. In accordance with the Joint Chiefs of Staff my purpose was to destroy his war-making capability, particularly in the strategic nuclear area."

The "possibility of preemption still seems to be in our strategic deck of cards," LeMay concluded, and indeed this is still the prevailing attitude within the Strategic Air Command today. "In a real situation, you don't compare going first to going second," a former Pentagon official said. "You compare going first with not going at all. If you're going to get into nuclear war, that's big time. When you go, go. Do it. Finish the job. Launching under attack just means that you've missed the moment."

"We have never as a matter of national policy accepted the notion of preemption," John Steinbruner said. "We have always as a matter of military realism planned to be able to do it. And that creates an inherent conflict between political authorities in Washington, if you will, and responsible military authorities down in the chain of command. It creates a conflict between our declaratory policies and our anticipated operational practice."

"For ever, really, the military planning concerning nuclear weapons has had almost nothing to do with declaratory doctrine," Barry Blechman, a former Carter Administration official, noted. There is "this basic disconnect" between the way the military thinks of nuclear weapons and the way the political leadership and the public think about them. "The military thinks of them as weapons, as they have to, and they have to think of how they will be used in war."

"If there is a nuclear war, the United States will be the one to start it," an Air Force strategist who has worked on the S.I.O.P. told me. This officer noted, with pride, that elaborate Air Force "timing studies" in which he participated had shown how certain forms of precisely coordinated attacks on the Soviet Union could greatly reduce U.S. casualties from the level they would be if the Soviets made the first move. If we struck first, there is the opportunity to destroy at least some of the Soviet missiles that could otherwise be used against us. The U.S. military victory may be a hollow one—given the tens of millions of fatalities we would still suffer when the residual Soviet missiles were fired off—but in the calculus to which the planning bureaucracy is accustomed, the numbers make going first look like a better bet than going second. Thus, contrary to all the statements about responding to Soviet attacks, the actual U.S. war plans, including all the versions of the S.I.O.P. that have been developed since 1960, also give the United States the option of making a massive first strike on the Soviet Union if war appears to be unavoidable. General Bennie Davis, the present head of SAC, refused to acknowledge the gap between stated national policies and current war plans. "This nation has always had and has today a strategy of retaliation, and I just can't conceive that we would ever be in a preemptive mode," he said. "I just don't visualize that." When I asked whether SAC would carry out a Presidential order for a preemptive attack, General Davis bristled, saying that it was a "hypothetical question" and "very highly speculative" and one that he would not discuss. "We can hypothesize all day and I'm not going any further." Other SAC officers, asked whether they were prepared to execute a pre-emptive attack on the Soviet Union, replied, "Certainly."

SAC's success in keeping a first-strike option included in the S.I.O.P. was also indicated in a Congressional hearing in 1980. Senator Charles Percy, probing the implications of Presidential Directive 59, asked Secretary of Defense Harold Brown about Pentagon preparations for "acting in anticipation of hostile action . . . rather than waiting to retaliate. Do we have a plan?" Brown replied, "There are options that cover that situation."

———

The Navy's attitude is markedly different. The Air Force has always emphasized massive preemption against military targets. This is a simple extrapolation from the "max effort" strategic bombing practices it used in World War II. It prefers counterforce strikes aimed at destroying enemy missile and bomber bases, not cities. Since submarine-launched missiles have not been accurate enough for pinpoint attacks on "hard targets," such as Soviet missile silos, Air Force doctrine has been partly designed to preserve a unique role for itself and to prevent diversion of strategic weapons funding to the Navy. The Air Force refers to its missiles as the country's "primary" nuclear deterrent.

The Navy, in contrast, has steadfastly regarded its nuclear submarines as assigned to a retaliatory strategy intended to guarantee "assured destruction" of Soviet cities and industry. The Navy has not wanted to yield the primary role in strategic deterrence to the Air Force, and its view of what ought to be done is closely related to the mission for which its ballistic-missile submarines are suited. (It does not take exceptionally accurate missiles to destroy cities, since a large nuclear bomb a few miles off course is still going to destroy all soft targets within a radius of several miles; random targeting of the Soviet Union, in fact, would probably kill as many people as pinpoint attacks since so much lethal fallout would be created.) The different policies of the two main services to which nuclear weapons are entrusted should not be mistaken for the first instance in which, as the historian William McNeill writes, "rival groupings of officers embraced rival doctrines, and used those doctrines as tools in their struggle for places in the military hierarchy."

Moreover, neither the Air Force nor the Navy has any particular enthusiasm for the academicians' notions about limited nuclear options —such as small-scale demonstration shots—or for controlled escalation. Nations do not wage war "by halves," said Paul Cambon, the French Ambassador to Britain at the beginning of the century, and this is the way those whose job it is to wage wars still regard their assignment. When the subject of limited nuclear war comes up, Richard Garwin noted, "all the military people say, 'That's not any kind of war I was ever in. There we used everything that we have, and there's no way that escalation can be controlled.' "

A NORAD General, concurring in this view, said, "Nuclear war is probably one of the most difficult things to control in the world. When you talk about the superpowers, the escalatory factors that would prevail are tremendous. Most of the military people will tell you that it's going to escalate by leaps and bounds until somebody gets a little sanity." He added that the rejection of limited nuclear options was a consequence of the elementary military logic, "If you start to shoot a few, the other guy can shoot his whole wad." Lawrence Freedman, Professor of War Studies at King's College, London, states this point very well in his lucid study, *The Evolution of Nuclear Strategy*:

> If the U.S. [limited nuclear war] policy was designed only as a reaction to plausible opening nuclear shots from the U.S.S.R., then a Soviet proclivity for large strikes renders it futile; if it was designed for opening shots for the U.S. then it could be folly, for it would invite a massive Soviet response without gaining any of the advantages of a first blow.

Another glaring problem with the limited nuclear war strategy is that nuclear submarines, which carry hundreds of warheads on their multiple-warhead missiles, are unsuited for such purposes. Once a submarine fires one missile, it risks revealing its position and being destroyed by the enemy. It is very hard for submarine commanders to rationalize limited nuclear options that would amount to suicide missions in which they use a tiny fraction of their weaponry, withhold the rest, and in the process allow themselves to be found and sunk. And, of course, once one sub fires all its missiles—which are enough to devastate the Soviet Union—the likelihood of keeping the war limited diminishes greatly.

The Navy's thinking was explained to me by a retired Admiral who is a specialist in command and control systems. "We have built a whole cottage industry of think-tanks" that have come up with unrealistic "rhetoric" about how U.S. weapons will be used, he said. "There's thousands of people spending millions of dollars annually writing all these things to each other. In simplest terms, a nuclear weapon is a devastating capability to apply power which is absolute as far as absolute can be. I don't care whether you've got multiple warheads, single warheads, whatever the throw weight is. Basically, you have a weapon that goes from Point A to B, whether it's an artillery shell, a rifle bullet, or a nuclear weapon. It's just the degree of damage that you can apply. But it's not clear, and I don't believe it has ever been clear, in the United States' eyes, as to how it's going to apply that nuclear weapon.

"We're not going to shoot first," the Admiral said—emphasizing a major point on which Air Force and Navy thinking diverge. He agreed with the Air Force, however, in dismissing the notion of controlled escalation and limited nuclear war. The theoreticians believe, he continued, that "if we shoot, we're going to have all of these options. And if we have all of these options, we're going to have all of these [command and control] organizations. And if we're going to have all these organizations, we're going to have all these procedures. Okay. That is understandable [but] the objective has been lost. The objective is you have a weapon, and if you have a weapon you should clearly understand in your mind that you are going to use that weapon if you come to that point of using it. And where is that point? The point is when you are attacked. . . . We will then shoot. But, by God, we're going to shoot and we're not going to sit there and Mickey Mouse it with option three and option four. We're going to take out the cities."

When the Reagan Administration's Nuclear Weapons Employment and Acquisition Master Plan was being prepared, CINCLANT—the head of the Atlantic Fleet—was asked to present a draft plan for what the Navy would do in a protracted nuclear war. The Navy ridicules the whole concept, as became evident when it presented the requested analysis at a formal Pentagon briefing. The naval officer making the presentation was accompanied by several of his colleagues, who sat in the front row. "They giggled as they presented it," a Pentagon official who attended the session observed.

Thus, in addition to the divergence between subtle U.S. declaratory policies and crude operational strategies, the Air Force and the Navy, the nominal executors of the present, limited war-fighting policy, disagree both with that policy and with each other on how nuclear weapons can or should be used. I asked a former Pentagon official, a civilian nuclear strategist who played a major role in the development of the current protracted war-fighting strategy, if he could give me the names of any senior military officers who agreed with it. I told him I'd not been able to find any. He seemed surprised by the question and, with some hesitation, mentioned three individuals. I noted that one was already on the record with doubts about whether limited nuclear options could be used and that the second declined to be interviewed on the subject. On further reflection, the strategist conceded that all three remained skeptical that nuclear war could be fought in any controlled way— that is, they disagreed with the central premise of the war-fighting policy.

It is possible, I suppose, to be loyal to the policy despite such reservations—in the same way it was possible for the White Queen, in *Through the Looking Glass*, to make it a practice to believe six impossible things before breakfast. It is difficult to avoid the impression, however, that the confusion surrounding U.S. nuclear strategy is less a calculated attempt to keep the Russians off balance than a reflection of the fact that the official thinking on this subject has always been remarkably muddled.

The great irony in the convoluted debate over the optimum nuclear strategy is that it is hardly necessary to have a sophisticated nuclear weapons employment policy in order to hold the other side at bay. What ordinarily keeps one from going into the ring with a boxing champion, after all, is not knowledge of his specific strategy. The fact that he has enormous strength, and any number of ways of clobbering a would-be opponent, is deterrent enough. The Pentagon, likewise, need not articulate an elaborate policy for responding to Soviet attack in order to assure deterrence, and it need not fear that the Soviets would interpret confusion about U.S. policy as an invitation to provoke a fight. Deterrence is not created by words. It is assured by thousands of weapons sitting silently in their silos and on board patrolling submarines.

Whatever plan the military adopts for using nuclear weapons obviously affects the kind of strategic command and control system it will require. For example, if the United States expected to make a preemptive attack on the Soviet Union if it appeared that war was unavoidable—as the Air Force would prefer it to do—then no elaborate early warning systems to detect missile attacks would be required, although there would be heavy emphasis on strategic warning indicators, such as reconnaissance and electronic eavesdropping satellites, as well as human intelligence, that might provide clues to Soviet plans. The President and SAC, striking at a time of their own choosing, would need nothing more than a simple communications system to transmit the order to U.S. forces telling them when H Hour would be and which S.I.O.P. subpart they were to execute.

If massive retaliation were the national policy, an early warning system would be needed. It would only have to function as a simple indicator that a Soviet attack was in progress, though. No detailed attack assessment capability would be required, since the number of incoming warheads would be irrelevant if no attempt at proportionate response was contemplated. A simple communications system could also be used, one which told SAC forces: "Fire everything now." Once the missiles were launched and the bombers were on their way, the command system would have nothing more to do. Accordingly, it need not be specially protected in order to survive multiple enemy attacks and, like paper plates and plastic forks, could be designed to be used once and disposed of. Moreover, from the Navy's point of view, no centralized communications system would be required to issue the necessary orders to nuclear submarines. A Soviet attack that cut off all messages to the subs on patrol would be enough to let the "revenge force" know what it had to do.

A strategy of proportionate response obviously demands greater attack assessment capability, and the newer, war-fighting/controlled-escalation doctrine demands an even more elaborate command system. If national policy is to be able to use nuclear weapons in wars that could extend for weeks or months, as indicated in the Defense Guidance Statements of Secretary of Defense Caspar Weinberger, this would require the warning and intelligence-gathering system to supply continuing data about ongoing attacks and counterattacks. More elaborate arrangements than an adviser in a Toyota Corolla would have to be put in place to give U.S. commanders data and advice on exactly how many Soviet warheads had been fired, where they were headed, and which Soviet silos still held missiles. A more versatile communications system would also be necessary, since instead of having to give only one order, commanders might be called on to give several—reprogramming and retargeting missiles, for example, in response to unfolding circumstances. The components of the command system, far from being throwaway apparatus, would have to be extremely well protected so that they could survive and function during extended conflict. This is all the more necessary since the command system itself would be a possible target for Soviet attacks.

Since strategic policy so dramatically affects command-system requirements, the more the policy changes—and the more confusion there is among the services as to what the policy actually is—the less likely will be a good matchup between nuclear weapon employment plans and the command system's capabilities. There are, as Desmond Ball observed, long "lead times" for designing and installing new command systems. Given the "extremely transitory" U.S. strategic doctrine, he said, there have been only "rare periods" when the command-system equipment being built actually fitted the stated purposes of the strategic policy makers.

Indeed, it was the gradual appreciation by civilian officials at the Pentagon of the widening gap between evolving strategic policy and the existing command and control arrangements that prompted the connectivity studies of the past few years. It had become obvious that the command-system hardware installed during the 1950s and early 1960s, and left essentially unchanged for the next two decades, as well as the S.I.O.P. itself, was far better suited to what the Air Force and the Navy preferred—massive preemptive attacks or massive retaliation —than to the subtler missions that the civilian nuclear strategists preferred.

There is, accordingly, an implicit message in the military's neglect of elaborate command-system requirements. It is not a simple case of "bad management" that is responsible for the apparent weaknesses in the current system for retaliating after a Soviet attack. Given the Air Force and Navy viewpoints on what ought to be done with nuclear weapons, the existing command system, despite its shoddiness in many respects, is good enough for the applications of brute force they have in mind. The military quite evidently has deep instincts telling it that whatever the civilian strategists may postulate, nuclear war will not consist of engagements that can be neatly programmed over an extended period from some central headquarters. Should the weapons ever be used, it will be in a desperate, all-out attempt to forestall an imminent assault by the other side or in a fit of murderous revenge for the destruction of our own homeland. That is what the S.I.O.P. is designed to provide, and no elaborate control mechanism will be needed to execute either of these major options.

By sticking with a relatively crude command and control system, the military has set its own nuclear weapons policy in concrete. It has, in effect, vetoed the controlled-escalation strategy that is so much at odds with ingrained military thinking. The civilian policy-makers at the Pentagon do not appear to have grasped the fact that their notions about surgical strikes and controlled escalation have been rendered irrelevant by the military's commitment to traditions that predate the nuclear age by a few millennia. The Air Force is simply not prepared to abandon its offensive plans or to exchange the bludgeon for the scalpel; the Navy is not prepared to do anything but respond to a Soviet attack with biblical fury.

However loosely planned the strategic command and control system has been, it has had one nominal goal: maintaining Presidential control over the use of nuclear weapons. The general subject of civilian versus military authority was extensively debated when Congress adopted the Atomic Energy Act of 1946. The Truman Administration took a clear stand: it wanted a new agency established, the Atomic Energy Commission (AEC), which would have physical possession of all nuclear weapons, handing them over to the military only at the President's personal direction. The military wanted no such thing.

Congress sided with the Truman Administration, and the new agency, through its Division of Military Applications, set up storage depots in which all nuclear bombs were kept under civilian guard. It is noteworthy that the Soviets adopted a similar procedure once they acquired nuclear weapons: KGB units, not the Soviet military, held on to the country's nuclear ordnance.

The Strategic Air Command, which was also created in 1946, began work on intercontinental bombers capable of reaching the Soviet Union.

Within two years, the first of the new bombers, the B-36 and the B-50, were delivered to the Air Force—empty. To the annoyance of the military, which kept lobbying for custody of the nation's atomic stockpile, the Air Force would have to send a pickup plane or van to an Atomic Energy Commission facility and await Presidential release authorization before it could get any atomic weapons.

The feeling within the Truman Administration about keeping military hands off nuclear weapons was expressed in a memo to the President in July 1948 by his Budget Director, James Webb, who wrote: "[T]he idea of turning over custody of atomic bombs to these competing, jealous, insubordinate services, fighting for position with each other, is a terrible prospect."

The Pentagon persisted in seeking to change the cumbersome weapons release process. After all, in a sudden crisis, logistical problems and the resultant delay in putting the weapons in the hands of those who might have to use them could prove costly. This was especially the case since the United States was relying on nuclear weapons to counter the advantage in conventional forces that the Soviet Union was presumed to enjoy in Europe. (The Soviet edge, according to recent analyses, may have been much less significant than it appeared to be in the late 1940s.)

By the early 1950s, the military began to get its way. During the Korean War, nuclear weapons were allowed to be deployed on certain U.S. Navy aircraft carriers. Other overseas deployments followed as the United States sought to bolster the ability of its Western European allies to deter a Soviet attack. The protocols for transferring nuclear weapons to the services were altered in 1952, and the new arrangements soon allowed the military to obtain weapons from AEC depots as easily as books could be withdrawn from public libraries. Within a decade after the Atomic Energy Act established putative civilian control of nuclear weapons, the nation's entire stockpile of nuclear weapons had been handed over to the military.

The nuclear arsenal, which grew rapidly during the 1950s, contained a diverse assortment of weapons. There were not only large "strategic" weapons—intended for use against the Soviet homeland—but also thousands of smaller "tactical" weapons intended for battlefield use in regional conflicts, such as war in Western Europe. Tactical weaponry included short-range nuclear missiles, nuclear artillery shells,

nuclear demolition mines, and other devices. Although much less destructive than strategic weapons, they were hardly small in comparison
with conventional bombs. Some of the junior-size nuclear ordnance
had explosive power approaching or exceeding that of the bombs
dropped on Hiroshima and Nagasaki. Some of the weapons carried
by fighter-bombers, for example, went up to one megaton in explosive
power—about eighty times as great as the one dropped on Hiroshima.

By 1960, thousands of strategic and tactical nuclear weapons were
deployed worldwide at U.S. Air Force bases and Army installations
and on U.S. naval warships. Not only did positive Presidential control
grow more tenuous as a result, but the risk of accidents also increased.
The Eisenhower Administration's attempt to solve both problems cen-
tered on special authorization codes that the President would have to
issue before nuclear weapons could be used. In theory, although the
weapons were in military hands, they could be activated only if the
President—reaching into his much publicized black briefcase—handed
out the secret combination.

Yet so rapid had been the growth of the arsenal, and so unsys-
tematic were the security procedures, that neither strict Presidential
control nor effective safety measures were actually achieved. This became obvious when the Kennedy Administration initiated a major
overhaul of U.S. nuclear policy in the early 1960s. Officials were aghast
at the gaps in the system for safeguarding the country's nuclear arsenal.
There is no shortage of hair-raising reports from this era—such as one
concerning fighter planes with fully armed nuclear weapons that AEC
officials found sitting on the edge of a runway at a European air base
with only a single armed guard standing by. Presidential control was
also undermined by ambiguous arrangements under which the authority
to use nuclear weapons in various contingencies had been delegated to
certain military commanders.

The Kennedy Administration made the restoration of Presidential
control and the prevention of accidental nuclear war the focus of its
program to improve the command and control system. The highest
priority was to perfect the technology and procedures to make sure
that the weapons could not be used without proper authorization from
the White House. The centerpiece of this effort was a device called the
"Permissive Action Link," or PAL. Several varieties have been devel-

oped, but the concept behind all of them has been the same: to build into each weapon, or attach to it, a lock that prevented it from being detonated. Only when the proper combination was fed in, in the right way, would the bomb's triggering mechanism work.

Simple PALS had four-digit codes, while more advanced ones required that up to twelve numbers be fed in before the weapon could be detonated. If a mistake were made in attempting to unlock a PAL, only a limited number of tries would be permitted. In addition, other security measures were developed such that any attempt to tamper with a PAL or with the weapon itself would cause the bomb's arming mechanism to self-destruct.

Procedural safeguards, as well as equipment like PALs, play a large role in the program that was created for maintaining positive control of U.S. nuclear weapons. The authorization codes themselves had to be kept highly secure, so that only the President or someone authorized by him would be able to give the order to execute an attack. At the receiving end, moreover, the officers who got the instruction to launch the missiles or deliver the bombs would have to make extensive checks to make sure the orders were authentic and that they carried them out to the letter.

At Whiteman Air Force Base in Missouri, the Strategic Air Command has its Missile Procedures Trainer. It is used in teaching and testing the officers who are responsible for firing U.S. Minuteman missiles, and the instructors there explained to me in detail the steps that have to be followed. The trainer is a replica of one of the hundred Minuteman launch control centers—called LCCs or capsules—that are staffed around the clock by two-man crews. The capsules are underground, like the Minuteman missile silos, in order to increase their survivability during a nuclear attack.

Normally, each launch control center will be in charge of ten missiles. (The missiles are at unmanned sites that may be many miles away; they are linked to the launch control centers by hardened underground cables.) Five launch control centers form a squadron which commands fifty missiles. Following the SAC "two-man rule," the two officers in each capsule must act together to fire a missile. The people assigned to this duty are covered by an Air Force Personnel Reliability Program designed to eliminate anyone with medical, psychological, drug, alcohol, or other problems that could interfere with his work. The average age of the Minuteman launch control officers is twenty-five, their average appearance and demeanor like that of an Eagle Scout.

When a launch order—an Emergency Action Message—is sent to the capsules, it arrives in code, and the two launch controllers must separately decode and validate it. They are tested regularly to make sure they will be able to do this quickly and accurately. The methods for interpreting and authenticating the code are kept in a double-locked safe, to which each has a key. The form of the message indicates that it has come from the President or another authorized member of what is referred to as the "National Command Authority." If the message is garbled or in some way defective, they will follow procedures to check it out. If it is a valid usable message, they will take no further steps to reconfirm it. Their standing orders are to execute it immediately.

A valid order will include a six-digit combination that the crew plugs into a positive enabling switch (its version of the PAL). There are sixteen million possible combinations, and there is no chance that the two officers in one capsule could find the right one by trial and error. Their capsule is connected to the other four in their squadron, and the minute anyone attempted to initiate a missile launch, alarms would ring in the other capsules. Each capsule has inhibit switches that can stop other crews from unauthorized launching.

In an authorized launch, each officer would insert a key into one of a pair of widely separated keyholes—the distance between them preventing either crew member from turning both keys by himself. The keys have to be turned at the same time, so it is impossible for one person to turn one and then run back and turn the other. Moreover, even when the crew in one capsule turns its keys simultaneously, this will not launch any missiles. The crew in a second capsule must also turn its keys. Hence, there is not just a two-man rule, but actually a four-man rule. In addition, since any of the officers in the five capsules can veto a missile launch by any one crew, there is normally a ten-man check on any missile firing. Should some of the capsules be destroyed, however, control will lapse automatically to the surviving ones, and a single crew, if necessary, can fire all fifty missiles assigned to the squadron.

The safeguards demonstrated at the Missile Procedures Trainer were far more extensive than those I had seen described in public. I discussed them with General Davis at SAC Headquarters. "As far as the United States is concerned, it is impossible, it is impossible to accidentally launch a nuclear weapon," he said. "Impossible. Just not humanly possible—or not machine possible—for an accidental launch. And for the Soviets, I'm very confident they have similar safeguards."

Desmond Ball, although a critic of many aspects of the command system, concurs in General Davis's view of the dependability of the positive controls that have been adopted. "People who talk about accidental use of nuclear weapons, I tune out," Ball told me. "There are many, many problems to worry about other than the idea that these things are going to get launched accidentally."

———

Presidential control over the U.S. arsenal has been enhanced greatly by the careful employment of PALs and related procedural safeguards. Yet there are still huge gaps in the application of these protective measures. As secure and impressive as the PALs, in theory, may be, more than half the weapons in the U.S. strategic arsenal are not actually equipped with them.

Nuclear-missile submarines, to be specific, carry almost five thousand warheads—twice as many as the Minuteman missiles—but have been exempted from the same kind of physical launch controls. The submarine missiles have no mechanical or electronic barriers against unauthorized firing—no PALs or other tamper-proof security devices—and can be fired without "go codes" from the President or his delegated representative. Submarine crews are, of course, supposed to await Presidential orders, but if no orders get through to them or they choose to revise or ignore them, they are physically able to go ahead on their own and launch their missiles. The Minuteman crews have a "fail-safe" mechanism in which the lack of orders prevents them from firing if the communications system fails; the "fail-deadly" firing mechanism for the submarines works in the opposite way.

This is not to say that a solitary submarine commander could decide on his own to start a nuclear war. "Without proper authority, it would take a coalition of a good number of people within a submarine to fire a submarine-launched ballistic missile, particularly with the warhead activated," Vice Admiral Gerald Miller told a Congressional panel in 1976—one of the few occasions on the public record when this subject has been discussed.

"It isn't as if just any small number of people can sort of pull this off," John Steinbruner explained. "There are very elaborate rules. Basically, it's not too far off to say that the whole crew has got to pretty much go along with this, and at any rate, more than just a couple of officers." "I am not concerned about the commander and the Exec starting to fire weapons while the rest of the sub crew stands around open-mouthed," a retired Admiral told me.

Some experts think that direct Presidential control, in the form of PALs, should be imposed on the submarines, however highly one may regard the Navy's competence and loyalty. The need for this, they say, is underscored by the magnitude of the destructive capability represented by the one hundred and sixty warheads carried by each Poseidon submarine, the mainstay of the current U.S. fleet. Richard Garwin, who has repeatedly urged the installation of PALs on nuclear submarines, says he has met with considerable institutional resistance. "Navy commanders take it as a matter of pride that they are gentlemen, like the British," he said. "And therefore they ought to be trusted to follow orders and launch their nuclear weapons—and not launch them otherwise."

Herbert York, another physicist and a former Defense Department official, also believes it is a dubious proposition to allow such powerful war-fighting machines to remain at sea without greater positive control over what they can do. "The PAL program is good as far as it goes, but it doesn't go far enough," York told Congress several years ago. It is not desirable to have a situation, he explained, in which "a submarine crew which somehow became falsely convinced that the world had already gone up in nuclear smoke could really trigger exactly that event."

There has been "no problem" to date with unauthorized action on the part of submarine crews, John Steinbruner said. "Good record. But you're facing a long time in the future, so it's something worth thinking about."

The Navy's pride notwithstanding, the major practical question about installing PALs centers on the availability of reliable methods for transmitting Presidential orders to submarines on patrol in the ocean depths—a complicated feat given the fact that most radio and other signals cannot penetrate very far into seawater. It is argued that the autonomy given to the submarines is needed to assure retaliation in the event the country is attacked and the President or other military officials are unable to get a message through. The submarine commanders must simply be trusted to follow the contingency plans that have been laid down to cover this eventuality, even though, it would appear, the plans are not very specific. If submarine commanders are unable to receive transmissions after trying all the appropriate methods, one official explained, "their orders are to go ahead in the absence of orders to do whatever they want." Presidential control obviously diminishes when there are no physical constraints but merely a set of procedures—thou shalt do this and thou shalt not do that—to keep the subs from firing their missiles.

Thus, despite great attention to the establishment of civilian control, there is reason to doubt whether this is guaranteed by the command system that has been improvised by the military. The fact that half the strategic forces can be fired without the President's direct order is some indication that the President may be a figurehead, an honorary commander in chief, as far as the actual use of U.S. nuclear weapons is concerned. Other fundamental problems that undermine his ability to control the rest of the strategic forces—not just the submarines—reinforce this suspicion.

4
DECAPITATION

The President's most frustrating problem in preparing to command U.S. forces during a nuclear war is that he may be among the first to die. The priority attached to killing him is a result of the simple logic that it is usually a lot easier for an enemy to bring about disarray by eliminating the other side's leadership than by trying to destroy its entire war machine. "From the military point of view, attacks on command and control are the most efficient way to use forces," a national-security adviser to President Reagan told me. "This goes clear back to the days when officers stopped wearing fancy uniforms, because the enemy found out that if you kill the officers, the troops don't act effectively together. The military principle is clear."

The Soviets have long recognized the decided advantage of a quick strike against Washington, D.C., and the major U.S. military command posts at the outset of a nuclear war. Soviet strategists have written extensively about the need to bring about the "disorganization of [the enemy's] state and military command and control." Writings on this subject by Soviet military analysts were reviewed by the Pentagon in the late 1970s, and officials came to the conclusion, according to Congressional testimony by General Van Doubleday, that "Soviet strategic doctrine indicates Soviet strategic targeting specifically includes U.S. command, control, communications, and intelligence."

One of the clearest indications of Soviet thinking on the subject was an article in a Soviet military publication written in 1966 by Colonel M. Shirokov:

> Under conditions of a nuclear war, the system for controlling forces and weapons, especially strategic weapons, acquires exceptionally great significance. A disruption of the control over a country and its troops in a theater of military operations can seriously affect the course of events, and in difficult circumstances, can even lead to defeat in a war. Thus, areas deserving special attention are the following: knowing the coordinates of stationary operations control centers and the extent of their ability to survive; the presence of mobile command posts and automatic information processing centers; the communications lines' level of development and, first of all, that of underground and underwater cable, radio-relay, ionospheric and tropospheric communication lines; field communications networks and duplicate communication lines; communication centers and the extent of their facilities, dispersion, and vulnerability.

The date of this statement—1966—is significant, because a major circumstance that encouraged the Soviets to give special emphasis to this mode of attack was the very large U.S. lead at that time in the number of nuclear weapons. Aiming the limited Soviet arsenal against U.S. military and political leadership "was a very natural thing for somebody running behind to do," John Steinbruner explained. "It was also a very effective thing to do, a way of compensating for their very real disadvantages in terms of the numbers and qualities of deployed weapons." Soviet strategy in that era, another U.S. military analyst wrote, could be summarized very simply: "attacking the weakest link."

Robert Berman and John Baker, in their study of Soviet strategic forces which was published by the Brookings Institution, noted the apparent logic behind the Soviet decision in the 1960s on the number of SS-9s to build to counter U.S. Minuteman deployments. Unable to produce SS-9s rapidly enough to match the U.S. missile for missile, the Soviets took a different approach: "relying on its SS-9s to provide a means of neutralizing the one hundred critical command-and-control links of the Minuteman force." By 1966, the Soviet SS-9s, each of which was assumed to have a monstrous twenty-megaton warhead, were able to destroy only about a quarter of the Minuteman launch control centers; by 1969, they were able to destroy most of them; by 1971, they were able, with a high probability, to destroy them all. Thus, long before SS-18 deployments, a window of vulnerability existed, although it was elements of the Minuteman command apparatus, not the Minuteman missiles themselves, that were at risk.

Soviet planning, which can now be carried out with the benefit of much larger forces, still includes provisions for strikes against the U.S. command system, but the Soviets by no means limit themselves to this small set of targets. Instead, Soviet writings emphasize the advantage of a first strike—a massive preemptive attack at the outset of a nuclear war—that includes the destruction of these facilities as part of a wholesale attack on U.S. strategic capabilities. The purpose of the attack is to cripple the U.S. nuclear war-fighting system to the greatest extent possible, thereby reducing the magnitude and the likelihood of a U.S. counterattack.

"By attacking the U.S. forces and associated command, control, communications, and intelligence system, and thus causing any U.S. response to be less coordinated, more ragged, and much more degraded than it otherwise would be, the casualties which the Soviet Union would be likely to suffer could well be less than half what they otherwise might be—perhaps 30 to 50 million fatalities rather than 50 to 100 million," Desmond Ball concluded in an analysis of Soviet strategic planning. "Indeed, if the U.S. National Command Authority and the other critical elements of the U.S. command and control system were to be successfully destroyed at the outset of any exchange, Soviet planners could well believe that it might be possible to limit fatalities and damage to much lower levels."

Soviet awareness of the potentially decisive importance of attacks against enemy leadership is suggested not just by their writings about how to attack the United States. There is a more practical manifestation of their thinking: their extreme sensitivity to the danger of similar strikes being launched against them. To protect their own high officials during possible nuclear conflict, they have built some two thousand underground bunkers capable of housing more than one hundred and ten thousand Soviet military officials and Communist Party leaders. Within the ring road that circles Moscow, Western analysts believe that at least seventy-five emergency relocation centers have been built, some of them several hundred feet deep. Other major Soviet cities and military centers have similar facilities. Some of the ones in or near Moscow are operational command posts linked to Soviet forces, but most are VIP shelters intended to increase the possibility that the top echelon of the Soviet state will survive.

Comparable precautions to protect U.S. leaders have not been taken. In Washington, neither the White House nor the Pentagon—where the National Military Command Center is located—is provided with such an array of shelters. (There is a bomb shelter under the East Wing of the White House, but it can only withstand a blast pressure of 25 psi; it would not enable the President to survive a direct attack on Washington.) In the 1950s, the Alternate National Military Command Center was built at Fort Ritchie, Maryland, but although it is underground, it, too, was not designed to withstand direct nuclear attack. Other main U.S. command posts, such as NORAD Headquarters, are correspondingly vulnerable. The buildings in the Cheyenne Mountain Complex can be sealed off from the main entrance tunnel by huge, twenty-five-ton blast doors—provided the hydraulic system to close them works. (The door failed to close, a government inspector told me, when he once asked to see it tested.) The buildings inside the complex also rest on hundreds of large steel shock absorbers to reduce the effects of nearby blasts. These precautions might have provided some protection against the kind of missiles the Soviets had in the 1960s—although some experts say privately that even then the shock-absorber system seemed rather dubious—but they offer scant protection against highly accurate SS-18s equipped with twenty-megaton warheads. "We must operate on the theory that anything that can be found can be destroyed," Lieutenant General Scowcroft said.

In 1961, Pentagon consultants proposed that consideration be given to building an ultrasafe command post for the President. A secret study by the MITRE Corporation looked into the possibility of putting such an installation somewhere between three thousand and ten thousand feet underground, much deeper than anything the Soviets are believed to have built. It was found that the survival of the President and his senior advisers might be assured indefinitely. They could have all the bottled water and food they needed. What they would be unable to do would be to talk with anyone else—all inputs to their cavern and every output from it being easily severed. Communications were found to be "an almost insurmountable problem," and the proposal was abandoned.

Another study completed the following year reinforced official awareness of the vulnerability of Washington and the national command system to Soviet attack. This now declassified 1962 study was prepared for the Army by the Stanford Research Institute and the Bell Telephone Laboratories. One of its major conclusions was that "the loss of the command function, either by direct attack on command [centers] or indirectly through the severance of communications, can prevent force employment or cause severe reduction in force effectiveness, resulting in disastrous consequences—for example, the possible defeat of the nation."

The study was quite specific about the small number of weapons that needed to be aimed at Washington and a few other targets to produce devastating results: "For example, it requires only 17 weapons to essentially destroy the national command or, as an optional target, 19 weapons to destroy the national communications and put the national command out of contact with the force." The situation two decades later is not much different, as the recent connectivity studies and Desmond Ball's analysis have shown.

It is noteworthy that the U.S. advantage during the 1960s in the number of nuclear weapons "was sharply mitigated in reality by command vulnerability, which was particularly acute at the time," John Steinbruner said. "The conceptions of the strategic balance that have prevailed over the past twenty years are seriously misleading, and the U.S. reading of the history of these two decades must be revised accordingly. None of the popular measures of relative U.S. and Soviet strategic capability—delivery vehicles, warheads, equivalent megatonnage, lethal area coverage, hard target potential, or post-attack force balances— takes command performance into account, even though it is undeniably a critical element of actual capability."

The much better protected Soviet command and control system, Pentagon experts believe, could absorb much larger attacks and remain functional. In addition to providing greater protection for their leadership, the Soviets have taken several further precautions. The United States has one hundred underground launch control centers to fire its Minuteman ICBMs—each hardened to withstand high blast pressure and equipped with power and supplies intended to keep it functional for a few days following a nuclear war. The Soviets, Desmond Ball noted, have three times that number of underground command posts to launch their ICBMs. The United States has three main very low frequency transmitters and six backup ones for communicating with its submarines on patrol; the Soviets, Ball said, have twenty-six such facilities. The United States is highly dependent on telephone communications and has only a small number of communications satellites. The Soviets have a much larger communications satellite system, composed of relatively simple satellites that can feed messages into an extensive network of receiving terminals at their various military headquarters, naval bases, and missile sites. Their telephone system has also been built with much greater attention to its wartime survivability.

There are some features of the U.S. command and control system that the Soviets lack—they do not have instantaneous photoreconnaissance capability, early warning or electronic-intelligence satellites in geosynchronous orbits, or very advanced computers. The United States has opted for technological sophistication, while the Soviets have chosen to concentrate on simpler, more redundant, and more durable hardware. To knock out the entire Soviet command system, Desmond Ball estimates, would require "more than two thousand" nuclear warheads. A Pentagon consultant familiar with U.S. studies of the Soviet command system said, "Most people you talk to would use figures in that ballpark." Even then, Ball said, "it would probably not be possible to isolate the Soviet [leadership] completely from the strategic forces or completely to impair the Soviet strategic intelligence flow."

———

The United States officially maintains that it would never consider a decapitating attack against the Soviet leadership and command network. The topic is very sensitive politically, since to acknowledge preparations for this kind of undertaking would disclose the first-strike option in the S.I.O.P. After all, a strike that paralyzed the Soviet command system would have a large potential payoff if it came *before* they had fired their missiles—and a negligible payoff if it came afterwards. There would not be much point in planning to disable their command system only *after* it had fulfilled its mission.

Nevertheless, U.S. military officials, even though they acknowledge the risk of the Soviets attempting to decapitate us, are reluctant to acknowledge the military logic of decapitating them. "We don't even consider such a thing," Donald Latham, the Assistant Secretary of Defense and the Pentagon's chief spokesman on command-system planning, told me. "Somebody would be 'decapitated' here if he brought forth a study that says let's go strike the Soviet Union first."

Many contingency studies on how to attack Soviet leadership have in fact been done by U.S. strategic planners. Leon Sloss, the Pentagon official who led a 1977–79 inter-agency Nuclear Targeting Policy Review during the Carter Administration, wrote in a summary of this work, "As a consequence of this review, increased emphasis in U.S. nuclear [weapons] employment policy was given to the targeting of enemy military forces and political-military leadership . . . [T]he Soviet military structure had always been targeted in our nuclear war plan. However, the Carter Administration's studies focused greater attention on destroying Soviet general purpose forces and the Soviet command structure . . . and suggested more effective methods of targeting these military objectives." The Congress was informed of the results of this review when William Perry, then the Under Secretary of Defense, told the House Armed Services Committee in 1979, "A relatively small percentage of the [U.S. strategic] forces are devoted to that [Soviet leadership] mission. That small percentage does not reflect a lack of priority on this objective. It only reflects the fact that there are fewer targets here."

The priority assigned to killing Soviet leaders is made clear in the documents that summarize the results of a series of "Internal Conferences on War Aims and Strategic Forces" that took place in 1979–80 under the auspices of TRW, a major defense contractor with strong connections to the Reagan Administration. The participants in these private sessions included General Bruce K. Holloway, the former Commander in Chief of the Strategic Air Command; Dr. Colin S. Gray, the leading advocate of the decapitation strategy and an adviser to the Pentagon; Dr. Benson D. Adams, a Pentagon expert on nuclear weapons policy; Dr. William Schneider, who is now the Under Secretary of State for Security Assistance; and a number of technical experts on nuclear force targeting, the MX missile, and Soviet politics. Dr. Francis X. Kane of TRW was the coordinator of the conferences.

General Holloway, in a March 31, 1980, memorandum to Dr. Kane, discussed his views on the "conclusions shared by most of the

group" as well as some of his own "impressions" on the issues that had
been discussed. The United States "war aims," he wrote, included "prevention of the loss of our way of life," "damage limitation," and the
"degradation of the Soviet State and its control apparatus to such an
extent as to make successful negotiation possible." In achieving these
objectives, "the importance of crippling the [Soviet] command and the
control system . . . assumes extraordinary proportions.

"Limited Nuclear Options," Holloway continued—the kind of
strikes associated with a strategy of controlled escalation—"are not
feasible. Only if we are able to reestablish unequivocally United States
strategic force superiority (in our minds and the enemy's) is there any
reason to believe that LNOs can lead to successful negotiated settlement. It would be quite the reverse; and regaining strategic superiority
in the proximate future is an extremely unlikely condition. (I believe
we all agreed on this.)"

The Holloway memo goes on to describe the kind of offensive
against the Soviet leadership that he believes must be the centerpiece
of U.S. war plans. "Degradation of the overall political and military
control apparatus must be the primary targeting objective. Irrespective
of whether we strike first or respond to a Soviet strike (presumably
counterforce), it assumes the importance of absolute priority planning.
Striking first would offer a tremendous advantage, and would emphasize
degrading the highest political and military control to the greatest possible degree."

As to the feasibility of killing Soviet leaders and thereby paralyzing
their war machine, General Holloway noted, "I am convinced that in
the Soviet system there is such centralized control that it would be
possible to degrade very seriously their military effectiveness for nuclear
or any other kind of war if the command control system were severely
disrupted. Major damage would be difficult to achieve and would require better intelligence than now possible (better reconnaissance and
better clandestine inputs) but it can be done. Moreover, it must be
done, because there is no other targeting strategy that can achieve the
war aims that underwrite survival."

"Can you imagine what the Soviets would think if they saw the
Holloway memo?' asked a former U.S. intelligence official with whom
I discussed the document. "A memo by the former Commander in
Chief of the Strategic Air Command? Can you imagine what *we* would

think if *we* obtained a comparable Soviet document describing their plans to attack our leadership?" Yet the Holloway memo, despite its bluntness, should actually be nothing new to the Soviets. It is based, after all, on the same premises as President Carter's PD-59 of July 1980 and President Reagan's nuclear war-fighting strategy document, NSDD-13, of October 1981. These two documents are top secret, and the versions of their contents leaked to the newspapers have never set forth more than a few fragments of the official policy. The only real shock of the Holloway memo is to see what may be inferred about the goals of a nuclear war-fighting approach set forth in black and white. What is particularly clear from the memo is that the notion of fighting long nuclear conflicts and controlling escalation is not really the point of the war-fighting strategy, at least as far as the military is concerned. As a member of one of the connectivity review groups noted, "Official policy suggests we're moving toward long-range war fighting. But in reality we're moving toward first strike."

Despite the Strategic Air Command's interest, since the late 1940s, in "counterforce" strikes intended to cripple the Soviet war machine, the technology to do this effectively has not been available. That technology is now being perfected, and the thrust of the Reagan Administration's Strategic Modernization Program is to incorporate this first-strike weaponry into the U.S. arsenal. Some of the super-accurate weaponry needed for attacks against hardened Soviet command posts and underground missile silos will be provided by the ten-warhead MX missile—which is three times as powerful and twice as accurate as the most advanced Minuteman missiles. The Navy's new Trident D-5 missiles will also be accurate enough for attacks against hardened targets. Instead of serving merely as a revenge force that can destroy Soviet cities, U.S. submarines will take on a war-fighting role. Equipped with the D-5 missile, they will have "a counterforce capability, even a preemptive capability," Richard DeLauer, the Under Secretary of Defense, said at the 1981 MITRE Corporation symposium. (His speech touched on such a sensitive subject that it was deleted in its entirety from the published transcript of the meeting, although recorded on videotape.) Mr. DeLauer's remarks, made in the relative privacy of an experts' meeting, represent one of the rare instances in which a high official has confirmed the Pentagon's intent to build weapons whose specific purpose is to permit a first strike on the Soviet Union.

A new navigational satellite, called NAVSTAR, will also help overcome the inherent problem that has prevented submarine missiles from
being used as first-strike weapons. The sub's chief limitation as a firing
platform has been that, unlike the silos in fixed, geodetically defined
locations, the precise position of the submarine at the instant it fires has
always been slightly uncertain. The NAVSTAR satellites will compensate for that. They can quickly feed into each missile, right after it
comes up out of the water, the exact navigational information it needs
to deliver its warheads right to their assigned targets.

The Pershing II missiles that the Administration began to deploy in
Europe in late 1983 are further high-accuracy instruments that could
be used in a strike on the Soviet leadership. The Pentagon insists that
Moscow is not within range of the missiles, except for its "western
suburbs." The Soviets dismiss this claim out of hand, just as the Pentagon, one imagines, would quickly brush aside any comparable Soviet
claim that an advanced new weapon would somehow fall just short of
the obvious target. Indeed, the Kremlin's particularly vociferous objection to the Pershing IIs, according to Barry Blechman, was notably
different from its usual rhetoric about U.S. weapons. Its opposition had
"an edge to it," he said. "They saw the Pershings as a threat to them—
personally."

The Reagan Administration has explicitly incorporated the strategy
outlined by General Holloway in the latest U.S. war plan—SIOP-6,
which went into effect on October 1, 1983. "Soviet leadership and
command and control and communications are targets," a Pentagon
consultant said. The SAC commander, General Davis, who was in
charge of developing SIOP-6, told me, "I think a fundamental issue
here is that most people really don't appreciate that the U.S. strategy
is one of counterforce. That is, it is not a mutual assured destruction
strategy or a city strategy. It goes after the Soviet military leadership
threat and, of course, . . . the land-based ICBM capabilities."

Colin Gray, a participant in the sessions at TRW and a defense
consultant whose view that "victory is possible" strongly influences the
Reagan Administration nuclear strategy, has summarized the merits of
decapitating strikes against the Soviet Union. In his view, an attack on
the Moscow-based leadership structure could have a paralyzing effect
on Soviet military operations and score a knockout blow that could
"cut off the head of the Soviet chicken."

There is thus a notable similarity between the statements of U.S. and Soviet military experts on the stratagem of decapitation combined with attacks on the enemy's nuclear forces as a preferred opening move in a nuclear war, should such a confrontation be forced upon them. Hence, when U.S. planners express concern about this kind of Soviet strike on the United States, they are not being paranoid. They are simply describing the possibility that the Soviets will do unto us what we have planned to be able to do unto them. A senior officer who has worked on the S.I.O.P. told me, "There is every reason to believe that U.S. and Soviet war plans are mirror images."

The connectivity studies have focused on particular scenarios that could be exploited in a Soviet attempt to decapitate the U.S. command and control system. Timing is obviously critical. The Soviets would want to give U.S. leaders minimal warning, lest they issue retaliatory orders while their power to do so remained intact. Since Soviet land-based missiles have a flight time to the continental United States of about half an hour, Desmond Ball said, "[i]t is generally presumed that any Soviet attack against soft command, control, and communications centers would involve the use of submarine-launched missiles, in which warning time would be minimal."

The surprise achieved by using submarine-launched missiles could be enhanced by firing them on what are called "depressed trajectories." That is, unlike normal trajectories, in which the missiles lob their warheads high up out of the atmosphere, the submarine missiles could be fired in somewhat lower flight paths. They would travel faster, although they would use more fuel. The latter is an important consideration in long-range attacks, but something that would not matter much if the missiles had only to traverse a short course to their target—a few hundred miles, say, from somewhere off the East Coast to Washington, D.C. The missiles on depressed trajectories could still be detected by U.S. early warning satellites, but the warning time would not be great.

The amount of warning time that would be available cannot be determined precisely, Desmond Ball concluded, "but for an attack on Washington it is unlikely to be more than ten minutes; indeed, it could well be less than five minutes." U.S. military officials agree with these estimates, and Richard Garwin believes that they may be optimistic.

"It's even worse than that, because if that's what they want to do, they don't have to use submarines," Garwin told me. "They use a nuclear weapon which is smuggled into Washington, and I think it highly likely if there's a Soviet nuclear attack on the United States, it will start without a missile launch but with a bomb exploded in the Soviet embassy. This was a problem we had in the 1950s, when the nuclear weapons were much bigger than they are now. It's a more serious problem in the 1980s when the world really is much more open and the nuclear weapons are smaller."

It would obviously be extremely risky for the Soviets to try to bring a nuclear weapon into the U.S. capital, a point that Garwin also made. "Of course, I'm sure we do everything we can to make sure people don't smuggle nuclear weapons into the United States, but the Soviets are very capable people, and if they thought they would survive a nuclear war or win a nuclear war—or help themselves significantly—then you might expect that they would use a smuggled weapon."

The danger posed by submarines is likely to increase, however, if the Soviet Union follows through on its threat to station additional ones off the U.S. coasts in response to the U.S. deployments of Pershing II and cruise missiles in Europe. Instead of the one or two Soviet submarines that have been kept on patrol off the East Coast, a much more consequential strike force could confront the United States.

Since 1957, the U.S. Navy has operated a Sound Surveillance System (SOSUS) which has a little-publicized but quite remarkable capability of tracking Soviet submarines. It does this by picking up the noise of their engines and propellers. Sound waves travel for thousands of miles underwater, and the Navy's thirty-six fixed underwater listening posts around the world feed the echoes from each sub into one of the largest computers that has ever operated. The data-processing equipment, located at Monterey, California, sorts out the distinctive sound of the Soviet subs—which are much noiser than those of the United States—from all the other noise in the background. The system allows the Pentagon to know, most of the time, where the Soviet subs are located. If any Soviet subs approach U.S. shores, the U.S. is able to place its own anti-submarine forces on alert in that area. The Soviets have no comparable means for the open-ocean tracking of U.S. submarines.

SOSUS stations in Maine, Canada, Great Britain, Portugal, Bermuda, and other locations have the ability to indicate whether a sudden increase in Soviet submarine deployment off the East Coast of the

United States has occurred. If so, the Pentagon would be likely to recommend major precautions—such as getting the Vice President out of Washington—to reduce the chances of a strike that could wipe out the entire national leadership. At least, that's how it would have worked to date. If numerous Soviet submarines are routinely deployed off the coast, instead of the lone one or the pair usually there, the strategic warning role of SOSUS will be reduced. The danger of decapitation attacks from these submarines will be a constant, high-level threat.

Another decapitation threat may, literally speaking, be on the horizon. The Soviet Union, following the lead of the United States, has been developing long-range cruise missiles—small, pilotless jet aircraft that fly at subsonic speeds and can be equipped with nuclear or conventional warheads. They can be launched from trucks, planes, ships, or submarines. Should the Soviets deploy sea-launched cruise missiles off the United States, this will pose a major new threat to Washington, D.C., and other targets near the coasts. "If we go ahead with sea-launched cruise, we can know that the Soviets will," Paul Warnke, the former head of the U.S. Arms Control and Disarmament Agency, said. "We'd have to consider every Soviet fishing vessel as a potential strategic delivery vehicle. You wouldn't know whether it was full of codfish or cruise missiles." The Soviets are reportedly developing a sea-launched cruise missile, which the Pentagon designates the SS-N-X-21, that can be launched from their Yankee- and Victor-class submarines, the type normally stationed off the U.S. coasts.

The danger associated with cruise missiles is all the greater since they cannot be detected by the present early warning system, which was designed to look for high-flying objects such as ICBM warheads and conventional bombers. An inherent limitation of the PAVE PAWS radars on the East and West Coasts, and of all conventional radars, is that they cannot see below the horizon. The earth curves, but standard radar beams do not. The farther one gets from the radar, the greater the blind spot—the zone in which low-flying objects can proceed undetected. At a distance of one thousand miles from the early warning radars, for example, anything flying at less than a hundred and twenty-nine miles above the earth's surface will go undetected. ICBM warheads, which on standard trajectories go about seven hundred miles out into space, can be spotted by current U.S. radars; even on depressed trajectories, the warheads still travel about five hundred miles above the earth. Yet cruise missiles, which skim a hundred feet above the ground or the open ocean, would not register on the radar scopes.

Nor can the early warning satellites over the Atlantic and Pacific pick up tiny cruise missiles in the lower part of the atmosphere. Their small jet engines give off infrared signals that are far too weak to be detected. It may be possible to deploy patrol aircraft along the U.S. coasts to try to provide warning of cruise-missile attacks. However, the small size of cruise missiles—some current U.S. models are as little as fourteen feet long and only two feet in diameter—would make them hard to track by airborne radars. The patrol planes could be equipped with heat sensors to try to detect operating cruise-missile engines, but the heat they produce is so trivial and easily masked by technical countermeasures, or even just the clouds, that spotting the missiles in this way would be difficult. Moreover, as a defensive maneuver, the criuse-missile engines could be shut off as the missiles approached U.S. coasts. The new missiles, that is, are so sleek that they can simply glide for ten or fifteen miles at a time, thereby evading efforts to detect them by picking up telltale engine emissions.

On an average workday, the President, the Vice President, the Secretary of Defense, the members of the Joint Chiefs of Staff, and other top officials will be in Washington. On a few well-known occasions, such as the annual State of the Union address, most of them will be in the same room. During a prolonged crisis, at least some of the key decision-makers could be taken to undisclosed locations. Evacuation would work less well if there were only a short warning time—or none at all.

For many years, the survival of the President and top military leaders has been predicated on the assumption that they could be quickly transported to Andrews Air Force Base in Maryland—some ten miles from the White House—where they could board a Boeing 747 that would become their flying command post. David Packard, Under Secretary of Defense during the Nixon Administration, was the prime mover behind efforts to acquire a plane that could function as the National Emergency Airborne Command Post. (The acronym "NEACP" does not roll off the tongue and has been transformed into the more pronounceable nickname "Kneecap.") Four Boeing 747s were converted for this purpose; the first was delivered to Andrews in 1974. It was assigned a ninety-member battle staff and kept on constant runway alert. The other three planes were kept in reserve at SAC Headquarters in Omaha.

The main flaw in the Kneecap program has been that the blast created by a single one-megaton nuclear weapon exploded over Washington would destroy all soft targets within several miles, including the White House, Andrews Air Force Base, and the plane itself. If the Soviets wanted to be extra sure of catching Kneecap on the ground, they could aim a weapon or two right at Andrews. Under Secretary of Defense Perry, speaking in his characteristically understated way, told Congress in 1979 that "the availability of this aircraft cannot be unconditionally guaranteed." Killing the President, the Secretary of Defense, and the members of the Joint Chiefs of Staff before they boarded the plane, or destroying the plane before they arrived, would be a relatively trivial task. Even without a smuggled weapon, the short flight time of submarine-launched missiles would allow the bombs to fall before Kneecap's passengers could be assembled and helicoptered to Andrews.

The practical difficulties in evacuating the President were demonstrated in 1977, when Zbigniew Brzezinski, President Carter's National Security Adviser, staged a mock exercise. "Brzezinski decided to play field marshal and asked to talk to the guy in charge of evacuating the President," a former Pentagon official said. He called for a helicopter to take him to Andrews, a drill that ended up as "a nightmare, just a complete disaster," according to one White House aide who participated in it. One part of the mishap was that "the helicopter that is supposed to be on alert at all times, to land on the White House lawn, almost got shot down by the Secret Service."

Six years later—a lag that says something about the decision-making pace at the Pentagon—a new plan has been developed for using Kneecap. According to Donald Latham in August 1983 testimony before Congress, the plane will no longer be based at Andrews. It will be kept on alert at an unidentified airport further inland. The new plan calls for it to be sent aloft in an emergency, and for the President to be helicoptered to a "marry-up point" with his command post.

The new procedure, like the one it replaces, does nothing to protect the President from a short-warning or no-warning nuclear attack against Washington. Mr. Latham did not explain how a helicopter is supposed to fly through what could easily be a barrage of large nuclear weapons landing on the city or exploding above it. (In the 1977 exercise staged by Dr. Brzezinski, concern about thunderstorms in the area was enough to cause several minutes' delay in getting the helicopter to the White House.) The new location of the Kneecap, moreover, proved difficult to keep secret. The day after Mr. Latham's testimony, Senator Daniel Quayle of Indiana, to the surprise of officials at SAC Headquarters, issued a press release lauding the stationing of the plane at Grissom Air Force Base in the Senator's home state. He explained to reporters that he had lobbied to have the plane stationed in Indiana in order to make sure that Grissom was kept open and to secure for the local area the benefits of the $4.6 million in additional spending generated by basing the plane there. Whatever the advantages to the Senator's constituents, the military benefits from moving the plane are not great. Soviet submarine-launched missiles could reach Grissom Air Force Base—and every airport within helicopter range of Washington that had runways suitable for a rendezvous with a jumbo jet—just a few minutes later than they could hit Andrews.

Top Soviet leaders, despite greater efforts to protect themselves, might also have difficulty surviving a direct U.S. attack against their capital. Indeed, they might find themselves no safer than some of their predecessors who decided, in the middle of the twelfth century, to build a fortress for their protection at the top of Borovitsky Hill, along the northern bank of the Moscow River. When Mongolian invaders struck the city less than a century later, they easily destroyed this special sanctuary. It was made of wood, and the attackers simply burned it to the ground.

Successive regimes found Borovitsky Hill an advantageous location, and fortifications on this site have been rebuilt many times in Russian history. In the fifteenth century, Ivan III put up a massive brick wall, which still stands, familiar to us today as the outer wall of the modern Kremlin. The wall is up to sixty-two feet high and as much as twenty-one feet thick. In the aftermath of a U.S. attack on Moscow, there would no longer be a Kremlin sitting atop old Borovitsky Hill. Actually, there would no longer be a Borovitsky Hill, this site having been usurped by immense bomb craters filled with the ashes of the Soviet capital.

The underground shelters that have been built will not guarantee absolute protection against incoming U.S. warheads. For one thing, like officials in Washington who would have little time to run for their helicopters, Soviet leaders may not have much of an opportunity to seek their underground hideaways. Missiles launched from U.S. submarines stationed in the North Sea could reach Moscow in minutes, as could the Pershing II missiles that the U.S. is deploying in West Germany. The distance from these launch areas to the Soviet capital is about six hundred to a thousand miles—a short-haul trip for missiles that fly faster than nine thousand miles an hour.

If the Soviet leaders do reach their designated sanctuaries, they may find that high-yield U.S. weapons exploded at ground level—as well as earth-penetrating warheads that burrow into the ground and then explode—can readily excavate the shelters and kill those inside. "The explosions will scoop out the shelters like a giant hand reaching into the earth," the physicist Henry Kendall commented.

The Soviets might hope to derive some benefit from their attempt to keep the location of the shelters secret. U.S. intelligence agencies, however, have paid close attention to the building of these installations —monitoring construction with powerful orbiting cameras capable of very detailed photoreconnaissance—and have identified many of the entrances to them. If the entrances have been detected, the Soviets might hope that the direction taken by the underground tunneling cannot be ascertained. They may also have secretly built alternate entrances. None of this matters too much. Although the Soviets may have secrecy on their side, the physics of exploding warheads gives certain advantages to the attacker. For the U.S. warheads, in order to kill the inhabitants of the underground tunnels, need not hit every segment of every tunnel. Blast waves propagate quite readily in tunnels—this is the reason the Air Force proposal to hide MX missiles in long underground tunnels had to be abandoned—and people miles away in other segments of the Moscow catacombs will be killed as readily by a bomb that drops on the tunnel entrance as by one that falls right on them.

In addition to attacking Moscow, a U.S. strike aimed at disabling the Soviet command system would have to include numerous other facilities, the locations of which appear to be well known to U.S. war planners. Thus, according to reports in the defense-industry magazine *Aviation Week & Space Technology* and other publications, the Pentagon has identified such key targets as: the headquarters of the PVO Strany, the Soviet Defense Command (an underground installation about thirty miles from Moscow); the main long-range radio transmitters that give orders to Soviet submarines (at Petropavlovsk, Vladivostok, Dikson Ostrov, Kaliningrad, Matochin Shar, and Arkhangelsk); the principal ground control stations for Soviet satellites (at Kalinin, northwest of Moscow, and at Yevpatoriya in the Crimea); and the principal Soviet early warning radars (near Minsk and Novgorod in the western USSR, near Irkutsk in south central Siberia, in the northwest near the Barents Sea, in Latvia near the Baltic, and in other locations around the country).

Photoreconnaissance is only one of the means of locating the elements of the Soviet command system. Some of the most important U.S. intelligence-gathering devices are orbiting electronic eavesdropping stations known as the Rhyolite satellites. Like the U.S. early warning satellites in high orbit over the Eastern Hemisphere, the satellites in the Rhyolite program, which are in similar orbits, send their data to a ground station in Australia. It is located at Pine Gap, a few miles southwest of Alice Springs.

The Rhyolites function, according to a former U.S. intelligence officer, Victor Marchetti, "like a vacuum cleaner" and pick up a very wide range of Soviet communications: telephone, microwave, radio, and satellite. They permit the U.S. to monitor everything from walkie-talkie communications during Soviet troop exercises to the emissions given off by Soviet radars. Detecting the latter is an "extremely important function of the Rhyolite program," Desmond Ball notes, because it "allows the U.S. to map the location of and hence to target their early warning (EW) stations, air defence systems, anti-ballistic missile systems, air fields, air bases, satellite tracking and control stations, and ships at sea. Recording the frequencies, signal strengths, pulse lengths, pulse rates and other specifications of these radar systems would in turn allow the U.S. to jam the transmitters in the event of a war; knowing their location would also enable U.S. bombers to evade the air defence systems en route to their primary targets."

It may take two thousand or more warheads to destroy the entire Soviet command system, but this may not be an insuperable obstacle for the United States. There are almost five times that number of weapons in the U.S. strategic arsenal. Aided by a great deal of intelligence data about the Soviet command system from Rhyolite and other sources, the U.S. military is acquiring the means required to undertake such an attack. (The Chinese have a small nuclear arsenal aimed at the USSR, and protection against this threat is probably the most tangible achievement of the Soviet shelter-building effort.) The U.S. strategic force is large enough to be able to attack command head-quarters and communications facilities without giving up the ability to attack a wide range of additional targets. New weapons, such as the MX missile and the Trident D-5 submarine-launched missile, are de-signed specifically to attack hard targets, such as underground com-mand posts, and in a crisis they will increase the temptation to attempt a decapitating strike against the USSR. Thus, as John Steinbruner commented, "if there are differences in the vulnerability of the [U.S. and Soviet command systems], these are relatively insignificant against the basic fact that both sides are extremely vulnerable."

———

The death of the President will not deprive the U.S. strategic command system of the means to execute a retaliatory strike. If no one but the President knew the go codes, and they could be lost with him, the United States could be crippled with obvious ease. "Prudence dictates that you're never in that situation," General Davis said. There has to be more than one finger that can be put on the trigger and, in theory, this has been provided for in two ways.

Devolution of authority—the passing of the President's office to the Vice President, the Speaker of the House, and others in the order speci-fied by law—is one method for ensuring continuity of government. According to the Constitution, there will always be "a President," at least until the list of sixteen designated successors runs out. Prepara-tions can be made so that the nominal successors are briefed on U.S. war plans and given a means to gain access to the authorization codes and the required communications channels so they can assume the role of Commander in Chief. In practice, though, since these officials also work in Washington most of the time, they would be likely to be lost with the President in any surprise attack.

In addition, as Lieutenant General Scowcroft stated, "assuming that there is a military command center still existing somewhere, they may have no idea who the President is or how to find him. If they find one or more successors, there's the problem of determining whether or not a given successor is the President." There would be the further problem, which he did not mention, of getting the military to accept whoever became President by default. The armed forces might readily follow a respected Secretary of Defense or Secretary of State or the Speaker of the House, one official commented. It was less likely, he added, that they would follow some random Cabinet officer with no established understanding of the complex military problem at hand. Scowcroft himself said in the unpublished part of his 1981 talk at the MITRE Corporation that except for the Secretaries of Defense and State, the civilian successors to the President were "almost completely unacquainted" with the complexities of strategic command and control problem.

Delegation of authority is another method for maintaining continuity of command. The statutory basis for this is quite fuzzy, since there is nothing, apart from the President's implied powers under the Constitution as Commander in Chief, to specify to what extent the President may hand over his authority to others. At any rate, there is no law at the moment preventing the President from making any arrangement he wants to appoint certain people he trusts to command U.S. nuclear forces should something happen to him. The advantage of explicit delegation is that those specifically charged with this responsibility—unlike a hapless Cabinet officer who is suddenly told that he or she is in charge—can be specially prepared to execute the S.I.O.P. The designated official or officials might also be protected in some way to improve their chances of surviving the President. They would also have to be given authorization codes and staffs that could assist them in issuing Emergency Action Messages.

"Well, there are contingency plans, I just really can't discuss them," Donald Latham told me, and that is about all the Pentagon will say about the subject. Over the years, officials have periodically hinted that some delegation of authority has taken place—to make sure the Soviet leaders recognized the fact. Thus, an Eisenhower Administration official told the *New York Times* in March 1955: "No one was going to have to hunt around in the ruins of the first onslaught for someone else to issue the order for an atomic counterbombing." Who the stand-ins for the President might be was not specified.

Desmond Ball, who said he is not privy to the contingency plans for delegating authority over nuclear weapons, commented, "This is probably one of the most closely kept secrets." He speculated, however, that "it may not be a closely kept secret. They may not actually have plans for it. It may be a question that is just deliberately left open." One official who is familiar with the delegation procedures cautions that it is difficult to make a hard and fast generalization about how they have been applied. "Delegation is a very personal thing," he said. "It varies from Administration to Administration." Some Presidents have permitted a relatively facile turnover of authority to various military commanders under certain contingencies; others have tightly limited the transfer of authority.

"Presidents by and large have been extremely reluctant to delegate," an adviser to President Reagan said. "As a matter of fact, some of them have refused even the most minimal preparation of their successors, even like handing them out a code which they can use to authenticate themselves. My guess is this President [Reagan], just because of his personality, is more relaxed about all those things than any of his predecessors, about holding everything unto himself, more willing to delegate."

A President does not have to decide the moment he assumes office whether to delegate the authority to execute the S.I.O.P. to a specified set of civilian successors or military officers. Since bolt-out-of-the-blue attacks are not regarded as likely, the President could choose to wait until there was some strong reason to take steps to prepare a successor, such as a period of greatly increased tension with the Soviet Union. Delegation could even be done as a last-minute step. A Carter Administration official noted that the President has three, not two, main options under attack: ride it out, launch under attack, or delegate under attack. Thus, the Soviets would have to recognize that while they might be able to kill the President, he could still decide—despite what Harry Truman said—to pass the buck.

Setting up new arrangements so that a civilian chain of command would survive a nuclear attack is one aspect of the contingency plans that have been made in recent years. The Carter Administration initiated programs to assure "the continuity of government," and made plans for evacuating key officials so there would be a surviving civilian leadership. The military, however, has its own chain of command, and senior officers have all the means—without the involvement of any civilian officials—to issue orders for a retaliatory strike. Logically, one would expect that the way to arrange this would be to have the go codes available at least to those in the military hierarchy who are already in trusted positions of authority over U.S. forces—starting with the Secretary of Defense, the Joint Chiefs of Staff, and the head of the Strategic Air Command. In fact, according to the transcript of a talk given at a 1980 seminar at Harvard by Raymond Tate—a former Deputy Director of the National Security Agency—all of these officials "in some sort of succession" have been given the authority. "The codes and devices are set up to allow that," he said.

"The public wants the President to be the only person that can use nuclear weapons—that he has a key that he hides in his underwear or something," a former Pentagon official said. "But that's not the way it is." Codes were definitely required to give the orders to use nuclear weapons, he said, but the President very definitely did not have the only set. Like Mr. Tate, he noted that the Strategic Air Command had the codes, and so did the National Military Command Center in the Pentagon (which is operated by the Joint Chiefs of Staff) as well as the Alternate National Military Command Center at Fort Ritchie. "The military is basically entrusted with nuclear weapons," he continued. "They're not treated like children. Controls are tight down below"— that is, there were tamper-proof electronic locks and double-key arrangements in the Minuteman launch control centers—"but loose at the top. Sergeant Bilko can't start World War III, but General Bilko can. There is an informal gentlemen's agreement at the top as to how business will get done, and they only tell the underlings very little, and don't tell the public anything."

The President's de facto sharing of authority over nuclear weapons with the military raises some tricky questions about whose say-so will prevail should the President and senior military leaders disagree. Different cases can be considered. At one end of the spectrum, there is the likely veto by the military of any capricious orders from the White House. "If the President should for some reason pick up a phone and say, 'OK. I've had it with the Russians. Let's go. In five minutes,' you can be pretty certain it wouldn't happen," John Steinbruner said. "People are not prepared to do that." During the final days of the Nixon Administration, the kind of implicit veto that can occur was applied when Secretary of Defense James Schlesinger instructed the commanders of U.S. forces not to obey any unusual orders from the White House without confirmation from the Pentagon.

At the other extreme, Steinbruner said, if there are "massive signs that a Soviet attack is under way, some explosions actually going on, the warning sensors screaming bloody murder and all that, at that point what the President says and doesn't say is very marginal. The President blinks an eye and says that's it. And even if he doesn't do it, and the pressures are great enough, chances are somebody in the military command would say he did it and nobody'd ever discover the difference." With the control arrangements now in place, Paul Bracken said, the President's real function is not so much to pull the trigger to launch the weapons as it is to act as a safety catch preventing others from firing the triggers they have. "There are plenty of people with the potential for jumping the gun," a Pentagon command and control expert said.

Senior military officials are reluctant to talk about their capability to veto Presidential orders, or to take any independent actions. "In my view, an irrelevant question," General Davis replied when I mentioned this subject. Other SAC officers said that the question was "very sensitive" but that it was perfectly obvious that "launch crews could decide not to turn their keys and theoretically you could move that behavior up the chain of command." It is also physically possible, since the authorization codes are in the hands of senior military leaders, for them to initiate missile launches without waiting for a Presidential directive. "The Constitutional problems are very severe and not faced up to," one senior military officer said.

The greatest potential conflict between the President and senior military leaders would involve a circumstance in which the President wanted to ride out an attack, and perhaps try to negotiate a cease-fire with the Soviets, when the military wanted to launch a counterattack. "You provoke the system and it's going to want to go, and it's going to be hard for anyone, including the President, to stop it," Steinbruner said. An official who recently reviewed the attack authorization arrangements noted, "If you focus on explicit predelegation, you miss ninety percent of the story." The military's "institutional ethos," he continued, was such that the lack of Presidential orders would make little difference. "In the absence of directives from the National Command Authorities, there would be retaliation if the United States came under attack."

A counterattack organized by the military would be dependent on the survival of at least one of the senior officials who have the means to issue properly coded Emergency Action Messages. However, these members of the senior military command mostly live and work in the Washington area or in other fixed locations known to the Soviets. Thus, while responsibility may be delegated to them, or assumed by them, it's not clear that they will survive long enough to use it.

General Davis, for example, works at Offutt Air Force Base and lives there, too. SAC does have a three-story underground command post, but it was never intended to survive a direct attack. It is only just below ground—under the front lawn of the main SAC Headquarters building—its bottom a mere forty-six feet from the surface. Although it can be scaled off to protect those inside from radioactive fallout, the facility cannot protect them from the blast of a weapon targeted directly at Offutt.

General Davis can choose to leave his headquarters and board his own flying command post, which is held on reserve for him. "I have various options that I can exercise, and one of those, of course, is to go aloft, to command SAC from aloft," he said. "However, I have twenty-four hours a day, three hundred and sixty-five days a year, a general officer airborne in the Looking Glass, the airborne command post, and one of the functions of that general officer is to survive to command the SAC forces and to receive and carry out, pass on and carry out, orders from the National Command Authority."

What General Davis did not add was that he himself and the General aboard Looking Glass, according to Raymond Tate's unusually explicit account of the delegation process, could assume the role of the National Command Authority. "So if all else goes, the airborne commands can take over and be the central authority, with all the capabilities—CINCSAC, Looking Glass, etc.," Tate said. "CINCSAC" is Pentagonese for the Commander in Chief of SAC—who is, at the moment, General Davis.

Others in the military chain of command—the "etc." in Mr. Tate's list—possibly include the Supreme Commander of U.S. forces in Europe and the heads of the U.S. Atlantic and Pacific fleets. They are as vulnerable as those whom they might be called on to replace. Hence, although authority, in principle, can always be delegated in an attempt to keep someone at the helm, there is no guarantee that it can be done smoothly or dependably following a major attack. It was one thing for then Secretary of State Alexander Haig, after the attempt on President

Reagan's life in March 1981, to stand up and declare, "I'm in charge here." Nuclear ordnance can create larger difficulties in maintaining national leadership than the .22-caliber bullet that struck the President did—especially if the strike plan is specifically aimed at the National Command Authority. The Soviets, who lack a constitution specifying an orderly chain of succession, and whose extremely centralized style of government makes extensive delegations of authority less likely, would possibly be in even worse shape than the U.S. following a strike against Moscow and their main command posts.

At the moment, the main U.S. hope for preserving centralized control after a Soviet attack hinges on the airplane that General Davis mentioned: the SAC Airborne Command Post, code-named Looking Glass. William Perry told Congress in January 1979 that "nearly all" of the U.S. strategic command and control systems would be lost after a nuclear attack and that the United States would be "totally dependent" on its airborne command capabilities.

5

LOOKING GLASS

Every eight hours, an EC-135 takes off from Offutt Air
Force Base in Nebraska or from Ellsworth Air Force Base in South
Dakota. A top-secret Looking Glass mission begins. The jet, a specially modified Boeing 707, carries a United States Air Force general, a battle staff, flight officers, and communications technicians.
They relieve a similar twenty-member crew in another plane that has
been flying in an undisclosed pattern above the Midwest, and that will
land after its replacement is in the air. These flights have been going
on continuously since February 3, 1961. Most of them originate from
Offutt.

If the Soviet Union were to launch a surprise attack on the United
States, the general riding in Looking Glass would probably become
the doomsday officer responsible for giving U.S. missile and bomber
forces the order to retaliate. According to the contingency plans that
Raymond Tate alluded to, which have never been discussed elsewhere
in public, that task would be very likely to fall to him since the White
House, the Pentagon, the Strategic Air Command's Headquarters at
Offutt, Kneecap, and other key command posts could be so easily
wiped out in an opening Soviet salvo. This is the reason for keeping
a Looking Glass plane aloft at all times.

SAC will not officially acknowledge the investiture of the Looking Glass commander as a potential surrogate for the President, but it does acknowledge that the plane is "the first place command goes" if SAC Headquarters at Offutt is destroyed. (There are alternate SAC command posts, at Barksdale and March Air Force Bases, but Looking Glass is the primary backup.) Officials also state that Looking Glass has all of the means to "build, process, and disseminate an Emergency Action Message"—the coded orders that direct the missile and bomber forces to execute the S.I.O.P., the nuclear war plan—and that it "has the authentication codes required to do that." The essential documents are kept in a double-locked, fire-engine red "clacker box"—so named because of the sound of the alarm that goes off when this steel safe is opened. The general in command and the chief of the airborne battle staff hold the keys.

A documentary film produced a few years ago in cooperation with the Air Force included a simulation of how Looking Glass would carry out the part of its assignment which has been described in public: relaying Presidential orders. (Some of the same footage was used in the ABC-TV film *The Day After.*) The officer in command, Major General C. R. Autery, was far more senior than the "dashing lieutenant colonel" to whom President Truman was unwilling to give the authority to use nuclear weapons. General Autery was certainly dashing, however—not necessarily a matinee idol, but someone definitely on the move as the plane tried to keep its location secret. He did not ham it up for the cameras and appeared calm, even a bit bored, as he acted out the role of conferring with his aides and passing on to the forces their instructions for going to war. He showed no more emotion ordering a nuclear attack on the Soviet Union than the average person might display ordering a pizza.

Under actual combat conditions, the situation would be more tense. Having been on board one of the standby Looking Glass planes recently, I suspect that the general on duty would be gravely concerned about his inability to make contact with U.S. nuclear forces and with the country's surviving military and political leaders. Although it was intended to be the flying switchboard through which the President and the Pentagon could transmit directives, the plane's ability to carry out this mission is in doubt. This was suggested in a number of homely ways, most notably when the battle staff mentioned, in passing, the problem they had with one of their critical radio antennas—its tendency to fall off.

Current hardware problems aside, even perfect communications gear will not solve the plane's most immediate quandary once a nuclear war begins: the lack of informed people with whom to talk. The plane will be included in the conference call with CINCNORAD in which he announces his attack assessment, if he has enough data to make one. The plane is dependent on him for this and cannot carry out a detailed independent evaluation of the nature and extent of any ongoing Soviet attack. Looking Glass has no direct tie-in with the early warning satellites. Nor can it get data directly from the radars in the Ballistic Missile Early Warning System. Looking Glass's only information from these sensors will be what has been relayed to it from NORAD, SAC Headquarters, or other ground stations. Once those have been destroyed, the staff on board will have no reliable means for assessing what is happening to the United States.

It would not make any difference if the raw data from the early warning satellites and radars could be fed directly to Looking Glass, bypassing all intermediaries. Looking Glass does not carry the kind of computers needed to process and interpret such information. Once its contacts on the ground are lost—which would happen very quickly in a major attack—Looking Glass will be operating in the blind.

Looking Glass, in theory, has four methods for launching the Strategic Air Command's Minuteman force. First, it can transmit the necessary Emergency Action Messages to the one hundred launch control centers, the underground command posts that each control a set of ten missiles. This would tell the two officers in each capsule which preplanned attack option to execute, and they would then fire their missiles at the prescribed targets. It is not necessary to send a hundred different sets of instructions. A single Emergency Action Message—"Execute Plan X," for example—will suffice, since the decoding process tells each pair of launch control officers receiving it what Plan X means for them. One launch control center, according to that plan, may have to launch all of its missiles; other launch control centers may not have to do anything.

Second, SAC has a fleet of auxiliary airborne launch control planes —of which Looking Glass is the flagship, so to speak—that provide a backup to the underground launch control centers. Looking Glass can give these planes the order to fire their assigned missiles. This method will be available only if there has been enough warning time to get them aloft, since they could be destroyed in a surprise attack by Soviet submarine-launched missiles. The Airborne Launch Control System planes are routinely kept on standby at Ellsworth Air Force Base and other SAC bases, not in the air.

Third, Looking Glass can fire the Minuteman missiles all by itself. It can do so by sending coded ultrahigh frequency (UHF) radio signals directly to the special cone-shaped UHF receiving antenna installed next to each silo. (This is also the method used by the auxiliary airborne launch control planes.)

Finally, Looking Glass can fire the rockets that belong to the Emergency Rocket Communications System (ERCS). These are a set of Minuteman missiles based at Whiteman Air Force Base in Missouri. Instead of warheads, they carry UHF radio transmitters in their nose-cones. The transmitters can broadcast a preprogrammed launch order for thirty minutes or so after they are boosted into a suborbital trajectory. The order, broadcast over two UHF frequencies, can be picked up by all launch control centers. Before sending the signal to fire the ERCS rockets, Looking Glass, if it wants, can feed revised orders into their transmitters.

In addition to launching the Minuteman force, Looking Glass can send messages to SAC bombers and can transmit directives to the Navy's TACAMO planes, which would then relay the orders to U.S. submarines. Since the TACAMO planes are seldom in a position from which they can reach the entire submarine fleet, the link between Looking Glass and the subs is tenuous. The connection between the SAC airborne command post and the bomber fleet is also problematical. As the bombers enter the Arctic region, they are supposed to get orders on the SAC "Green Pine" network. This consists of radio beacons set out in a chain extending from the Adak in the Aleutians to Keflavik, Iceland. Looking Glass can feed messages into the Green Pine beacons, but the beacons themselves can be destroyed fairly easily—the Soviets can home in on their emissions—and they are capable of only relatively short-range message transmission.

As a backup, Looking Glass can relay messages to the bombers by using a cumbersome procedure referred to as a "hand-off." According to the S.I.O.P., schedules have been arranged for SAC bombers to take off from various bases and head off in a line down their assigned attack corridors. Looking Glass can pass orders to one of the auxiliary airborne command posts, which then relays it to the last bomber to take off from each base. The bomber at the end of each line can pass on the orders to the bomber ahead of it, which does the same, finally delivering the orders all the way up to the lead plane. The hand-off only works as long as the bombers remain within radio range of one another, and as long as the last bomber is still close enough to Looking Glass or one of its auxiliaries. This puts considerable time pressure on Looking Glass to issue orders while this plane-to-plane hand-off method is still available. The necessity for a better means of communicating with the bombers has been recognized.

Looking Glass is an important component of the strategic command system apart from the role of its commander as a backup Commander in Chief. Even if the President is still alive, a SAC command post will be vital to the execution of a retaliatory strike. Kneecap, the President's own command plane, does not have all of the means required to coordinate the launching of the Minuteman force. For one thing, it depends on SAC for information on the status of SAC forces, and it will have to obtain this data from Looking Glass if SAC Headquarters at Offutt is destroyed. Otherwise, Kneecap has no idea of the resources available. Moreover, while Kneecap is able to broadcast orders, it does not have two-way communications procedures set up with the launch control centers to get an acknowledgment. It relies on Looking Glass to do that. Unless those in charge know which launch control centers and missiles are functional, they will have no way to determine the likelihood that their attack plan can be executed. If the kind of attack they want to order is not feasible, they will not know it and will lack the opportunity to select an alternate course of action.

The Presidential command post, moreover, does not have the capability to launch U.S. ICBMs if the launch control centers have been destroyed or incapacitated. Kneecap, unlike Looking Glass, does not carry launch control officers and is not set up to send orders directly to the Minuteman silos. Kneecap is also unable to launch the ERCS rockets by itself. Only Looking Glass and the auxiliary planes in the SAC airborne command and control system can do so.

There are important safety catches in the delegation of authority to Looking Glass. The general in charge of Looking Glass cannot issue

Emergency Action Messages on his own whim. There are procedural checks and balances, and several crew members must work together with him to issue launch orders. The battle staff on board has separate teams, to make sure the two-man concept applies. The rest of the crew, as on a submarine, must also cooperate in sending orders to the launch control centers or directly to the missile silos.

Moreover, should Looking Glass desire to send a launch order to the silos—bypassing the launch control centers—further physical safeguards will be involved. The firing mechanism installed in the silos will not allow Looking Glass to fire at will. The principal safety feature is a "hold-off switch"—a device that prevents the airborne launch control planes from gaining access to the firing mechanism unless the two SAC officers in the launch control center agree or have become isolated from the silos assigned to them.

In routine peacetime circumstances, the lockout device is always on, but in a major crisis it could be shut off. There are two ways this can be done. The officers in the launch control center can simply be ordered to turn off the switch and to turn over control to Looking Glass and the other airborne control planes. The trigger aboard Looking Glass would then be "set." The hold-off switch also has a timer, and if the launch control center is destroyed or its links to the Minuteman silos are severed, the timer will automatically allow Looking Glass and the auxiliary launch planes, after a predetermined period, to take over.

Whether any of the means available to Looking Glass for launching U.S. missiles will succeed depends on the performance of the communications systems that are stuffed into every nook and cranny of the plane. Like any airplane, Looking Glass depends heavily on radios for both transmitting and receiving messages. It has the extra capability of being able to use a very large part of the radio range, all the way from very low frequencies (VLF) to ultrahigh frequencies (UHF). It is also able to use the Air Force Satellite Communications System (AFSATCOM), which uses UHF frequencies, although it is unable to use the Defense Satellite Communications System (DSCS), which uses super-high frequencies (SHF). (Kneecap can use SHF, and this is one of the few differences between the communications systems on the two planes.)

To issue an Emergency Action Message, Looking Glass does not rely on one preselected frequency but on several that are used simultaneously. "We shotgun the message on all available communications systems," one battle staff leader said. This is prudent, since all of the various radio frequencies available have inherent limitations, and once nuclear weapons have started to detonate over the United States, further complications with radio transmission and reception will arise.

With standard very high frequency (VHF) and ultrahigh frequency (UHF) channels—the kind used, for example, by television stations and commercial aircraft—one problem is their range. These radio signals go in a straight line, and for anything beyond the horizon—which is about two hundred to three hundred miles away from a plane flying at the altitudes used by Looking Glass—other modes of communications must be used.

For long-distance transmission on a day-to-day basis, Looking Glass relies on four "ground entry points." These are facilities that link the plane with the military's nationwide telephone system. The four relay stations, which are operated by AT&T, are in Lyons, Nebraska; Fairview, Kansas; Hillsboro, Missouri; and Lamar, Colorado. These go-betweens take the radio messages from Looking Glass and pass them along over the land-lines that are leased to the military; similarly, they broadcast messages up to Looking Glass from everyone else tied in to the defense communications system.

If a Soviet attack occurs, the four ground entry points used by Looking Glass—as well as the few dozen other major switching centers that handle the bulk of U.S. military communications—will be prime targets. The plane will then have to fall back on more cumbersome means of communications.

Looking Glass can still try to use standard radio frequencies, but it must rely on SAC radio relay planes to pick up and retransmit its messages across the country. These planes are supposed to keep Looking Glass in touch with the scattered SAC missile and bomber bases and with the Pentagon, NORAD, and Kneecap. This message route also has its potential problems, such as the difficulty of getting the relay planes into the air before they are destroyed on the ground—none of them are normally kept in the air—and keeping them in range to pick up and rebroadcast messages to and from Looking Glass.

The conventional radio frequencies available to Looking Glass suffer from a further weakness: some of them are easily blacked out by nuclear detonations. This was one of the lessons of the atmospheric nuclear weapons tests of the 1950s and early 1960s. A few one-megaton weapons—the size carried by typical Soviet ICBMs—detonated two hundred miles above the United States would block high frequency transmission for hours. The test designated *Starfish Prime*, which took place on July 9, 1962, used one such warhead detonated above Johnston Island in the South Pacific. It cut off HF transmission across the Pacific, all the way from Australia and Japan to the West Coast of the United States, for half an hour. A barrage of such weapons, fired at intervals, could extend the blackout of these frequencies for longer than the plane could be kept in the air.

Higher frequencies, such as UHF, are less susceptible to blackout, but there are other problems in relying on them. For one thing, since UHF can only be used for short-range (line-of-sight) transmissions, only a fraction of the Minuteman force and SAC bomber bases around the country will be within direct range of Looking Glass and the auxiliary airborne command posts at any given time. UHF transmissions between Looking Glass and the auxiliary airborne command planes, and between Looking Glass, Kneecap, NORAD, and the Pentagon, will be dependent on the proper deployment of radio relay planes. Moreover, UHF transmissions with the bomber fleet will end as soon as the last bombers going down their attack corridors pass below the horizon.

UHF communications also depend on the ability of the launch control centers to receive messages on these frequencies. The launch control centers are supposed to have survivable UHF antennas for this purpose. These antennas are normally kept below ground, inside a pipe, and can be raised and unfurled, like an umbrella, when necessary. Keeping them withdrawn protects them against nearby nuclear blasts. However, such explosions can cover the area with dirt and debris. To counter this, the antennas are attached to heavy detonator-controlled springs that can push them up through whatever may be on top. A complication with these pop-up antennas has been observed in tests. The springs that raise them up are so strong that the antennas are frequently not just thrust up a few feet into position: they are accidentally launched. The antennas are not tested often, since too many of them get lost.

UHF transmissions from Looking Glass can also be sent out via the Air Force Satellite Communications System. This is one way for the plane to keep in touch with Kneecap, for example, and with the portion of the SAC B-52 bombers that have AFSATCOM receivers. (These devices are one of the improvements being made to overcome the problems with the "hand-off" arrangement.) The satellites are orbiting message repeaters, devices that receive signals from one source and retransmit them automatically. However, the AFSATCOM satellites are susceptible to Soviet jamming—they do not incorporate sophisticated anti-jamming protective equipment—and the AFSATCOM receivers on the ground at various SAC bases would be unlikely to survive an initial Soviet attack.

The unavailability of high frequency radio and satellite communications would force Looking Glass to rely on various backups, such as very low frequency transmissions. The plane's VLF antenna, which is the one that occasionally drops off, does not do so through anyone's carelessness or from simple happenstance. The difficulties with this device result from the physical strain put on it when it is deployed. The antenna in question consists of a heavy, copper-jacketed steel wire that is twenty-eight thousand feet long—more than five miles—and weighs almost a ton. It is unreeled behind the plane when necessary, attached to a stabilizing drogue that is intended to keep it from whiplashing around. In peacetime, the antenna is never used over land, in order to avoid possible injuries to the public should it separate from the plane. However, following a nuclear attack, it becomes a key part of what is called the Survivable Low Frequency Communications System. Connected to a powerful transmitter aboard the plane, it broadcasts long radio waves that can travel thousands of miles. It is very difficult for an enemy to jam such signals, another advantage over conventional frequencies.

Unfortunately, it is also hard to fly the plane with such a heavy antenna trailing behind it and to keep the wire from oscillating. Because of the considerable drag the antenna creates, even when it is only partially unreeled, the plane must keep to straight and level flight, or to very gradual turns, in order to keep the antenna stable. If it does start to whiplash, it can pull itself loose or force the crew to cut it. (The co-pilot and the antenna operator have devices for doing this.) Air turbulence, which can cause the wire to become uncontrollable, is the most frequent reason for the loss of the antenna. The plane does not carry a spare.

Despite all its problems, the low frequency antenna is very important to the present communications capability of the plane: it may be the last-ditch method for conveying orders to the launch control centers, each of which has a buried VLF receiver. It is also an important means for keeping in touch with Kneecap, the Navy's TACAMO aircraft, and the B-52 bomber force (which is currently being outfitted with VLF receivers, another way of eliminating dependence on plane-to-plane hand-offs). However, whereas high frequency transmissions can convey a great deal of information in a short amount of time, low speed is an unavoidable characteristic of all VLF transmissions.

"It could conceivably take twenty minutes to send the kind of [Emergency Action] messages we're talking about," a SAC communications officer explained. Another SAC technician noted that "different units may be tasked to receive at different rates, which requires Looking Glass to rebroadcast on different frequencies. We may have to retransmit at different speeds; in addition, the slower the speed, the better the possibility of reception." A further complication is that although it is relatively difficult to jam VLF transmissions, that does not stop the Soviets from trying. They have powerful VLF jamming stations, and this forces changes in the way messages have to be transmitted. "We can beat Soviet VLF jamming, but we have to reduce the data rate," one expert noted. "We have to repeat ourselves. For example, the message 'ABC' would have to be sent 'A-A-A-A-A-A, B-B-B-B-B-B, C-C-C-C-C-C.' "

Since Looking Glass has only one VLF antenna, and since each transmission may take several minutes, the time required to broadcast a comprehensive message to the forces on these frequencies may be appreciable. These time delays will create a critical problem if, as the Pentagon assumes in many of its scenarios, the Minuteman force and the launch control centers are vulnerable to Soviet ICBMs. In that case, the missiles and the command centers could be destroyed before VLF launch orders got through. "A lot of us are less than comfortable with the Looking Glass VLF system," an Air Force communications adviser told me.

The Emergency Rocket Communications System at Whiteman Air Force Base is another method for broadcasting Emergency Action Messages, but it is one of the oddest arrangements in the whole command system. These rockets have been put in what the Pentagon believes to be highly vulnerable fixed locations—one of the Minuteman missile fields. In the standard attack scenarios, they are considered to be the first thing that goes. Desmond Ball said that he was astonished by the decision to place the communications rockets at Whiteman. After all, it would be trivial, he noted, to equip every satellite the U.S. government launched with a simple device that could be activated to spread an Emergency Action Message to all U.S. military bases. Satellites in high orbits would face none of the risks of imminent assault to which the present emergency rockets are exposed. With such obvious ways of arranging the facile transmission of orders, Ball said, it was really quite bizarre to be dependent on "silly, gimmicky" arrangements such as communications rockets based where they were most likely to be destroyed.

Of all the potential communications problems facing Looking Glass, the most complex ones are posed by the phenomenon known as electromagnetic pulse (EMP). A side effect of all nuclear explosions, it has become the focus of major Pentagon attention within the past decade or so. At issue is the concern that every piece of modern electronic circuitry—from digital watches to computers to the entire national electric power grid and telecommunications system—might suddenly stop working as soon as a few large Soviet weapons were detonated somewhere high above the continental United States. These weapons might zap all sensitive electronic equipment in the country with an unprecedented electrical jolt.

The EMP issue, which is easy to sensationalize, is difficult to resolve. This is partly because little detailed information on the subject is available in the open literature. It also reflects a situation in which a high degree of technical complexity combines with a lack of data to produce a wide range of opinions among scientists. "There's a lot of uncertainty, a lot of conclusions based on theory, and a whole set of simplifying assumptions," one government consultant told me. "Many of these [EMP] issues are controversial and judgmental," a former member of the Defense Nuclear Agency, which is responsible for testing the effects of EMP on various kinds of military equipment, said. "A lot of times there is not enough data. There is a lot of speculation." Another government official who has reviewed the EMP problem remarked, "You can't put two EMP experts in a room and have them agree on anything."

The last observation is a bit extreme, because the experts do at least agree on the fact that EMP is a real phenomenon, even if they part company in assessing its implications. The simple physics of EMP is not in dispute. Every nuclear weapon gives off various kinds of energy. Some of that energy is in the form of gamma rays. If a large weapon is detonated close to the ground, most of the damage is caused by the resulting heat and blast and by the extensive radioactive fallout. The prompt gamma rays and associated electromagnetic disturbances are relatively trivial in comparison with all the other effects of the weapon.

However, if a large nuclear weapon is detonated at high altitudes— a few hundred miles above the United States, say—the gamma rays assume an altogether different significance. The energetic gamma rays would interact in the upper atmosphere, creating intense electromagnetic radiation that would spread for a thousand miles or so in every direction. It could bathe the entire country is an electrical storm that could potentially affect much of the nation's communications and electronic circuitry. Unlike lightning bolts, which are highly localized, the EMP phenomenon would have broad-ranging effects, which would be especially pronounced since the EMP disturbance is formed locally wherever the gamma rays strike the top of the atmosphere. This means that the voltage from the burst does not diminish much even at great distances from the point of the explosion.

The possible repercussions of EMP are all the more dramatic because of the way in which power lines, telephone lines, antennas, and other equipment can "collect" it. If a length of wire is exposed, say, to an electrical field of ten thousand volts per foot, then two feet will be hit with twenty thousand volts, three feet will be hit with thirty thousand volts, and so on. "The longer the lines, the more current they will pick up," a Pentagon consultant on EMP explained. If the lines in question happen to be telephone lines that lead into central switching centers, which route messages from one place to another across the country, the accumulated EMP could seriously damage the backbone of the nation's telecommunications system. Most of the experts to whom I've spoken believe that the land-lines upon which the Department of Defense depends for critical messages are highly susceptible to disruption from EMP. This is partly due to the new technology that has been introduced in recent years.

Older electronic equipment, such as the radio and television sets of yesteryear that used vacuum tubes, and systems that normally operate at high voltages are not expected to be affected much by EMP. Modern integrated circuits, on the other hand—the kind installed in everything from hand-calculators to mammoth computers—work at very low voltages and may be affected by the sudden high-voltage jolt from high-altitude nuclear detonations. "Chips and this low-power microtechnology burn out when one lights a match a mile away, so to speak," General Richard Ellis commented.

Such extreme pessimism about EMP is questioned by many who have studied the problem. It is not that they dismiss EMP altogether. The issue is whether EMP will cause wholesale destruction of the nation's communications and electronic circuits or whether the effects will be more limited. "EMP is a middle-size problem," a Pentagon adviser told me. "It is not the case that one weapon will wipe out all electronic circuits."

A government official who has extensively studied the problem said, "The more I look at EMP, the more I find it to be overstated. The fifty thousand volts per meter figure"—a standard estimate of the strength of the pulse—"is a worst-case estimate. It's not realistic. EMP is more a problem of disruption than destruction. EMP might create actual total loss of a critical transmitter, and on a selective basis it can be very important in terms of outright destruction." The overall effect of EMP, he continued, is more likely to be "disruption in which circuit breakers get flipped, lines go down temporarily, you have to repeat messages, and so forth." This did not mean, he cautioned, that EMP would not create major problems. "For time-sensitive operations, such as getting the bombers off the ground, you can't afford much disruption. In a context in which minutes or seconds can be important, minor disruption can translate into major degradation of [command] system capability."

A balanced assessment of the effects of EMP requires recognition that many things can be done, and have been done, to protect critical equipment against it. Various forms of shielding can be installed to deflect the pulse, and critical equipment can be designed to reduce the chances of disruption. The Minuteman missile silos and launch control centers, as a case in point, and the missiles themselves, have been extensively safeguarded against EMP, officials note. The cables that link the launch control centers with the silos are inside massive lead sheaths and buried about six feet deep. Large surge arresters are put in to prevent the pulse from damaging equipment. "Minuteman was probably the first system to approach the EMP problem systematically," a government contractor who worked on the Minuteman communications system said.

Some officials concede, however, that it is hard to test the effectiveness of all of these precautions. The "silos and LCCs are EMP-hardened. They have filters, for example, put in to detect EMP and to shut down the electronics for a microsecond to protect them from the pulse, but they are not really tested," one analyst said.

In any case, the application of protective measures against EMP has been somewhat hit or miss, and much of the equipment in the command system is unprotected or inadequately protected at present. Thus, of the four E-4 planes originally put into service in the Kneecap program, only one of these airborne Presidential command posts (designated the E-4B) was EMP-hardened. The others (designated E-4A) were ordinary Boeing 747s, although they are now in the process of being upgraded to the E-4B configuration. (The Soviets reportedly have surveillance means to determine whether the Kneecap plane that happens to be on standby at any given time is an E-4A or an E-4B.)

The task of protecting the E-4 planes from EMP is extremely difficult and expensive (more than a hundred million dollars per plane), since the technique used is to harden the entire hull of the plane to prevent damaging levels of EMP from getting inside the aircraft. There are some two thousand penetrations on the plane's fuselage, and plugging them against EMP is a major undertaking. Even when this is done, "the uncertainties concerning the response of the aircraft to EMP are overwhelming," one official noted.

Some of the variables that will determine what happens are the angle at which the EMP burst hits the plane, what equipment is on or off at the time, and whether the trailing wire—the five-mile-long VLF antenna with which Kneecap, like Looking Glass, is equipped—is deployed. That antenna would be a giant collector of EMP. In principle, certain things can be done—such as installing spark gaps and surge arresters—to prevent the wire from delivering EMP into the plane, but how well they will work is hard to determine. The "general consensus," one expert told me, is that "the E-4B has passed the test. People are satisfied that all that could be done has been done, although that is not to say that confidence is extremely high."

The Air Force operates a special EMP test-bed at Kirtland Air Force Base in New Mexico. The centerpiece of the apparatus is a mammoth wooden trestle—held together with wooden bolts, rather than metal ones—that is surrounded by antennas designed to produce electrical bursts similar to EMP. Planes can be rolled out onto the trestle, zapped, and the effects on their equipment determined. The trestle is intended to help determine what EMP will do to planes in flight. Another facility at Kirtland tests what will happen to planes parked on the ground. Testing apparatus is also available to determine the EMP hardness of warheads, missiles, radios, and other equipment.

The E-4A and one of the Looking Glass EC-135s have been tested at Kirtland, as have other planes such as the Navy's TACAMO and the SAC B-52 bombers. The results of the tests have not been made public. An Air Force spokesman at Kirtland said, "We never talk about what we find out." One thing he did mention, however, was that the E-4B has not been tested there and is not yet scheduled to be tested. The lack of such testing seems rather odd, since it would appear to make sense, before going to the enormous expense of converting the E-4As into E-4Bs, to determine how effective the additional protective measures are. The necessity for such testing is underscored, one Air Force adviser noted, by the kinds of surprises that have already occurred in the experiments done on the EMP hardness of various pieces of military equipment. He noted, "In EMP testing, nothing that you expect to break breaks. It's the wires you didn't think of that cause problems." Why the E-4B has not been tested, and why the Air Force is proceeding to acquire further E-4Bs without such testing, is not a subject that the Air Force is willing to discuss.

The EC-135s that have been on the Looking Glass mission since 1961, unlike the newer E-4 Kneecap planes, were built before the implications of EMP were appreciated. "The one continuing weakness of the EC-135 is its lack of EMP hardening," a special report to Congress noted in 1981. "EMP could create a terrible problem for Looking Glass," a former Pentagon official explained. The main difficulty would be caused by the disruption of the land-lines that Looking Glass hooks into via radio. This would badly damage its communications with the main ground command posts. The plane itself would be less directly affected by EMP. This is not so much the result of deliberate hardening against EMP—the plane has very little of that—as of happenstance.

"Generally the EC-135 is not considered to be that vulnerable, primarily due to the age of the electronics," one official explained. "It doesn't have a lot of modern microcircuits. The EC-135's airworthiness is quite high. Components may fail, but there's quite a bit of redundancy." Some of the newer equipment that has been installed on Looking Glass, he noted, such as the terminal that allows it to use the AFSATCOM satellite, is EMP-hardened. "The primary EC-135 problem is in some of the communications components. Some are robust and others have an unacceptable probability of failure due to EMP. There are plans to correct this. The planes are now in a period of initial hardening against EMP. In the next five years, the entire fleet ought to be hardened sufficiently to withstand EMP."

A worrisome problem that will remain with the plane's EMP protection concerns the long VLF antenna. There is no way that piece of equipment can be tested at the Kirtland facility. "You get into some of the variables that affect susceptibility to EMP and you throw up your hands," a government analyst noted.

At the moment, the EMP factor means that uninterrupted transmission of emergency orders from Looking Glass using the main SAC communications systems—which depend on leased telephone lines—can be guaranteed for only a half hour or less following a Soviet attack. This is the time it would take the Soviets to set off high-altitude detonations above the continent. The worst hypothesized effects of EMP may not matter too much, of course, since the central components of the command and control system—such as the Pentagon and the small number of AT&T switching centers—can be destroyed very easily anyway, and just as quickly, by direct Soviet attack.

———

Looking Glass, according to all of the studies of the present command system, is the command post most likely to survive a surprise attack. The mobility of the plane, and its secret flight pattern, obviously help make it more difficult to destroy than any of the fixed headquarters.

Still, there are questions about how long it could remain in the air following a nuclear attack on the United States.

Part of the problem involves the dust and debris that would be put into the air by Soviet nuclear detonations. To destroy hardened underground Minuteman silos, the Soviet warheads must go off on the ground, as close as possible to their targets. Those ground-bursts will put billions of pounds of soil into the air, the explosions creating the kind of discharge associated with large volcanic eruptions. There will also be huge conflagrations resulting from nuclear detonations, and these fires will put additional material into the air. Jet aircraft engines cannot operate if they are choked with such debris. Commercial airline traffic had to be diverted over a large region downwind of the Mt. St. Helens volcano after it erupted in 1980, and the aerosols lofted up all the way into the stratosphere by nuclear detonations would create comparable difficulties for Looking Glass and the other planes in the SAC airborne launch control fleet. This would be compounded by the fact that the detritus from the nuclear explosions would be highly radioactive—and none of the SAC planes can afford the weight penalty associated with heavy shielding.

To some extent, the dust problem can be obviated by keeping Looking Glass and the other planes upwind of the Minuteman bases. This will protect them, at least initially, although once the fallout from a large attack is spread across the country by the prevailing winds, the planes are likely to be caught in it. In addition, keeping the planes away from the missile bases involves the complication that they may then be out of range to use the UHF radio frequencies that are their only means of directly launching Minuteman missiles from their silos.

Radioactive dust is not, in any event, the only phenomenon that could knock Looking Glass out of the sky. More direct means of attacking the plane may be used, its location being a less than well kept secret. The plane flies at a normal cruising altitude of between twenty-six thousand and forty thousand feet. Commercial airliners use this part of the air space as well, and it is necessary, in order to avoid collisions with them, for Looking Glass to be under the supervision of the civilian air traffic control system. The battle staff explained to me that they have to check in with the air traffic control stations along their route, doing so over radio frequencies that anyone can monitor.

Simple radio direction-finding equipment can therefore be used to locate the plane. The plane also appears on the air traffic control system radar screens, and anyone with access to those can learn the plane's position. It is also possible that the Soviets, using so-called "ferret" satellites, can track the plane by monitoring its radio transmissions and that the Soviets can find it with spaceborne radars.

Once its location is known, Looking Glass can be targeted as part of an attack on the entire U.S. command system. According to Richard Garwin, Soviet missiles could barrage the region where they believed Looking Glass to be. If the plane were located, they could try to estimate how far it could travel within the fifteen- to thirty-minute flight time of their missiles to that region, taking into account the fact that each weapon they fired could destroy any plane within ten miles or so of its detonation. If the Soviets had the ability to retarget their warheads in flight—using a satellite monitoring Looking Glass to direct the warheads against it—their chances of destroying the plane would be even better.

"I do not believe that military command posts in aircraft provide survivability," Garwin said. "Putting their command and control in an airplane, as in Vietnam, enhances the status of pilots but it does not do the job as well as mobile ground-based command posts."

Looking Glass can fly for eleven hours on its normal fuel supply—half the plane's gross weight at takeoff is fuel—and it can be refueled in the air, by tanker aircraft, to extend its flight time up to an estimated thirty-six to seventy-two hours. At that point, SAC officials say, its engines would fail for lack of oil. The Pentagon's recent studies of how to fight a protracted nuclear war noted this problem and others, such as the lack of any real plan for what to do when Looking Glass had to land. Finding an airport that was neither bombed out nor covered with fallout would be one difficulty, and another would be the unavailability of auxiliary power supplies to keep the plane functioning. Finding a method for relaying long-distance messages would be still one more problem, since the plane's long VLF antenna, for example, is only designed for use in the air.

Some of Looking Glass's endurance problems could be solved fairly readily. Installing somewhat larger oil tanks could keep the planes in the air longer. The Air Force is not always eager to fix problems in such direct ways, however. "The Air Force wouldn't mind buying a new airplane simply because the oil reservoir on the old one is too small—or 'because the ashtrays are full,' as we used to say," Garwin commented.

Nevertheless, with all the exigencies of a nuclear conflict, Looking Glass may remain functional as the national command post for no more than a few hours after Soviet missiles are launched against the United States—however well lubricated its engines may be. Indeed, when all of its potential problems in communicating are taken into account, the ability of Looking Glass to transmit orders may deteriorate as quickly as fifteen to thirty minutes after an enemy attack begins— the time it would take the Soviets to knock out the ground installations on which it depends. The plane might be more survivable, in principle, than any fixed command posts, but Looking Glass can only order a retaliatory attack on the Soviet Union during the brief grace period before its communications capability disappears. Thus, having this plane in the air does not greatly alter the hair trigger posture of the U.S. command system.

Nor does the plane greatly increase the likelihood of being able to control the rapid escalation of a nuclear war. To the contrary. As one study of the Looking Glass mission concluded, "[T]he predicament of being trapped in an aircraft that cannot return to the ground without inviting destruction almost guarantees that the General will order attacks with everything in his power before landing."

Looking Glass, it is important to note, has no tie-in with the "hot line" to Moscow. The U.S. terminal for it is in the National Military Command Center in the Pentagon. The Soviet receiving station for the hot line is in the Kremlin. Both ends of the hot line could be severed readily, especially if both sides executed the decapitation maneuvers they have both so carefully planned. No provision for a surviving hot line has been made, yet the current U.S. strategy of controlled escalation presumes that a nuclear war can somehow be terminated on terms favorable to the United States. Some form of contact with the Soviets, and some kind of negotiations, will have to take place. But who will be able to represent the United States? How will they communicate with the other side? Whom will they talk to? Without a reliable means to carry out high-speed negotiations, a strategy of controlled escalation has a rather fundamental problem. "The United States has no business having a war-fighting policy if we have no ability to call them off," one official said. "How do you call off a war? How do you accept the Soviet surrender? Or give them ours?"

Since Looking Glass, for want of any other surviving central command post, may have to carry out any such negotiations, I asked General Davis how those on board would be able to communicate with the Soviets. "Well, there are many ways. Looking Glass has a significant communications capability," he replied. "It does not have a hot line as the hot line exists today between the National Military Command Center and the Kremlin, but there are many ways to communicate through a series of satellites, so paths could be found, I'm confident. We could get word."

Communications experts are less sanguine. If communications with the Soviets were that easy, there would be little need in the first place for the existing hot line. Moreover, once one or both sides had been battered by an attack, the residual message links even within each country, and between each country's forces and its central command posts, would be limited. The prospects for quickly establishing a connection between Looking Glass and Soviet military leaders in some unknown bunker therefore do not appear to be great. Both sides, in addition, would be fearful that in the process of communicating they might give away the locations of their headquarters and surviving commanders, thereby facilitating direct attacks upon them. Neither side may have the ability, while carrying on negotiations, to keep its own forces under control—for example, to prevent isolated submarine commanders from lashing out at the other side.

Lieutenant General William Hillsman, the former Director of the Defense Communications Agency, disagreed with General Davis about the ease with which links with the Soviets could be established. Between the U.S. and Soviet military establishments today such connections are essentially nonexistent, he said, and they would be very difficult to establish in the middle of a nuclear war. Apart from trying to reach them on the telephone, he said, "our ability really to communicate at the division commander level, to the corps commander level, or a corps commander, there is probably no way to do that."

Without surviving central commands, the decapitated United States and Soviet military establishments would be reduced to the status of pea-brained dinosaurs. Each might still have giant thermonuclear claws and tusks, but no sure means of deciding where to swing its tail, or even

of knowing whether it was still connected to extremities. It seems unreasonable to expect that two essentially headless creatures, in their
death throes, would be able to carry on much of a dialogue on how
they might bury the hatchet. Yet the ability of the two sides to carry
on negotiations to end an ongoing nuclear slugfest is presumed by the
present U.S. policy of controlled escalation. The policy is exceedingly
dangerous since leaders adhering to it, in Paul Bracken's words, "might
end up bumbling into a nuclear war with a vague belief in its con-
trollability." Any U.S. leaders who think a nuclear conflict can somehow be deftly managed—and stopped before it has gone too far—might
find it a sobering experience to serve a few missions as VLF antenna
operators on Looking Glass.

6
THE COMMUNICATIONS GAP

Every June, the major companies in the defense-communications business hold their convention in Washington. The get-together at the Sheraton Washington Hotel—the industry's equivalent of the Cannes Film Festival—is sponsored by the Armed Forces Communications and Electronics Association (AFCEA). On display is the latest in military communications and information-processing equipment, ranging from small field radios and radar-jamming devices to hundred million dollar communications satellites. It is all for sale. In between banquets and seminars, the hardware is looked over by top U.S. military officials.

Little of the impressively sophisticated communications equipment exhibited at the AFCEA convention will be found aboard the EC-135s assigned to the Looking Glass mission. Those planes, which have been in service for more than two decades, have not benefited from routine upgrading to keep their communications capability anywhere close to the state of the art.

Nor do the much newer Kneecap planes, which went into service between 1974 and 1980, have anything close to current-generation equipment. The original specifications for the four Boeing 747s that were to be used as Presidential airborne command posts called for them to be outfitted with much more advanced communications and data-processing equipment. The first three planes (the E-4A version), however, were simply given the same communications sets as the older Looking Glass planes. The one E-4B got a little extra equipment— such as an additional satellite terminal and a higher-power VLF transmitter as well as (yet untested) EMP hardening—but it was otherwise unimproved.

Should the battle staff on any of the E-4s, for example, want to prepare revised targeting plans per the President's instructions, their sparsely equipped flying command post will not offer them much in the way of computer assistance. Dr. Gerald Dinneen, the Assistant Secretary of Defense in the Carter Administration, told Congress that Kneecap "has a bunch of file cabinets. If they want to generate various options, they have to go to the file cabinets and do things basically by hand."

The military has not regarded the lack of computers on Kneecap with the dismay shown by Dr. Dinneen, an engineer who had been at MIT's Lincoln Laboratory and who joined Honeywell after leaving his civilian post at the Pentagon. Command and control equipment that may be shockingly primitive by the highest engineering standards is not necessarily worrisome to either the Air Force or the Navy, since neither service has any interest in fighting slow-motion nuclear wars that require moment-by-moment management by a central command authority. The main options preferred by the services should it come to a nuclear confrontation—preemptive attack or massive retaliation— can be executed without the assistance of the President and his aides sitting in front of flying computer consoles.

Still, the disdain felt by the Strategic Air Command and the Navy for the civilian strategists' notions of limited nuclear options is only part of the reason for the lack of up-to-date equipment on the Looking Glass and Kneecap fleet. After all, the obsolescence of the military's communications systems is hardly a problem just with these airplanes or with the strategic command and control system. "If you think we're in trouble in strategic connectivity, we're in terrible trouble in the battlefield theater area," General Ellis, the former Commander in Chief of SAC, told a Harvard seminar in 1982. Indeed, a review of the military's overall handling, or mishandling, of communications technology is essential to understanding why such large gaps in strategic command and control occurred in the first place and have persisted for so long.

"You might be amused by some of the exposure I had to NATO command and control," General Ellis said. "In 1971 I was sitting happily in Wiesbaden, Germany, as vice commander in chief of U.S. Forces Europe, and unexpectedly I was sent to Ismir, Turkey, as commander of the Sixth Allied Tactical Air Force. That is the easternmost projection of NATO's air power. . . . My communications—when I walked into my office, I'll never forget the terrible shock. The phone looked like a World War I instrument. I picked it up, finally somebody answered, and he sounded like he was on the other side of the world. And I said, 'Who is this?' and his voice said, 'I'm your secretary.' He was right outside the door."

Billions of dollars are spent each year on communications equipment for the military—the kind of gear on display at the AFCEA convention. Still, there are inordinate delays in getting it into the field and assembling it into a system that works together satisfactorily. Lieutenant General John Cushman, the retired former head of U.S. forces in Korea, has conducted an exhaustive study of the delays in upgrading the military's communications system. "The obstacles are not financial —in fact, billions of dollars which have been provided have been wasted—but are primarily organizational and institutional," he concluded. Cushman pointed to the "almost impossible bureaucratic superstructure and funding/approval process" within the Pentagon that creates "an all-encompassing thicket" impeding needed command and control improvements.

Cushman's report, published in July 1983 under the auspices of the Harvard University Center for Information Policy Research, focused on the communications systems deployed in the U.S. military's main theaters of operation. Cushman found, "For the typical senior commander, allied or U.S., whose forces must use these systems, they represent the largely unplanned splicing together of ill-fitting components which have been delivered to his forces by relatively independent parties far away who have coordinated adequately neither with him and his staff nor with each other. And they neither exploit the present capabilities of technology nor does the system for their development adequately provide that future systems will."

Cushman provided detailed examples of the inadequacy of the

present communications hardware. The standard combat radios with which the U.S. Army is equipped, the VRC-12, he notes, "are based on technology of the early 1950s." The Pentagon is still buying thousands of these radios each year, despite the fact that they do not provide the kind of secure, jam-resistant communications that would be needed in combat against an enemy whose forces were outfitted with elementary communications interception or jamming equipment. (Vietnam, he noted, in which U.S. troops were pitted against forces that did not have such equipment, has misled Pentagon planners badly; the command and control situation in a NATO/Warsaw Pact war would be very different.) The process of acquiring newer radios that might be equal to the Soviet electronic warfare threat began in the 1960s, but replacements for the VRC-12 have not yet been put into the hands of the troops. "The lengthy development cycle" for the new radios "is not unusual," Cushman found. "The Army's typical best cycle for development and fielding of its command and control equipment is twelve to fourteen years, and it is usually longer."

So long are the delays, for example, in getting computers into the field, that the commanders at many U.S. military bases, Cushman reported, are going out—using money from "training funds"—to buy Apple and Radio Shack personal computers rather than waiting for the custom-made military computers whose development is snagged somewhere in the Pentagon's complex equipment procurement bureaucracy. These "black market" acquistions, as he calls them, may solve temporary problems, but they suffer from a major drawback: the ad hoc computer setup at one base may not be able to link up easily with the homemade computer installation at the base across the road, or with the central computers at various headquarters, thereby delaying the passing of critical combat messages.

The most noteworthy contributor to the command and control problem, Cushman commented, is the wide gulf between the "providers" and the "users": the offices in the Pentagon, which oversee development and production of communications gear, and the commanders out in the field who would have to use it in combat. The procurement bureaucracy within each service dominates the hardware acquisition process, he says, and has a "ten-to-one ratio of influence over the users." Instead of spending years developing custom-made, superdeluxe systems, he believes, the services ought to make better use of available off-the-shelf technology and get it into the field quickly. His exhortation is not immediately appealing to the procurement bureaucracy, which has no strong inclination to adopt streamlined purchasing arrangements that would largely put itself out of business.

Other experts share the view that lack of funding hardly accounts for the present shortfall in the military's command and control capability. "I think it is hard to make the case that not enough money has been spent in the command and control and communications area," Charles W. Snodgrass, a former staff member of the House Appropriations Committee, noted. "I fundamentally don't believe that the problem of command and control is budgetary. If this country can't buy a good command and control system for five billion dollars, I don't think it can be bought. . . . So I don't think that lack of resources is the reason this country has not been able to build an effective command and control system. I think it's more the nonbudgetary issues: fighting for turf, the separation of the military services, the competition between the civilian and military sides of the Pentagon, and with the civilian agencies such as NASA."

Even the suppliers of communications equipment to the Pentagon are remarkably candid about the situation that exists, suggesting that the Pentagon is deriving no more practical benefit from the advanced communications equipment it is buying than an illiterate would get from an encyclopedia. James M. Osborne is the former vice president and general manager of the Government Communications and Automated Systems Division of RCA, and he was program manager for the special communications system installed for launching the Minuteman missiles. The present Pentagon procurement bureaucracy, he told me, is unable to specify what it wants, unable to oversee the production and development of what it has ordered from the communications and electronics industry, and unable to make good use of the equipment it gets. "Finally, we deliver the equipment over to our customers—late, and at an exorbitant price. We hand it over to people who don't have the capability to operate, repair, [and] maintain it, so in the end the intended use of the equipment is subverted. It's just not what we want."

At the AFCEA convention, I spoke with retired Rear Admiral Jon Boyes, the president of this defense-industry organization. With so much advanced communications technology available to the Pentagon, one would think that reliable and timely orders could be delivered, I noted. An Air Force spokesman had told me that the United States now had the capability to communicate back and forth "from President to foxhole" using the new technology. Admiral Boyes cautioned, "Let's go back to the famous incident of the *Mayaguez* affair in the Thai Gulf."

The *Mayaguez*, an American merchant ship, was seized by the Cambodians on May 12, 1975. President Gerald Ford dispatched U.S. forces to rescue the crew. The communications backup for the operation was a fiasco, with U.S. forces on the scene unable to communicate with each other. "The carrier planes had UHF, and the Marines had VHF, and the Air Force had to bring in UHF so that everybody could talk," Admiral Boyes explained. Another complication was with the link back to Washington. The Pentagon was having problems with one of its satellites and had to borrow a NATO satellite to send voice messages to Hawaii; from there the messages could be sent through a U.S. Defense Communications System satellite to Thailand. However, some of the messages had to be routed through Clark Air Force Base in the Philippines. Security broke down at that point, because orders were passed out to the Air Force and the Navy "in the clear"—unencoded and over channels that anyone could monitor. The Cambodians learned how many Marine helicopters there were and where they were going. As a result, forty-one Marines were killed and fifty wounded when the helicopters landed.

The irony of it all was that shortly before the Marines attacked on May 14, Cambodian radio had announced that the *Mayaguez* and its crew would be released—just as the Cambodians had freed the crews of Panamanian and South Korean vessels seized a few days earlier. The Marines, at great cost, succeeded in boarding a deserted ship, because the crew they were attempting to rescue was on another boat that was bringing it to the U.S. destroyer *Wilson*. The captain of the *Wilson* informed the White House that the men from the *Mayaguez* were safe, and President Ford ordered all offensive operations to a halt. The most disturbing aspect of the entire incident was that bombing of the Cambodian mainland continued for nearly an hour after the President called it off. One shudders to think what the implications would be if the confrontation had taken place, say, in Europe, and the order to cease hostilities involved nuclear instead of conventional bombs.

Such concerns are increased by the awareness that NATO nuclear forces are coordinated primarily by a nonsecure telephone system and a radio backup, called CEMETERY NET, that is subject to immediate disruption in the event of a nuclear conflict on the Continent.

I asked Admiral Boyes whether the kind of communications problems experienced during the Cambodian incident in 1975 had been rectified. "After the *Mayaguez* affair was all over, we attempted to set up a program for joint common voice communications equipment, and the thing is still stumbling around in the bamboo," he replied. "I would say in the positive sense, which is the way we should address it, it is being improved upon. And whereas I am not pessimistic about it, we have a long, long way to go in our command, control, and communications."

A special Congressional panel that reviewed the command and control problem a few years after the *Mayaguez* incident estimated that "it will take at least twenty-five years" to replace "the existing kludge of tactical communications equipment." I have yet to find a dictionary with the word "kludge" in it, but I think I can understand what the authors of that report were talking about.

One engineer at the AFCEA convention looked out over the equipment displays as we spoke, and commented on the array of new communications systems being developed under Pentagon auspices. "How they're going to fight a war with all this gear is beyond me," he said. "They'll be tripping all over themselves." His own company is building one of the latest systems intended to convey the launch order to U.S. strategic nuclear forces.

The Pentagon's ineptitude in exploiting communications technology has been obvious for some time. The Kennedy Administration, for example, found that far from being at the forefront of the computer and telecommunications age, the services were relying on essentially the same technology used during World War II. "During the Cuban missile crisis, Kennedy discovered that worldwide communications was 'deficient,' to put it euphemistically," a Pentagon adviser said. The situation today is not vastly different—satellite programs notwithstanding—and in one sense the ability to exploit communications and electronics technology seems to have fallen off badly.

The flexibility displayed in World War II—when the Allies rapidly developed the means to confound German radar, to confuse German radio navigation systems, and to jam German communications—is not a virtue of today's Pentagon planning bureaucracy. Such high-speed innovativeness is quite foreign to today's peacetime military. "I think we are not well organized to do the same sort of jobs that we did during World War II," Lieutenant General Hillman Dickinson said. "We have a long way to get back to that capability, or even to begin to create it."

In 1962, hoping to overcome the glaring shortfall in communications capability, the Kennedy Administration established the Defense Communications Agency to try to coordinate the development of an upgraded system. A directive was also issued that year establishing the Worldwide Military Command and Control System and the National Military Command Center in the Pentagon. No technological leap forward occurred when WWMCCS was set up. At birth it simply consisted of the widely scattered defense communications facilities that already existed, which, by administrative fiat, were henceforth expected to be operated as a system. The communications gear to be used and the procedures to be followed in the future were unspecified.

The armed services, which prefer as much as possible to stay with their traditional missions—fielding armies, sailing ships, and flying airplanes—gave little attention to making WWMCCS an effective communications tool. True, the revolution in electronics and communications technology was hard for them to ignore—who can forget the role of radar in the Battle of Britain?—and lip service was paid to it. "If there is a World War III, the winner will be the side that can best control and manage the electromagnetic spectrum," Admiral Thomas Moorer, the former Chairman of the Joint Chiefs, stated.

The services persisted, nevertheless, in seeing sophisticated electronic equipment and communications devices as add-ons to conventional equipment rather than as urgently needed technology that greatly changed the concept of modern warfare. There was also little enthusiasm for WWMCCS because of the feeling that centralized control over military operations was implied by a centralized communications system. "Many military commanders think the worst thing that ever happened was the establishment of the National Military Command Center in the Pentagon," Charles Snodgrass commented. "The field generals in many cases have been delighted that it has taken so long and has been so inefficient and didn't work because, again, what fun is it to be a four-star general . . . if any time a real war starts Lyndon Johnson goes over the bombing list every night and tells you what you can or can't bomb? You didn't go to West Point twenty-five years ago and train your whole professional life to have somebody look over your shoulder." He added, "And you can find very respectable military opinion which says that the Iranian raid failed because the commander is so busy looking back over his shoulder and talking to Washington under the spotlight that he isn't able to take the chances he needs to take."

General Richard Ellis, a proponent of enhanced communications, admitted that his outlook was not always shared by his colleagues in the military. When equipment such as communications satellites came along, he noted, "[p]eople saw it then (and I guess some still do) as a mixed blessing, because it put Washington in immediate contact with the battlefield commander. Battlefield commanders normally aren't interested in that."

No commanders are less interested in being kept on a short leash from Washington than those of the Navy. The Navy traditionally operates as a vehicle for projecting power over wide areas and is used to having considerable independence. Naval commanders have their assigned mission and do not feel that they need continuous contact with the Pentagon or the White House in order to carry it out. Communications with nuclear submarines on patrol are naturally quite difficult, but this is not a situation that submarine commanders lament.

"The Navy's basic view," Desmond Ball said, "is that you put the subs to sea, the subs are secure, the submarine commanders are competent, they know their job, and they don't need day-to-day orders from Washington. They're not in the business of playing any finely tuned nuclear war. If a nuclear war comes and the subs have to be used, then the submarine commanders will take responsibility for that. And having all these other [communications] gadgets and gizmos are not of much interest to them." The TACAMO program, which offers little in the way of effective post-attack communications with the submarines on patrol, is apparently just a way to maintain the color of civilian control. In practice, the submarines retain the kind of autonomy the Navy cherishes.

————

In addition to service tradition and pride of command, there are major practical reasons for the unenthusiastic response to WWMCCS and advanced communications technology. A dominant factor has been the worry that this equipment is expensive and competes for the funds available for the services' highest priority purchases: more planes, tanks, and ships. Lieutenant General William Hillsman said that in the continuing in-house battle over the Pentagon budget, if something "doesn't fly, go under water, or go with treads with a big gun on the front of it, it's likely to get cut, if you're not careful to kind of watch where the ball is, in what court, and try to save it at the last minute." A general who has worked at NORAD said that the problem with communications gear is that it's hard to get funding for things that "aren't shiny and make a lot of noise and smoke."

Complicating the allocation of resources to command and control is the troublesome syndrome of cost overruns in the procurement of other equipment. When the cost of a new fighter plane skyrockets, for example, the Air Force has a choice: cut back on the number of expensive new planes it will purchase or divert money from other areas, such as maintenance and spare parts for existing planes, to pay for them. This latter option—which the Air Force has routinely exercised —cuts the combat readiness of the Air Force and involves, in effect, a compromise between the current security of the United States and the promise of increased security in the future. "Now, try telling a tactical commander who's got seventy-two airplanes sitting out on the ramp but hasn't any munitions to go with them, no spares at all to keep them flying, that what he really needs is command and control and communications," Air Force General Robert Marsh said. "You know he won't go for it. It's a matter of priorities."

The battle for a piece of the Pentagon budget involves ferocious nonstop competition among the services and their various program offices, as well as complex interactions among thousands of contractors and a plethora of Congressional committees and subcommittees. The stakes are enormous: individual careers, the places of the services in the military hierarchy, hundreds of thousands of jobs, billions of dollars of profits, substantial campaign contributions. "That's real money you're dickering for," General Dickinson remarked.

Human nature and the incentives to which large bureaucracies and business organizations respond do not guarantee that what best serves the national defense becomes the deciding factor—or even a dominant consideration—in allocating Pentagon resources. Felix Rohatyn, the investment banker and head of New York City's Municipal Assistance Corporation, watched bemusedly not long ago when various city, state, and union officials clashed over the manner in which an unexpected surplus would be spent by the city. He quipped, "As soon as there is a whiff, a whiff of anything remotely relating to money, everybody goes off the wall."

Rohatyn was speaking about a fight over a few hundred million dollars. When the divvying up of a three hundred billion dollar annual defense budget is at issue, the self-interest of all parties involved is stimulated—uncontrollably. General John Vessey, Jr., the Chairman of the Joint Chiefs of Staff, has spoken of the need to give everybody in the Pentagon "appetite suppressant pills." He did not identify the magic ingredient that could moderate the immoderate ambitions of each service and defense contractor for ever larger programs and budgets.

At the June 1983 AFCEA convention, I asked Admiral Boyes about the driving forces affecting the acquisition of command and control equipment by the Pentagon. "We're caught up in a lot of parochialisms between the services constantly fighting," he said. "We're caught up with the parochialisms in the intelligence community, and the communications people, and the computer people all looking out for themselves, designing their own systems. That's the issue to me."

As the investigation of Pearl Harbor revealed, interservice rivalry like that between Admiral Kimmel and General Short was not a form of healthy competition but a divisive force that undermined the nation's security. Such behavior on the part of the turf-conscious services continues, as a June 1983 investigation by the General Accounting Office revealed. The government auditors were studying how well certain military equipment had been tested. They were examining, in particular, the common failure to do sufficient research to determine if these systems would stand up against Soviet defenses, such as surface-to-air missiles. (Cutting back on funds for tests is another way to divert resources needed to cover the cost overruns in major procurement programs.) The Air Force had hired a contractor to do some tests and gave it Air Force intelligence data about the way in which a certain Soviet defensive system appeared to work.

The Army, it turned out, had also hired the same contractor to build working replicas of the Soviet system. The Army, however, had more than just intelligence information: it had somehow or other captured the actual Soviet defensive system in question. Nevertheless, the Army did not share this valuable information with the Air Force, which, the GAO reported, only learned of the fact "through unofficial sources."

There is a strong feeling of "us" and "them" within the services, General Cushman noted—the nasty, aggressive, expansionistic, ever-threatening "them" usually being the other services, not the Soviet Union. He said that this outlook "can be extraordinarily inhibiting to effective planning for coordinated multiservice action." In some cases, there are good technical reasons for conflicting views. The Army, for example, being more interested in communications among battalions on the ground, might find one frequency band or technique best for this purpose. The Air Force, on the other hand, might be influenced by the advantages of other frequencies or technologies for air-to-air communications. They might differ, accordingly, on the optimal system for air-to-ground hookups. Such technological considerations, however, are hardly the dominant impulse behind the warped sense of service loyalty that can lead one service to withhold potentially vital intelligence information from another.

According to many observers, in-fighting among the services has had the disastrous effect of delaying the installation of new communications equipment that is needed to enable all U.S. forces to work together in combat. "Look at the [NATO] European military forces today," Admiral Boyes said. "We're still struggling about how do we put AWACS"—the advanced airborne radar and surveillance aircraft—"together with the Navy together with the Army. We're doing it, but it's a painful process. The Air Force and the Navy have been fighting over JTIDS"—the Joint Tactical Information Distribution System—"for years. JTIDS is, you know, a remarkable way of using modern electronics techniques to pass massive amounts of information, and the Navy and the Air Force have been fighting that problem for ten years. One service says I need these characteristics, and the other service says I need these characteristics, and the basis of the dispute is primarily who's going to be in charge. That's the basis of the feud. . . . Ultimately, you're talking two elements that all men face, and that is power and money.

"Contractors, by the very nature of marketing, are parochial," Admiral Boyes continued. "They want to sell a piece of equipment that they have put money into so they can get to the bottom line which is, properly, profit. So they get involved with the service, and they will sell an idea to the service, and then everybody becomes polarized in the service as that's the way we've got to go. Ideas that come out of laboratories, unless they have a sponsor, will die. So a company has to make some very quick decisions, perhaps on a new type of chip or a new technique, and that becomes a commitment to getting that sold, regardless of what other good ideas are on the shelf."

"Everything is so single-interest," Richard DeLauer, the Under Secretary of Defense and the head of the Defense Resources Board, explained. One reason that defense needs, rationally defined and analyzed, do not dominate the budget process, he said, is that there is "no integrated military point of view." Each service is out for itself and "there is no consensus." The Army, DeLauer noted, wants to cut forces, not readiness; the Air Force wants more planes, not readiness; and the Navy wants more big ships over everything. All three services are enmeshed in a continuing struggle, with a common viewpoint occurring only on the rarest of occasions—as when the Joint Chiefs of Staff, without the customarily protracted interservice negotiations, quickly opposed a proposed cut in military salaries.

In principle, defense budgeting should reflect an appraisal of defense needs and a weighing of alternate means to meet them. That is what primers on sound management, and common sense, would suggest. No one familiar with the defense procurement process believes that this is how the Pentagon budget is prepared. "Well, it really boils down to this: what are the real needs? What do I really want to do? What are the alternatives?" James Osborne, the former defense industry executive, noted. "An endemic problem I ran across in most of the programs was that someone had forgotten to do that."

Instead of rational planning, there is what one senior military officer called "a hidden context" in the decision of how to allocate resources. The Joint Strategic Target Planning Staff, he said, which makes up the U.S. strategic war plan, and for which he worked, does not study the kind of targets that, for compelling military reasons, the United States should be able to attack in the event of war. "We don't buy weapons to cover targets, we buy weapons independent of targets—because they are symbols of strength, because the Air Force wants new missiles or the Navy wants new submarines—and then we look around to find targets to shoot at. It's the inverse of the sensible way to do it."

A Pentagon budget analyst expressed the view that one would search in vain to find any military logic behind most Pentagon spending decisions. "The defense budget is an enormous amount of pork," he said. "It gives the President enormous power. It gives Congress enormous power. It represents the biggest concentration of wealth in the economy." According to official pronouncements, the high level of spending is a response to the dangers posed by the Soviet military establishment. The "Soviet threat" was simply "a marketing device," he said, used to sell the miscellaneous projects of the services. There are dangers posed by the Soviet military establishment, he said, but there was still only a weak correlation between the nature of Soviet capabilities and the way in which U.S. military programs were organized.

"There are certain proofs to determine how serious you are about the threat," this Pentagon official said. "If we're so serious about defense, why don't we reinstate the draft, stockpile more weapons in Europe, increase training, build shelters for [NATO] planes, disperse materiel from ground storage sites in Europe?" The emphasis on massive long-term projects—supercarriers for the Navy that won't be available for a decade or more—rather than on increases in the readiness of current forces is a definitive indication, he believed, that self-aggrandizement by the services, rather than compelling defense needs, dominates the Pentagon budget and planning process.

Decision-making on major Pentagon programs is compromised by more than just a lack of objectivity in weighing alternatives—or, in many cases, the general disregard of all alternatives to a program that has already attracted a powerful constituency. From a procedural perspective, the process of deciding what to do is so convoluted that decisions of any kind—even bad ones—are seldom forthcoming. "The problem is, everything moves at the speed of a glacier," Richard DeLauer said. "You take one step forward and three steps back, then you do four steps, and after a week's gone by you've made a step. . . . For every guy who says yes, there are three guys who say no. That's the kind of situation we face."

The battles among the services are fought in a complex review and budgeting process that involves not just the Pentagon but also the White House, the Office of Management and Budget, the General Services Administration, and what Mr. DeLauer called "a jillion" Congressional committees. Good ideas can easily get lost; bad ideas can easily find powerful backers; every idea can be delayed and delayed. The process of winning approval for a new piece of equipment and getting it built and deployed can be so cumbersome that it is practically guaranteed to be obsolete by the time it is put into service. A 1982 review of current military technology by the Institute of Electrical and Electronic Engineers illustrated this situation when it noted that the latest Air Force fighter planes had control systems that used microelectronic chips less advanced than those installed in ordinary hand-held calculators and digital watches.

"We try to evaluate the needs, translate the needs into programs, and follow them through all the oddities of the decision process—which I'd guess I'd best describe as a series of poker games," General Dickinson said. "Because very few decisions are ever made all at once in Washington. If you get a decision made it simply gives you the right to ante one more time in the poker game. That continues clear on through the process until the budget is final, and even then it's subject to additional reprogrammings, and things can fall out from under it later in the year even after you've had it approved by Congress. Certainly there are many, many fingers in the pie, and, as I say, very few have any overall system responsibility or authority."

Once a decision is nominally made, Mr. DeLauer lamented, that is rarely the end of the matter. There are many advocates and "for every winner there are four losers," he said. "You never hear from the winner —he doesn't even call you up and say thanks—but all the losers start wanting to change everything around." DeLauer noted that one of his predecessors at the Pentagon, Gerald Dinneen, got money from Congress for upgrading command and control systems "and bingo, the minute the Services got it the priorities changed, the rate of implementation changed, a whole bunch of things got changed."

Even the President, General Dickinson said, had a hard time getting his personal communications needs satisfied by the procurement bureaucracy. He explained, "It's hard to understand how the President could become a disadvantaged user, but he really was. His Presidential airborne command post was removed from the Air Force budget time after time because the programmers in the Air Force were more interested in fighter squads."

To correct this resource allocation situation, insofar as it related to command and control systems, the Defense Science Board recommended in 1978 that a central office be established in the Pentagon to manage the development and acquisition of new communications systems. The idea did not go over well. The obvious problem was that such a powerful new office would take away from the services their strongly valued independent control over major procurement decisions. As a compromise, a "directorate" on command and control and communications was set up within the office of the Joint Chiefs of Staff. General Dickinson was the first director, and General Herres is his successor. Both have been able to inject suggestions into Pentagon decision-making on command and control. Yet their kibbitzing is no substitute for managerial control, which neither of these Generals, nor any central office in the Pentagon, exercises over the billions of dollars in expenditures that are made annually on communications equipment. "It's very difficult to get the services to agree to have us in their programming knickers," General Dickinson said.

The net result of the services' spending priorities and decision-making methods, the Congressional Budget Office concluded, is that "though nuclear forces have developed substantially in the last decade, the command, control, and communications system has undergone little change."

The Pentagon's difficulties in integrating new communications technology into its accustomed operations have ample historical precedent. The University of Chicago historian William McNeill has studied how various military establishments have dealt with changes brought on by scientific and engineering progress. He has analyzed, for example, the situation that began in the mid-1850s, when "patterns of both naval and land armament that had remained almost stable since the seventeenth century began to crumble away, exposing admirals, generals and statesmen to the acute discomfort of having to face the possibility of war under conditions and with weapons of which they had no direct experience. This put a premium on imagination and intelligence among naval and military leaders and drastically penalized the old bluff disregard for anything that smacked of thinking."

The naval arms race of the early twentieth century, McNeill likewise found, involved a "rush of new technology that cascaded upon the [British] Royal Navy" and put "strains on morals, money, and managerial organization; it also began to get out of control itself. By the eve of World War I, fire control devices"—for aiming naval guns—"had become so complex that the admirals who had to decide what to approve and what to reject no longer understood what was at issue when rival designs were offered to them. The mathematical principles involved and the mechanical linkages fire control devices relied upon were simply too much for harassed and busy men to master. Decisions were therefore made in ignorance, often for financial or personal or political reasons."

The strains on today's military decision-makers are, if anything, getting even more severe as the rate of technological change increases. A Congressional panel that reviewed the command and control system a few years ago expressed "a concern that borders on dismay" over the Pentagon's attempts to purchase advanced communications equipment. A "shortage of competent management personnel" had led to "several disastrous procurements of communications equipment which might have been averted if professional communicators had been in decision-making management positions."

Computers, for example, play a major role in the present command and control system. Automated data-processing equipment has been in widespread use for only two decades, and the underlying technology is advancing so rapidly, one computer expert noted, that "1978 is the equivalent of a hundred and fifty years ago as far as today's computers are concerned." Yet, as a government communications specialist told me, "today's colonels—who are in charge of major computer programs—when they went to school eighteen years ago, computers were no big deal." As a result, when the need to make key decisions arises, they cannot rely on their own independent technical judgment—and they may not even be able to understand the complex issues that, as program managers, they are responsible for resolving.

James Osborne said that as a defense contractor he witnessed a "people problem" that arose all the time when the pace of technological change bedeviled hapless Pentagon decision-makers. In industry, he said, each general manager of a high-technology operation realizes that the engineers on his staff "have a three- to five-year half-life." That is, the field is changing so quickly that unless there is continuous retraining, an engineer's skills will become obsolete very quickly. "If the engineer can't absorb the training, you get rid of him or put him into some other job where his technical knowledge doesn't matter. The government has no comparable forcing function. There's nothing to require people who don't know what they're doing to give up their positions. They're invulnerable.

"Unhappily," Osborne continued, "you don't see many technically astute military people. Very few people demand the kind of technical proficiency that [Admiral Hyman] Rickover"—the developer of the nuclear-powered submarine—"had on his staff. There are very few guys like Rickover." As a result, "the government people don't have the capability to write [equipment] specifications—the job is handed over to industry—and the manufacturing systems are getting very sophisticated, but contract administration is beyond the capability of the government."

Osborne also noted that when someone in government with technical skills does raise questions about what one of the services or contractors is doing, that is the quickest way to get off the career path to a bigger job. "Don't make too much noise, smart guys simply don't rock the boat. That's the rule. To go up in command, don't cause controversies." Getting into the boat, on the other hand, and rowing hard in the officially sanctioned direction, is the obvious way to promotion. One implication of this, a Pentagon official observed, is that the larger and more gold-plated the program you're involved with, the better your chances of advancement. "Not one goes from colonel to general by managing a thirty thousand dollar program," he noted. "The way to do it is to manage a three billion dollar program." Obvious, badly needed, but unglamorous repairs are likely to be brushed aside by aspiring officers who are looking for the kind of large-scale undertakings that can make their careers take off. These programs usually take so long to carry out, moreover, that if one falls apart, the colonel who pushed it through is likely to be long gone—and probably a general—when it all goes sour.

The Congressional panel that investigated the Pentagon's maladept use of communications technology noted some of the effects of career advancement practices on the command and control problem. Military promotion has traditionally depended and, the panel found, largely still depends on holding line jobs—commanding ships or planes or troops—not on serving in specialized technical fields. As Raymond Tate, whose national security assignments included a stint as Deputy Assistant Secretary of the Navy, explained, "No military officer whose goal is to make three or four stars is ever going to get caught dead being a comm or EW [electronic warfare] officer, or running an intelligence unit, because that is not the way you do it." This means, he adds, that "one of the big problems with electronic warfare and command and control in two of the services is, quite frankly, the lack of understanding of the seniors involved—not because they aren't brilliant people or well-qualified military commanders"—Mr. Tate still works as a defense consultant—"but, in my view, because they have not acquired personal understanding through the services' training and assignment process."

The technological illiteracy of several senior military commanders was embarrassingly revealed in a top-secret exercise called EWCAS— Electronic Warfare/Close Air Support. The exercise simulated the conditions that are expected to prevail in the "electronic battlefield." Reviewing the results of this drill, the General Accounting Office noted that "military commanders do not fully appreciate the intricacies of electronic warfare or its potentially devastating effects." This was demonstrated during the exercise, one of the government auditors reported, when it became obvious that the field commanders—Lieutenant Colonels, Colonels, and some of the Generals—failed to appreciate the effects that forms of electronic warfare could have on the performance of their forces. They would simply send their planes into combat with no consideration of the fact that enemy missiles could home in on the signals they were emitting and destroy them, or that enemy jamming could cut off communications between the planes and their command centers. Standard exercises and war games had not prepared them for these problems. The exercises to which they were accustomed usually assumed perfect communications and no interference from enemy electronic warfare units.

The military commanders' lack of knowledge about the new technology at their disposal makes it very difficult for them to make sensible choices, but this is not a new situation for decision-makers. "Do you know what the definition of a 'responsible position' is?" a physicist and leading member of the Manhattan Project once asked me. "It's one in which you make important decisions on things you know absolutely nothing about. I know. I've held many responsible positions in my career."

————

The Pentagon's missteps with advanced communications technologies are evident in its attempt to exploit one of the most powerful new tools: satellites. In contrast to the highly successful program for deploying spy satellites—which was run by the National Reconnaissance Office in cooperation with the Central Intelligence Agency and the National Security Agency—the military has been left to its own devices to establish a system for defense communications.

The Soviet launch of a Sputnik satellite in 1957 was an early spur to the Pentagon. The Army countered with Project Score, which was intended to produce something that could at least rival the eighty-four-pound Soviet device that broadcast a pinging noise as it orbited the earth. The U.S. effort met with early success, and in 1958 President Eisenhower was able to broadcast his Christmas message on a new U.S. communications satellite.

Subsequent progress was slower. A decade later, the Department of Defense had managed to deploy only small, relatively simple communications satellites with very limited message-carrying potential. It then embarked, in 1969, on what it called Phase II of its Defense Satellite Communications System (DSCS). Unlike the earlier satellites, which moved in relatively low orbits, the new ones were intended to be placed in geosynchronous orbits that would allow a single satellite to relay messages continuously over a wide area of the globe; four such satellites could provide worldwide communications capability.

The DSCS II program did not proceed very smoothly. The first pair of satellites, launched in November 1971, operated erratically and finally failed. After a major redesign, two more satellites were launched in December 1973, one deployed over the western Pacific and the other over the Atlantic. The Pacific satellite operated satisfactorily but its Atlantic equivalent developed problems. A further pair of satellites was sent up in May 1975, but a failure of the third stage of the launch vehicle prevented them from attaining their orbits and they were lost. A Congressional review of the program in 1977, written when the DSCS "system" consisted of only a single operational satellite, observed, "The various unique requirements placed on a purely military satellite make it more costly and complex than a commercial satellite; but, in view of the remarkable performance record of commercial communications satellite systems, one cannot help but conclude that the Department [of Defense] has not taken full advantage of the operating experience, technical expertise, and management philosophy which reside in the private sector."

Further defense satellites were subsequently launched, and they now constitute a working global communications network, although one that has severe limitations. Its message-carrying capacity, for one thing, is inadequate and would result, in any crisis, in what one official termed a "desperate shortage" of secure communications channels. Moreover, as one senior Pentagon communications adviser explained, the DSCS satellite system will work reliably only in a benign environment. "It's not built for wartime," he said. "It has little physical survivability and is not hardened against nuclear blast effects or EMP. It can also be jammed."

All these problems could be corrected by means that are currently known, this government adviser said, but he estimated that it would take ten or fifteen years to deploy such satellites. Since the technology to solve the problems was already available, I asked why it would take that long. He replied, "You should read General Cushman's report."

––––––

To the extent that the DSCS satellites could play a useful role, they would do so in crises in which, for example, the President and senior military officials needed to obtain information and issue directives regarding U.S. forces' involvement in a conventional war in Europe, the Middle East, or the Pacific. How well the communications system worked would depend, of course, not just on the satellites but on the WWMCCS computers and ancillary apparatus that feed information back and forth through the orbiting relay stations.

The performance of the Pentagon's worldwide communications system has been tested periodically. The results are not normally made public, and those that have been are less than encouraging. In *Prime Target*, a 1977 exercise that received some notoriety in subsequent newspaper accounts, an attempt was made to measure the reliability of the WWMCCS computer network. The Honeywell computers at the National Military Command Center in the Pentagon and at various major command posts in the United States and abroad attempted to exchange information. There are a lot of potential things that can go wrong in such a complex system. The set of instructions that tell the computers what to do is some seventeen million lines long, and serious mistakes in them, as well as any flaws in the hardware, can cause the machines, as the computer people say, to "crash." This can involve anything from brief interruptions in data processing or message transmission ("soft crashes") to total computer breakdowns that cause the loss of massive amounts of data ("hard crashes").

The scorecard for Operation *Prime Target*—whose publication was later attributed by Pentagon officials to a disgruntled employee of the Defense Communications Agency—showed that the headquarters of the U.S. European Command was involved in 124 attempted message transfers over the WWMCCS computer network, of which 54 ended abruptly due to computer failures; the Atlantic Command tried almost 300 times to obtain or transmit data, with 132 failures; the Tactical Air Command tried 63 times, with 44 failures; and the Readiness Command (popularly known as the Rapid Deployment Force) was involved in almost 300 attempted computer-to-computer conversations, of which only 43 succeeded. The Pentagon's multibillion dollar command and control system worked, overall, only a little better than a third of the time.

Subsequent tests of the WWMCCS computer network have been performed, although the Department of Defense, which is sensitive about the subject, has not published any detailed results. After additional exercises in 1980 and 1981 called *Proud Spirit*, and another trial called *Poll Station* in 1981, the Pentagon commented, "While the performance of WIN"—the WWMCCS Intercomputer Network—"in previous exercises was less than desirable, recent statistics"—which were not made public—"show that significant performance/reliability improvements have occurred."

A General Accounting Office investigation of this assertion concluded that there were "several exercise artificialities" that boosted the WWMCCS computer system's apparent reliability. Among the factors that enhanced system performance was the helping hand of Honeywell. It provided extra computers—to prevent the "saturation" that could otherwise occur in the WWMCCS system—and additional engineering support at fifteen WWMCCS sites. Also, the rules of the exercise were changed. A satisfactory performance was defined to mean the delivery of information from one military base to another regardless of the length of time it took. "They said it was a 'success' if the message ever got there," a government auditor discovered. The additional test results notwithstanding, GAO still maintained that WWMCCS was essentially the same nonfunctional system it had always been.

The running battle between the GAO and the Pentagon over WWMCCS now seems to have run its course, with Major General D. L. Evans, the new head of the WWMCCS system, finally throwing in the towel. In a keynote speech at the 1983 AFCEA convention in Washington, he acknowledged that "with hindsight, which all of us know is 20/20, this first WWMCCS [Honeywell] buy . . . was a wrong way to approach the command and control problem." He continued, "In the intervening years WWMCCS ADP [automatic data processing] has become—some say—the principal avocation of GAO and Congressional staffs. There are a total of eighteen GAO/Congressional reports on WWMCCS ADP in existence. One more is currently in progress. As you might expect these reports were very critical of the current WWMCCS ADP systems." General Evans conceded, "By and large the criticism was well founded."

Twenty-one years after President Kennedy's directive establishing the Pentagon's worldwide communications system, General Evans said that "we have only taken baby steps in providing commanders with the information needed to make decisions. . . . Ten or fifteen years ago, I was reasonably confident the Department of Defense was at the forefront of computer and communications technology [yet] the world of information processing began to accelerate. Price went down while performance went to new heights. But probably more important, the information processing industry in this country blew right by DOD. We were so busy regulating our laborious acquisitions of old technology, we nearly missed the train." He promised that new efforts would be made to transform WWMCCS into "the effective and efficient command and control system so desperately needed," and he invited the industry's help in figuring out how to do this.

One of the industry representatives at the AFCEA convention that General Evans was addressing told me, "I'm totally convinced that nothing works in the military except the bomb."

7

WHITE MAN'S MADNESS

With every change of Administration there is a rapid re-shuffling of the top positions within the federal government. Job turn-over at the Pentagon is all the more frequent because of the constant rotation of officers who want to move up the chain of command—career advancement requiring that those aspiring to general officer or flag rank have a broad range of command billets.

Robert Everett, the president of the MITRE Corporation and a senior Pentagon adviser on command and control systems, has watched Administrations and commanders come and go. He has observed "what the African colonials used to call 'the white man's madness'—big changes every time a new administrator came to the colonies. One would be an agricultural bug and say, 'The boll weevils are eating up all the cotton plants by the roots. Pull out the cotton roots, that's how to solve that problem.' So the natives would run out and pull up the cotton roots. The next guy would be a civil engineer and he would say, 'We need roads. So forget that boll weevil nonsense and get on with road building.' And they would go along with whatever the new thing was, because they didn't want to spend their time in jail.

"Similarly, in the command and control function," Everett contin-ued, "every incoming commander's background, environment, personality, whether he likes staff or hates staff, whether he's an authoritarian or not—his whole style, his whole being will dictate to one hell of an extent his and his staff's command information requirements. A lot of thought has been given to this, to identify basic information requirements. As we get down to tactical [combat] situations we arrive at some constants—things that tend to happen over and over. But that only gives us maybe ten percent of the [command and control] needs. There's still the other ninety percent that's going to change with every new 'white man' who comes in."

On January 20, 1981, the Reagan Administration took office, and one of its priorities was "rebuilding" America's defenses. This was said to be necessary as a result of years of "standing still" while the Soviet Union had been racing ahead. (Actually, the United States had more than doubled the size of its strategic nuclear arsenal between 1970 and 1980.) The main problem, President Reagan believed, was a lack of money in the Pentagon budget, which he promptly sought to correct with a five-year program that would provide $1.5 trillion to reinvigorate the Department of Defense. There was little effort by the White House to define exactly how the money ought to be spent, with most of it allocated to programs in the pipeline or already proposed by the services on what are commonly called their procurement "wish lists." The spending program appears to have been guided by the kind of self-serving suggestion offered to the Administration by Hans Mark, the outgoing Secretary of the Air Force. He advised his successors, "We need everything, as soon as possible."

David Stockman, the Director of the Office of Management and Budget, said that the expenditures recommended by the services were exempted, for all practical purposes, from independent review. The Administration also put off any effort, before embarking on a military buildup, to negotiate an arms control agreement with the Soviets. The President said that the country first had to build up its forces in order to improve its bargaining position.

The Reagan Administration's large but loosely managed allocation of funds to the Pentagon is reminiscent of the manner in which Great Britain poured money into a naval arms race with Germany at the beginning of this century. Winston Churchill, who was a participant in the process, wrote of one decision made in 1909, "In the end a curious and characteristic solution was reached. The Admiralty had demanded six ships: the economists offered four: and we finally compromised on eight." The Germans went ahead with their own naval buildup. "Fearing to be taken advantage of at the conference table, they preferred to stay away altogether and depend on an ever growing Navy to frighten the English into coming to terms," Barbara Tuchman wrote in *The Guns of August*. The two nations came not to terms but to war.

"Bismarck had warned Germany to be content with land power, but his successors were neither separately nor collectively Bismarcks," Tuchman continued. "He had pursued clearly seen goals unswervingly; they groped for larger horizons with no clear idea of what they wanted." A number of observers, including people who strongly urge improvements in America's military preparedness, make similar observations about the lack of overall planning on the part of the would-be Bismarcks who have influenced the Reagan Administration's policies for dealing with the Soviet Union.

Former Secretary of Defense Melvin Laird cautioned the incoming Administration, shortly after the 1980 election, that the country needed a military "buildup" but not a spending "binge." James Osborne, the defense contractor and communications specialist, noted, "I'm for a lot of what Reagan wants to do, but I'm against pouring the money into DOD, which doesn't have the capacity to articulate, specify, quantify, and control how money gets used." Jon Boyes, the AFCEA president, summarized the views of many sympathetic observers of the Administration when he commented, "You know, the problem becomes one of the political bosses depending upon the military leadership to tell them just how much is enough. And that's a bit like telling a child you can go to the candy store. But how much is enough?" What was needed, Admiral Boyes said, was "a very perceptive, astute, and sophisticated leadership that sits down and understands the national objectives. You cannot depend on any parochial group to discipline itself on how much is enough."

The Soviet Union has the option of trying to match or counter U.S. military initiatives. Whatever the United States tries to do, the Soviets can also try to do—or undo. Pushing ahead with "more of everything" will not lead to any net improvement in the security of the nation or to any permanent military advantages if appropriate Soviet countermoves are undertaken. This does not seem to have greatly influenced Reagan Administration planners. Their practice has been to calculate the desirability of a proposed piece of military hardware according to a peculiar accounting scheme in which its utility is not discounted by realistic consideration of possible Soviet countermoves. This is a major blind spot in the planning process, given an adversary whose technical capabilities are, to a first approximation, very close to our own. Yet with its concern about the United States' having engaged in "unilateral disarmament" during the 1970s, the Administration somehow thinks it can get away with unilateral rearmament during the 1980s.

Richard DeLauer, the Under Secretary of Defense, demonstrated the Pentagon's neglect of likely Soviet countermoves in an article he wrote on the revolution that is taking place in defense electronics. DeLauer advocated full-speed, across-the-board exploitation of the new technical possibilities. He did not comment, though, on how the same or related technologies, exploited by the other side, might affect the overall military situation. As for the Soviet use of the same electronic wonders, he said that this meant merely that "the United States must 'run faster' and simply let the devil have the hindmost." Conventional principles of sound management suggest the riskiness of this strategy. In business, a program of unrestrained production, combined with a total disregard of what the competition is doing, would be the shortest imaginable route to bankruptcy. In national defense, the consequences may be no less disastrous—although for the individual defense contractors, such as TRW, the major electronics firm for which DeLauer worked for twenty-three years before his appointment as Under Secretary of Defense, the prospect of an open-ended spending program naturally has some appeal.

In October 1981, in his first effort to define the priorities in the unprecedented peacetime military buildup he proposed, President Reagan spoke to the nation in a major televised address. Much of the subsequent attention and debate focused on a small number of controversial proposals he mentioned, such as the MX missile, and on the overall size of the proposed budget. The item that was formally listed as the number one priority in the Administration's "Strategic Modernization Program" received little attention. This was an eighteen-billion-dollar five-year plan for improved strategic command, control, communications, and intelligence systems—a program which Charles Zraket of the MITRE Corporation, and other Pentagon consultants, expects to grow into a thirty- to forty-billion dollar undertaking.

Much of the money in the strategic command system upgrade—although the President did not say so—was to go to programs already initiated by the Carter Administration. They were begun as a means to provide the command and control infrastructure needed to implement the war-fighting nuclear strategy set forth in Presidential Directive 59 of July 1980. Mr. Reagan, without any substantive revisions, was also keeping that Carter policy intact. In October 1981 he reaffirmed this strategy when he signed a top-secret National Security Decision Directive—NSDD-13—which, like PD-59, called for developing the means to use nuclear weapons in a protracted nuclear war.

The kind of command system the Administration planned to build was not described in the President's speech. Nor have subsequent Pentagon reports and testimony before Congress provided many more details on what is being done to alter the existing command and control apparatus to support the new U.S. nuclear strategy.

————

To try to learn more about what the Reagan Administration planned to do, I talked with Donald Latham, the former RCA and Martin Marietta engineer who is now the Pentagon's principal spokesman on command and control programs. Various experts in the field recommended that I seek him out, although they said it would be more for the experience of seeing how the Administration approached the issue than for substantive insights into command and control technology. Mr. Latham has a high reputation within the defense-communications industry, whose programs he champions, but a number of technical specialists question whether the three hundred and forty programs he has packed into a command and control improvement effort actually fit together in any coherent and logical way. The experts do agree that command and control deserves a high priority; where they part company with the Administration is in their assessment of how well the programs now under way meet urgent command and control needs.

The first time I met Mr. Latham was in Detroit in May 1983, after he talked at a symposium on command and control sponsored by the American Association for the Advancement of Science. He spoke very rapidly during his formal presentation and used dozens of charts projected on a screen to catalogue the various Administration initiatives. There was little technical explanation of what the particular command and control programs he mentioned were supposed to accomplish, or why, among the various options available to the Administration, they had been selected.

Instead, Mr. Latham spoke to the scientists' group in broad terms about what he referred to as the two phases of the Administration's command and control upgrade. Phase I is essentially an attempt to patch up the more obvious defects in the existing system. It consists of the kinds of things that one might do to repair an old house whose plumbing, roof, wiring, and so on badly needed to be replaced. EMP hardening will be added here and there, fifteen new ECX planes will replace the twenty-nine converted C-130s that the Navy uses for the TACAMO mission, new computers will be put into NORAD, and various other improvements will be made in the existing apparatus.

Phase II of the Administration's program is the effort to build an "enduring" command and control system that will permit the United States to do more than just retaliate in the event of a Soviet attack. Its stated purpose is to give the Pentagon the means to fight a nuclear war that could last for weeks or months.

Phase I, however, will not necessarily be completed before Phase II —the headings are very misleading. The services have their own priorities, and command and control programs are not necessarily at the top of the list. The Navy, for example, has already tried to divert hundreds of millions of dollars that are supposed to go for new TACAMO planes to support its ambitious ship-building program. The Defense Resources Board, headed by Mr. DeLauer, sanctioned this, although Mr. Latham's office has been trying to get the funds put back so new planes can be purchased to improve communications with submarines. The Defense Science Board's recommendation for a single office in the Pentagon with managerial authority over the command and control effort continues to be ignored. The individual service procurement offices, not the planners in Mr. Latham's offices, still buy all command and control and other equipment. Since some eighty percent of the command and control upgrade involves multiservice programs, an immense bureaucratic wrangle can tie up even the simplest acquisitions. In addition, a notable influence on the services' priorities is their interest in making the next advance with various new technologies rather than making repairs at existing installations. This is the reason for putting some of the exotic Phase II programs ahead of mundane Phase I chores. The confusion that stymies the Administration's overall command and control program, according to one Pentagon official who worked on the plans for the undertaking, results from the habit of throwing money at problems without first thinking about the kind of solutions that really make sense. The command and control planning was "not a very focused business," he said. "It was not an intellectually rejuvenated" military program under the Reagan Administration but just a routine case where "everybody who had a hobbyhorse came in and got money for their hobbyhorse."

The communications experts with whom I've spoken are essentially unanimous in their approval of efforts that fall into the general category of Phase I. In particular, there is broad agreement that a command system that can survive at least the initial stages of a major nuclear attack would be a welcome relief from a fragile command and control system that prompts the United States to maintain its forces on a hair trigger. "There are a few command and control and communications holes that I think can be legitimately patched up without wasting money and without doing something which is strategically silly," Desmond Ball said.

Opinion divides sharply, however, on the feasibility—and desirability—of Phase II. "People have their hands full right now to develop systems to detect attack and get [Emergency Action] messages out to the forces," a participant in one of the connectivity studies observed. Many of the programs now under way, he continued, "are designed to give us higher confidence in the ability to perform the basic mission," rather than an "enduring" command and control capability that would enable the U.S. to fight nuclear wars for weeks or months. "The programs unfortunately have been cast rhetorically in a framework that's not real." Another senior Pentagon consultant said of the eighteen billion dollar command and control program, "Off the record: the actions are supportable, the rhetoric is terrible."

Other observers are not so sure that the Administration is focused on pragmatic steps to repair the existing system and not misled by grandiose nuclear war-fighting plans. Richard Garwin commented, "Very often people will say, 'Let's try to do this more difficult thing and then the less difficult will fall out. It will happen automatically.' Not at all! When you try to do the more difficult sometimes you don't accomplish anything. So that's what I'm against."

After his presentation in Detroit, I interviewed Mr. Lathan, and in that session and in follow-up conversations with him, I attempted to have him speak more directly about exactly what the Administration is doing, and why. "Well, the concept is, let me call it more appropriately, I would want to term it surviving and enduring command control," he said in our first talk. "And under that umbrella title there are a number of initiatives to provide survivability and endurance to the command and control functions. Specifically, communications centers, decision centers, intelligence assessment centers, and so on. And so the form of these will take shape in time." That was about as detailed a description as he would give of the hardware in which the Administration plans to invest many billions of dollars.

In my next session with Mr. Latham, in his office in the Pentagon, I said that I wanted to ask for more specifics about the Administration's program, but he responded by saying, "The thing that bothered me about when we were talking there in Detroit was that the thrust of your questions was often to areas that, number one, were sensitive from a security point of view, and number two, seemed to me to be of almost total academic interest to the general public." He suggested that we leave such "boring" subjects to "people who are professionals in this area" and limit our discussion to a general "top down view of what we're trying to do and where we're trying to go and what all this Presidential initiative and so on to improve command and control really means to American security, deterrence, and things like that."

The most interesting topic about which Mr. Latham was willing to speak was the type of Soviet threat to which the U.S. command and control system might have to respond. Most of the experts with whom I've spoken believe that the fragility of the present command and control system exposes the United States to the risk of a Soviet attack aimed right at the main command posts and message-relay centers. Mr. Latham does not share the experts' concerns about decapitating strikes. "I think it's a very far-fetched, extremely high-risk thing than anybody would ever try, and so I tend to dismiss those kinds of approaches to strategic war." He added that he did not believe the Soviets would be tempted to escalate a conventional war in Europe to involve the use of tactical nuclear weapons. They would fear, he said, that the United States would retaliate using strategic nuclear weapons.

If these scenarios were ruled out by Mr. Latham, what then did he regard as the kind of danger the United States faced from the Soviet

Union? He replied, "The thing that would probably be the most threatening thing to the Soviet regime would be to see that their power structure is crumbling. Internally. That there is internal dissent. Some of the huge power centers have split out from under them. Or there is revolt within the Soviet Army itself. The ethnic Russians against the nonethnic Russians, so to speak." As a result of "some horrendous loss of control and power by the ruling Communist Party and all its elite," he continued, "this crumbling of the Soviet empire, however that would happen, that kind of thing might provoke an act of desperation against whatever they sensed was causing it. Probably Western society. I don't know."

I found the scenario used by Mr. Latham to illustrate how the Soviets might, in his words, irrationally "lash out" at the United States fairly bizarre. How billions of dollars of improved command and control apparatus and the other programs in the Strategic Modernization Program were supposed to shore up our deterrent against such attacks was equally mystifying.

Even though Mr. Latham's public rationale for the command and control upgrade may seem unclear, there is at least one obvious— if unstated—explanation for a large part of the program. The major first-strike option in the S.I.O.P., with its focus on killing Soviet leaders, is responsible for perhaps as much as half of the entire undertaking. The money is going for some of the Pentagon's most secret projects—the "black programs" about which virtually nothing is ever said, even to Congress. These programs, run by Pentagon departments such as the National Reconnaissance Office, involve a variety of surveillance methods for gathering massive amounts of intelligence data about the Soviet Union. Some of the information that is gathered is critical to the successful execution of a first strike. After all, if the Soviet leadership is to be targeted, its location must be known at all times. Thus, the new emphasis in the S.I.O.P. on this goal calls for a large expansion of the already impressive electronic eavesdropping capability of the Rhyolite satellites and of the KH-11 satellite program, which provides real-time photoreconnaissance—that is, instantaneous, high-resolution pictures of Soviet territory. Keeping track of Soviet leaders is a difficult enough task in peacetime, and if they are being moved about in a crisis, the planes or helicopters or limousines carrying them must be tracked; alternatively, the secret command posts in which they attempt to hide must be pinpointed—for example, by satellites that are able to intercept orders from these emergency headquarters and thereby permit their locations to be identified. The leadership can then be targeted and destroyed.

In addition to killing Soviet leaders, the new intelligence-gathering systems the Pentagon is developing are expected to play a key role in the follow-up strikes that would be made after an initial U.S. surprise attack. For U.S. planners have thought not just of a single, knockout blow against the Soviets but of how to go about a series of strikes aimed, first, at killing the leadership and hobbling the main strategic forces and, second, at destroying residual Soviet nuclear missiles. If a certain portion of the Soviet missile force, for example, survives the U.S. first strike, SAC planners want to be able to know instantaneously the locations of these still-loaded Soviet silos. They would then quickly retarget U.S. missiles and fire them off to destroy the remaining Soviet ones. Similarly, if U.S. intelligence can determine which empty silos the Soviets may be attempting to reload, those silos can be destroyed before the Soviets are in a position to use them in a counterattack against the United States.

Thus, while some of the improvements in command and control that are being made may enhance U.S. retaliatory capability, other parts of the program have more aggressive aims. It is possible, accordingly, in reviewing what is being done, to try to determine, from the nature of the undertaking, its defensive or offensive goal. Not every program fits neatly into one of these two categories, of course, for there are many "hobbyhorses" that the services are promoting without, as far as anyone can tell, any clear rationale.

―――――

Although security restrictions prohibit an analysis of the black programs in the Administration's command and control upgrade, the other hardware that is being developed can be described. Of great value in assessing these projects is a nine-hundred-page program-by-program report written by Thomas Sweeney of DMS, Inc., a Greenwich, Connecticut, firm that does market studies and forecasts for the major defense contractors. The December 1983 DMS survey of the Administration's spending plan, intended to show its clients the market opportunities that exist, is the clearest and most complete description of how the Pentagon intends to allocate the six percent of the total defense budget that will go to command, control, and communications over the next few years.

The command and control system planned for the future, like the one in place today, will be heavily dependent on a very small number of early warning satellites. Advanced Defense Support Program satellites (numbers 14 through 17) underwent a critical design review in May 1983, and they are supposed to be deployed over the next few years using the manned Space Shuttle. The launching of intelligence satellites has been slated as one of the shuttle's primary missions, although the problems experienced to date with this mode of satellite deployment may lead to use of more conventional rocket launchers. (The first tracking and data-relay satellite launched from the space shuttle went awry and, after months of delay, was finally maneuvered into geosynchronous orbit; the next two satellites launched from the shuttle, a Western Union communications satellite and an Indonesian communications satellite, were both lost; additional satellites have now been launched successfully, but continued reliance on the shuttle remains in doubt.)

The new early warning satellites, for which TRW and Aerojet Electro Systems are the major contractors, will differ from current ones in three major ways. First, they will have more sophisticated sensors. Instead of a rotating telescope that focuses infrared signals down onto two thousand lead sulfide detectors, the latest models will have what is called a "mosaic focal plane" consisting of eighty thousand sensors. The new models will not scan the Soviet missile fields a few times per minute but will stare uninterruptedly at each Soviet missile silo. Current satellites can identify the general area from which missiles are launched, but not the individual silos. For warning purposes, this makes little difference. All that counts is that the Soviet launches be quickly detected. However, in the new offensive Pentagon nuclear strategy, the more refined data from the advanced DSP satellites plays a key role. It indicates which Soviet missiles may have been held in reserve and permits them to be targeted in subsequent U.S. salvos.

Second, the revamped early warning stations are supposed to be able to do more on-board computing and more "station-keeping," such as making sure they are properly positioned in the right orbits. Increased autonomy will mean that instead of just collecting raw data and sending it to a specialized ground station, which has to process the information and compute how many rockets have been launched, the satellites can do some of the calculations and analysis themselves. The satellites could thus bypass today's readout stations and send their already processed data to the key command posts. Thus, the DSP satellites that look for submarine-launched missiles and report their findings to the ground station at Buckley Air National Guard Base may in the future be able to report directly to the Pentagon, SAC Headquarters, NORAD, and Looking Glass. However, the amount of on-board processing that can be done will remain limited for many years, and there will still be a need for some time to come for Buckley and other ground stations that can make sense of the data collected by infrared sensors on board the satellites.

Third, the DSP satellites of the future are expected to have the ability to transfer data quickly to other satellites rather than having to go directly to ground stations. This will compensate for the vulnerability of some of those ground stations, although it will not entirely do away with the problem. Ultimately, the satellite will have to transfer information to ground stations or command posts of some type, any or all of which may be susceptible to various forms of Soviet attack or sabotage.

Hundreds of millions of dollars have gone into development of new early warning satellites, and almost three billion dollars will be spent to deploy them as replacements for the three DSP satellites now in orbit. The technical features planned for this next generation of DSP satellites will have certain advantages over the present equipment, assuming that everything performs as designed. Still, there is reason to wonder whether a system consisting of such a small number of satellites —each of which is an exposed and essentially defenseless object in space—is really the best way to fulfill early warning requirements.

Satellites, after all, as one NORAD specialist explained, are "very fragile and can't stand a lot of bumping around." On station, which for the DSP satellites means a fixed orbit, they can be subjected to assaults from electronic jamming, laser or nuclear weapons, and attacks by homelier but also quite destructive devices. Among the simplest but potentially most effective anti-satellite (ASAT) weapons are space mines—"little fellow travelers," as Richard Garwin calls them, that follow other satellites around and can be programmed to explode on command from the ground to destroy their quarry. Space mines, which would follow within one hundred feet or so of their targets, need weigh only a few tens of pounds, Garwin said, and can use conventional explosives to pummel nearby satellites with shrapnel. (Other types of space mines, which would stand farther off, could also be deployed.) A several hundred million dollar early warning satellite or communications satellite, therefore, could be knocked out of service by a relatively cheap and simple weapon. This suggests, in Garwin's opinion, that continued dependence on a tiny number of early warning satellites makes little sense. These "fancy" satellites, he says, have "more capability and less robustness than would be required to serve reliably in nuclear war."

As an alternative to the vulnerable DSP satellites in the Administration's program, Garwin proposes: *(a)* that "lots of infrared warning satellites be deployed, not just a few, because space mines will take care of those if the Soviets want to destroy them"; *(b)* that many "dark satellites" also be put in orbit (satellites that aren't operating but that could take over immediately if something happened to the principal ones); and *(c)* that "many, many, many, that is, thousands of balloons" be put up in the same kind of orbits. These orbits, he adds, need not be geosynchronous but can be intermediate ones a few thousand miles in outer space. The decoy balloons, he says, can be "mixed in with the replacement satellites, which themselves are inside balloons. They are to confuse the other side so he cannot identify the replacements for the working satellites. The ones that are working can be identified because they're transmitting radio signals." The net result of this kind of arrangement would be a highly redundant warning system with little susceptibility to the obvious countermeasures that can incapacitate the few DSP satellites now scheduled for deployment. Desmond Ball and other command-system experts support such schemes for large numbers of simpler early warning satellites, although there are a number of possible versions. Ball suggests, for example, that the no-frills infrared warning satellites may be so inexpensive that instead of deploying decoys it may be just as easy to put up lots of additional backup satellites.

None of these programs has any appeal to the Administration, for they are inconsistent with both its defense-spending largesse and its nuclear war-fighting strategy. If one wants a "shoot-look-shoot" capability—that is, to be able to attack the USSR, assess the consequences of that attack and their counterattack, and then plan and execute further strikes—it is important to have the new DSP satellites. Their capability to pinpoint the still-loaded Soviet silos is regarded by Administration strategists as their most important feature. Garwin's proposed satellites, intended purely for warning purposes, would not be designed to provide more than a reliable indication of Soviet missile launches and a reasonable estimate of the number. The Administration strategy demands more information. The cost of getting it, however, is dependence on a small number of superdeulxe satellites. If they are successfully jammed or destroyed by space mines or other means, instead of getting an abundance of early warning data the Pentagon will not get any. The Administration program under way entails this all-or-nothing gamble.

The expected vulnerability of the new DSP satellites is made all the more acute by the Administration's refusal to engage in talks with the Soviet Union on the banning of anti-satellite weapons. The Soviets have proposed a complete ban on all such weapons and a cessation of all testing of prototypes. Negotiations between the United States and the Soviet Union on a treaty to eliminate ASAT weapons took place in 1978 and 1979. Robert Buchheim, the U.S. representative at the negotiations, said at the scientists' conference in Detroit that substantial progress had been made in the talks, especially on the question of how to verify such an agreement, and he urged their immediate resumption. The Reagan Administration, however, has declined all invitations from the Soviets, and the promptings of U.S. arms control experts, to resume them.

Instead, the Administration has eagerly proceeded with the development of U.S. ASAT weapons to be used against Soviet satellites. (The first new U.S. ASAT, carried aloft by an F-15 fighter, was tested in late 1983.) The Soviets, Pentagon officials note, have been testing ASAT weapons since 1968, whereas the United States stopped testing them in 1963. The Air Force believes that it will be able to catch up with the Soviets, and that the new F-15 system will be far superior to the cumbersome rocket-launched ASAT that the Soviets have tested (with unimpressive results). The Navy also wants a U.S. ASAT capability to be developed for use against Soviet satellites that monitor the whereabouts of U.S. ships. The Pentagon believes it can win the ASAT race and, if it has thought about the consequences of losing, appears willing to accept that risk. Once again, the military's priority is on offensive, not defensive, thinking.

The Administration's approach to ASAT weapons is similar in many ways to the Nixon Administration's handling of the MIRV issue during the negotiation of the SALT I Treaty. The United States, in the late 1960s, had already developed the technology for missiles with multiple, independently targeted warheads, but the Soviets proposed that a ban on MIRVs be included in the SALT Treaty. This was not much of a concession on their part, since they did not yet have the capability themselves. U.S. negotiators, on orders from the White House, refused to bargain away the U.S. lead in multiple-warhead technology.

The failure to include a ban on MIRVs in the SALT I Treaty will go down in history books as one of the worst mistakes ever made in American diplomacy. For the insistence on maintaining the U.S. edge in MIRV capability meant that the Soviets would be allowed, whenever they caught up with the United States and perfected comparable technology, to deploy it themselves. That happened very quickly, and the large Soviet SS-18 missiles deployed in the mid-1970s were equipped with up to eight or ten multiple, independently targeted warheads— numerous and potentially accurate enough to destroy the one thousand U.S. Minuteman ICBMs. Thus, in exchange for the temporary advantage of deploying MIRVed Minuteman missiles a few years ahead of the Russians, the Nixon Administration permitted the entire U.S. Minuteman force to be put at risk. Technically, there would have been no way, without MIRVs, for the Soviets to make an effective attack against the Minuteman force.

"I wish I had thought through the implications of a MIRVed world," Henry Kissinger said in 1974, although this was a somewhat disingenuous account of what had happened. Leading arms control specialists had personally briefed Kissinger on the MIRV issue, they have said, and forty U.S. Senators from both parties brought this matter to his attention in a very direct way: in the interest of achieving a MIRV ban in the SALT Treaty, they introduced a Congressional resolution calling for a moratorium on the testing of MIRVs while the treaty was being negotiated.

A U.S. refusal to negotiate a ban on ASAT weapons is sure to prove every bit as short-sighted as the decision on MIRVs. There is undoubtedly some potential advantage in shooting down Soviet military satellites (although their photoreconnaissance, warning, and electronic eavesdropping devices now in orbit are much less sophisticated than those of the United States). But there is also a major advantage in not allowing the USSR to develop and deploy the weapons that can incapacitate *our* satellites, especially since we are—and, according to Administration plans, will remain—so dependent on a small number of critical ones. Thus, where does the *net* U.S. advantage lie—in allowing satellites of both sides to operate under a rule of law, or in fostering an era of vulnerability for all satellites?

"I like keeping the satellites we have more than I want to destroy the satellites they have," Richard Garwin said. An ASAT treaty is the only way to reach this goal, but this option has been summarily dismissed by the Administration because of the purported difficulties of verifying such a treaty. Robert Buchheim, however, maintains that progress on that subject was made in the 1977–79 talks with the Soviets and that the effort to work out the details of an enforceable treaty should be resumed promptly. After all, the U.S. has an advanced space tracking capability—a worldwide system that keeps tabs on all the satellites that have ever been launched—as well as the capability, with present DSP satellites and other intelligence equipment, to monitor the test launching of Soviet ASATs. This would make it very difficult for the Soviets to run without detection a secret ASAT testing program that kept knocking satellite after satellite out of the sky.

The underlying reason for the Administration's resistance to an ASAT treaty appears to be not so much technical concern about verification as it is the bureaucratic priorities that are involved. The Air Force is beginning a massive effort to militarize outer space, an undertaking that received full Presidential sanction in Mr. Reagan's "Star Wars" speech of March 23, 1983. A new Air Force Space Command has been established, its mission including not just anti-satellite weapons but the deployment of space-based ballistic missile defense systems advocated by the President. "We expect a large, permanent, manned orbital space complex to be operational by about 1990," Richard DeLauer said, adding that it would be "capable of effectively attacking . . . ground, sea, and air targets from space."

In the context of the Pentagon's plans for seizing "the new high ground" of outer space, a ban on anti-satellite weaponry would be a major impediment. An ASAT treaty, indeed, would be the first step in putting the Air Force Space Command out of business and stopping the flow of hundreds of billions of dollars that are proposed to be spent on space weapons in coming decades. The lack of an ASAT treaty could make all of the new early warning devices and space-based command and control apparatus ineffective. But its commitment to an offensive strategy has determined the Pentagon's outlook, and obstinacy, on ASAT negotiations.

Ground-based radars will continue to play a role in the future U.S. early warning system. The existing BMEWS and PAVE PAWS radars, after extensive modifications, plus a set of additional PAVE PAWS radars and several new radars to detect bombers, will be used.

As one might expect, the old radars in Greenland, Alaska, and England are scheduled for major overhauls. They were built long before the age of MIRVs and were not designed to track large numbers of small warheads. Accordingly, the radar bandwidth, the radar range resolution cells, and other features must be changed to allow them to discriminate one tiny fast-moving object from another, to track the incoming warheads more precisely, and to predict where they are heading. New computers, such as Control Data Cyber 170-720 processors, will be installed as part of the upgrade.

The PAVE PAWS radars, built in the late 1970s primarily to look for submarine-launched missiles, need less upgrading. They will get new computers—to try to improve their ability to come up with an accurate count of incoming warheads. The power levels at the Otis and Beale PAVE PAWS sites will also be increased. Currently, only about eighteen hundred of the five thousand small antennas on each of the two "faces" of these radars are actually powered.

Additional PAVE PAWS radars are being planned to expand the ocean areas that come under radar surveillance. Otis and Beale provide coverage of northern Atlantic and northern Pacific waters, respectively, out to a range of three thousand nautical miles. An older FPS-85 radar at Eglin Air Force Base in Florida, a converted piece of equipment that used to be part of Cape Canaveral's space-tracking system, is currently responsible for monitoring Caribbean and Central American waters. To improve coverage against long-range Soviet submarine-launched missiles coming from southerly directions, the radar at Eglin will be replaced by a PAVE PAWS radar. It will probably be sited at Robbins Air Force Base in Georgia. Another, similar radar is tentatively planned for the Southwest, at Goodfellow Air Force Base in Texas. A PAVE PAWS radar will also be built at Thule, Greenland, to increase the capability of the most forward-based of all the early warning sites.

The multibillion dollar radar building and refurbishing effort will not be confined to missile detection. The Air Force plans to replace the entire Distant Early Warning network that watches for Soviet bombers. The network now consists of thirty-one radars set out in a chain from Alaska to Greenland. The DEW Line, as it is called, has significant gaps, little ability to detect low-flying aircraft, and suffers from routine malfunctions in its antiquated equipment. Thirteen new, longer-range radars will therefore be built, together with some three dozen unattended short-range radars.

More ambitious, and expensive, than the new DEW Line radars will be another kind of radar that the Air Force is developing. Since ordinary radars emit straight beams and cannot see below the horizon, only high-flying aircraft can be detected, and only when they are within a few hundred miles. However, a concept called Over the Horizon–Backscatter (OTH-B) radar has been proposed to overcome this limitation. One can, with mirrors, see around corners. Similarly, the OTH-B radar will use the technique of bouncing radar signals off the ionosphere, and capturing the signals that come back, to pinpoint objects that are far over the horizon and even flying at low altitude. The ionosphere is the electrically charged part of the atmosphere, and bouncing radio waves off it has been used, after all, as the principal means of long-distance radio communications. Why not try the same thing with radar beams?

All of these improvements to current radar warning systems, at least at first look, seem to have merit, especially to the technical specialists. One friend of mine has spent much of his career, and free time, designing and using various kinds of sophisticated equipment. Whenever he sees a broken piece of apparatus, his immediate reaction is to see if he can repair it. His concern for a troubled piece of machinery is like that extended to a sick child. Many engineering experts respond with this kind of sympathy when they look at the current radar setup.

Their ideas on how to fix the problems are also stimulated by the billions of dollars that would accrue to their companies from such projects.

Still, it makes sense to ask whether it is *worth* fixing or expanding the present radar warning system, and to what extent. As the Defense Science Board task force on command and control noted in its major 1978 report, "Early on in our study it became clear that the major difficulties in developing, acquiring, and deploying command and control systems are not primarily technical, but conceptual (What should the system do?) or administrative (How do we organize the required resources?)." Rear Admiral Paul Tomb explained that what this meant, at least in part, was that the Pentagon should not just make technical repairs in the present command and control system for the sake of making technical repairs. It should first determine whether it really needs the system in question and how much difference in its performance the changes will make. Tomb said that the Pentagon should "make sure they aren't doing Band-Aid fixes on dead horses. In other words, I want to make sure that we come up with a good architecture so we're building towards something." He said that obviously some "Band-Aids" were needed. "Horses get scratched and you fix that. That takes money, but not big money." The Pentagon, however, should not "waste a lot of money on splints and bandages when we ought to shoot the horse.

"I've found in the services," he continued, "that there are a lot of wounded horses lying in the bottom of file drawers someplace. And you come in with some money, and they pull out this drawer and out comes this little colt that—you know, it's got three legs instead of four—and we're going to try to have him win the Kentucky Derby! It isn't going to work. So I say no. Shoot that horse and get something that's going to do something. It may cost more. You may have to buy a brand new thoroughbred. But you're going to win the race."

What, then, is the point of upgrading existing radars and expanding the overall radar system? The new radars, like the present ones, will operate at a few fixed sites that are undefended and, for all practical purposes, undefendable. The same kinds of direct nuclear or nonnuclear attacks, or sabotage, that can destroy or disable the current radar installations will also be able to put the new ones out of business. The dynamic blast overpressures—the major shock waves from nuclear detonations—created by a single one-megaton bomb exploded within miles of any present or planned radar installation would destroy it as easily as one can blow out a candle. Thus it will make little difference what ingenious new warhead-counting computers the radars have if they won't be able to operate at all in combat circumstances such as these. Unlike missiles, which can at least be buried in hardened underground silos that could withstand the overpressures from all but extremely close nuclear detonations, the radars will necessarily remain large, above-ground installations that only operate, in wartime, at the enemy's pleasure. If anything, the deluxe features that will be added to the present BMEWS and PAVE PAWS radars will provide more reason for the attacker to make sure to knock them out. The expensive upgrade that is planned will be for naught.

The BMEWS radars, conceived and designed in the pre-satellite era, were the principal early warning system against missile attacks when they went into operation in the early 1960s. After the first early warning satellites began operation a decade later, the status of the radars changed: from primary warning stations, they were downgraded to backups to the satellites. Instead of trying, at great expense, to upgrade the radars, it might be better to phase them out. It does make sense to have backups for the present satellite warning system—but that can just as well be provided by more satellites. The kind of highly redundant and highly survivable network of warning satellites proposed by Richard Garwin would seem to be a far more cost-effective way of detecting missile launches. Large radars, along with many other fixed installations, would appear to have had their day.

The billions of dollars that will be spent on radars intended to spot enemy bombers involves an even more dubious decision than the plan for missile-warning radars. The Soviets, to begin with, have relatively few long-range bombers. Unlike the U.S. Air Force, which is passionately devoted to the manned bomber, the Soviets, as Sputnik proved, were much quicker to see the coming of the missile age. Indeed, right after World War II the Soviet military—aided by its team of captured German rocket scientists—moved ahead much faster than the United States to build long-range missiles. The ICBM, which the Soviets were the first to test-fire, is one of the few instances in which they have bested the United States in the competition in strategic technology.

Except for what looks like a token commitment to bomber development, the Soviets have continued to put their priority on missiles. Whereas the United States has more nuclear weapons in its bombers than on its strategic missiles, fewer than four percent of Soviet strategic nuclear bombs have been put on manned aircraft. It makes sense for the Soviets, as they have done, to build a massive anti-bomber defense system. That comports with the kind of threat they face from the United States. Correspondingly, it makes little sense for the U.S., facing a Soviet force consisting of a relatively small bomber component, to put much priority on strategic defenses in this area.

It is difficult, moreover, to think of a circumstance in which the Soviets might want to use bomber sorties in any opening move against the United States. The Pentagon has made much of the capabilities of the so-called Backfire bomber that the Soviet Air Force first acquired in 1974. The threat posed by the two hundred or so Backfires in the Soviet arsenal has been portrayed in the report, "Soviet Military Power," that Secretary Weinberger has issued periodically. The latest version of the report shows the continental United States dangerously within range of these swept-wing bombers. A map that covers almost a full page in this document shows the Backfire bases in the USSR and the direct route the planes can fly over the northern polar regions to the United States.

However, if one notes the asterisk on this Pentagon map, one finds that the ability of the Backfires to cover targets in the U.S. has been displayed with the qualifying assumption that the attack is staged not from their usual bases but from forward bases in the Arctic. The text notes that "most" of these bombers "are based in the Western USSR although over the last few years the Soviets have deployed a sizable number in the Far East." These geographical details, as well as the Pentagon's knowledge of them, are very important. Unless the bombers are first moved to staging areas in the Arctic—more than a thousand miles, in some cases, from their normal bases—they cannot carry out the hypothesized missions against the United States. They would be out of range.

In addition, the fact that the Pentagon intelligence system is already capable of keeping track of these bombers is an indication of how little we need new early warning radars in Canada's frozen reaches. The Central Intelligence Agency and the National Security Agency are already able to receive satellite reconnaissance reports on what is happening at Soviet bomber bases. The Rhyolite satellites and other electronic eavesdropping devices also allow the United States to monitor such things as the communications between Soviet pilots and their ground controllers. (This was revealed during the Korean airliner incident in September 1983, when the United States released transcripts of the radio messages passed between Soviet pilots.) It is hardly plausible that the Soviets could confidently assume that the massing of the Backfire bombers and refueling planes in Arctic bases would go unnoticed. Given the already extensive intelligence-gathering system that can locate the bombers, the new conventional radars to be installed on the DEW Line would seem to be superfluous.

The case for the advanced Over the Horizon radars is weaker still. These radars depend on the ability to bounce signals off the ionosphere. However, among the best-known and most spectacular features of the Arctic region are the electromagnetic anomalies that occur there and cause such periodic displays as the aurora borealis, or northern lights. The ionosphere is notably unstable in this region, and since it can move about so dramatically there would be great difficulty in using it as the intermediary medium in a radar system. Current Air Force plans call for deploying the new radars only on the East and West Coasts of the United States. As Air Force General Bernard Randolph conceded in testimony before a Senate subcommittee, "Because of performance degradation from auroral effects, the OTH-B radar is not suitable as a North-looking surveillance and warning system."

In other words, the OTH-B device will work except in the direction from which Soviet bombers are most likely to come. The device has other problems, too, Richard Garwin notes, since it is much more readily jammed than conventional radars and, because of its narrow bandwidth, cannot use the kind of anti-jamming features available to broad-band radars. The Air Force still intends to proceed with it, however. A DMS Market Intelligence Report noted, "This program has taken just about every road but the straight and narrow one to get to where it is today. Problems resulting from the Auroral effect involving instability of the ionosphere in the Arctic regions almost caused the program to be canceled in FY'78. However, then-Secretary of Defense Rumsfeld intervened and the program received $4 million. When the Air Force had just about made up its mind to shelve the effort, DARPA"—the Defense Advanced Research Projects Agency—"came to bat with beefed-up experimentation. The Air Force evidently expects the OTH-B to be a major part of future anti-bomber defense."

The report also noted that Congress was "pulling in the reins, but the program isn't in danger. It's just going to take longer to complete." Congress has already allocated more than a hundred million dollars for OTH-B, and almost a billion dollars, it was estimated, will be spent over the rest of the decade on this new radar project.

Whatever kind of sensors are relied upon for early warning, the information they obtain must be sent back to NORAD and the main U.S. military command posts. This is the next essential task of the command and control network. The early warning radars have depended on land-lines to tie them in to the rest of the defense system. The arrangement is subject to direct attack and to the effects of EMP. This situation will be corrected, it is hoped, by the installation of satellite transmitters at each of the radar sites. The radar operators can therefore bypass the land-lines, or supplement messages on them, by sending data via the Air Force Satellite Communications System. The satellite transmitters at each radar site, however, would be subject to direct attack or sabotage, and would in any event be destroyed in a determined effort to knock out the radar installations. This new communications gear, since it could be destroyed so easily, is not much of an answer to the data-relay problem that exists.

Communications with the other main sensors in the early warning system, the DSP satellites, depend on the three highly vulnerable fixed ground stations at Nurrungar, Australia, Buckley Air National Guard Base in Colorado, and at the Simplified Processing Station in Europe. To rectify this situation, six mobile ground terminals, or MGTs, are being built as backups.

The MGTs, like the existing ground stations, will process raw data from the satellites in order to determine how many Soviet missiles have been launched. Unlike the ill-fated Simplified Processing Station built in Nebraska in the late 1970s, the MGTs are supposed to be truly mobile. The computers, satellite terminals, satellite transmitters, power supplies, and associated equipment for them will be put on vans that can be moved from place to place. Soviet photoreconnaissance satellites are expected to have great difficulty locating them, given camouflaging that will make them look like ordinary large trucks. They are also supposed to be able to change location faster than the estimated Soviet "intelligence cycle"—that is, the time it takes the Soviets to gather and process satellite reconnaissance photographs. (Unlike the United States, the Soviets do not have instantaneous photoreconnaissance capability; instead of electronically relaying pictures to ground stations, Soviet satellites have film packets that are dropped back to earth, retrieved, and then processed.)

"The MGT is a real qualitative improvement over SPS," one government expert said. "It is a sound concept and a sound piece of hardware." Another expert expressed the fear that since "the Air Force is not attuned to operating in the dirt in peacetime, the MGT will end up as smaller versions of SPS but still not really mobile." This difference of opinion should be settled soon, as the MGTs start to go into operation.

Even with the planned degree of mobility, the MGTs will not be able to operate while they are moving around—they will have to be parked and set up first—and once they are operating, and transmitting, Soviet electronic reconnaissance satellites could pinpoint them. They could then be destroyed. Thus, while MGTs may increase the ability to get data from the early warning satellites in the opening phase of a nuclear war, they will not have the capability to endure a protracted nuclear conflict.

In addition to gathering data from the early warning satellites, the ground stations must be able to transmit whatever information they obtain back to U.S. leaders. In the short run, the DSCS satellites will remain the principal means of sending data from Nurrungar and any Eastern Hemisphere backup stations to the continental United States. The vulnerability of the DSCS satellites to jamming or other forms of attack, as well as the vulnerability of the intermediary ground relay stations that must be used—since the satellite is out of range of NORAD, SAC Headquarters, and other command posts—will cause continuing problems. However mobile and reliable the ground stations may become, there will be no net improvement in the amount of data getting back to NORAD as long as the communications hookup remains so fragile.

———

The Pentagon has planned to improve the present military communications network by moving to an ultrasophisticated new satellite known as MILSTAR. Now under full-scale development by Lockheed, General

Electric, and Raytheon, the first one is scheduled to be deployed late in this decade. It will operate three times farther out in space than present defense satellites, at much higher than geosynchronous orbit, and at much higher frequencies. The present DSCS satellites work at super high frequency (SHF), but MILSTAR will use extremely high frequency (EHF), although it will also have some capability to use lower frequencies to be compatible with existing UHF satellite transmitters and receivers.

MILSTAR will have a variety of technological enhancements, the DMS survey noted, including "state of the art techniques for jam-resistance and physical survivability. Key features include higher frequencies, band-spreading, onboard signal processing, end to end encryption, nulling antennas, nuclear and laser hardening. . . ." The list of advanced features continues, and, according to Donald Latham, the MILSTAR program is the "single highest priority" in the Administration's strategic command and control program. It is referred to within the Pentagon as a "brickbat" priority, which means it has officially been put on the Master Urgency List of important national defense programs.

Actually, MILSTAR, in various incarnations, was proposed long before the Reagan Administration took office. As one former Pentagon official noted, the new program is merely the latest justification for an Air Force project, once called STRATSAT, that has been sitting around for years looking for funding. MILSTAR, he continued, reminded him of the multibillion dollar continental warning system begun by the Air Force in the 1950s called SAGE. "The technical people got very excited about it," he said. "But it required an immense computer at one place. If you knocked it out, you knocked out the whole system. The same thing could be said of MILSTAR. The same thing could be said of that Marine barracks in Beirut."

MILSTAR will have some useful features that present communications satellites lack, Desmond Ball said. The Soviets do not, at the moment, have the technology for jamming the EHF frequencies that it will exploit. "One should not make the assumption that that's necessarily always going to be the case," he added. Similarly, current Soviet ground-launched ASAT weapons, which are useful, at best, against satellites a few hundred miles above the earth's surface, will be unable to pose any threat to MILSTAR, which will operate sixty to seventy thousand miles out in space—more than a quarter of the way to the moon.

Still, we are at the beginning of an arms race in space that, if the Administration's position against an ASAT treaty does not change soon, will permit the Soviets to develop and deploy anti-MILSTAR weaponry. One of the simple space mines that Richard Garwin described can be launched and orbited close to each MILSTAR satellite. The mine will follow it around like a little dinghy trailing behind a big boat. A signal to the space mine just before H Hour, or whenever the Soviets chose, would promptly knock the target MILSTAR satellite out of commission. The United States could, of course, make an even fancier MILSTAR, giving it the capacity to attack or maneuver away from space mines. The Soviets, one can surmise, would respond by making more aggressive and tenacious space mines. Three satellites are supposed to make up the global MILSTAR communications net. "All it is really doing is adding three extra aim points to the things the Soviets have to knock out," Ball said.

Instead of a communications system dependent on a few very expensive, high-tech, high-capacity satellites, Ball suggests that consideration should be given to a communications system based on large numbers of "dumb" satellites. "A very simple relay system," as he describes it. "Cheap. You can proliferate them in large numbers and you can probably carry twenty up in each shuttle. You might be able to carry more than twenty up in a shuttle and just disperse those around.

"The other alternative is not sending up multiples of twenty satellites, but simply just shove UHF transponders"—devices that take a signal, amplify it, and retransmit it—"on every satellite that goes up. Everything that NASA launches. On anything that's launched by the U.S. government, insist that a small transponder, which is not going to add to the weight, is not going to compromise its other technical capabilities, be added." With such a large satellite system, he said, the Soviets would have to attack everything in space, not just a few special satellites, in order to cut off message transmissions.

A Pentagon communications consultant, who happens to have worked on the old SAGE system, looks at MILSTAR in similar terms. He referred to it as another case in which "technological imperatives" had gotten in the way of military logic. "They look at the next big advance they want to make technically," he said. "Why would I just go off and buy a pedestrian thing off the shelf? If you're in the development business, you want to keep developing. There's no reason in the world why they couldn't have stayed at SHF"—the present DSCS frequency—"and made that jam-resistant." For example, the nulling antennas to be put in MILSTAR—equipment that blocks the signal intended to jam the satellite—could just as easily be put on future DSCS satellites, he noted. Other simple things could be done to improve the present satellite communications system, such as making better use of existing government and commercial satellites, he added, but they are bypassed in order to keep the development bureaucracy happy. "It's nutty to have thirty or forty commercial satellites up there not being able to use them," he said. That's not done because "the satellite communications mafia sees it as a threat to its budget."

The MILSTAR lobby, he said, makes various claims about the military utility of the new satellite. "They argue that they need a narrow beam so the signal from a submarine can't be detected unless you're right on top of the sub." This advantage was specious, he noted, because it was already so hard to detect a submarine broadcasting on present SHF frequencies. It takes only a few seconds for a sub to deploy an antenna and send a message at SHF, since this frequency can carry massive amounts of information in a short burst transmission.

As to the proposal by Ball, Garwin, and others for a highly proliferated system of orbiting relay satellites, he said, "That's the only concept that makes sense if you're interested in building a survivable system." The control mechanism would be a bit complicated, he cautioned, but the real problem with the proposal is that the Pentagon does not want to make a step backwards toward simpler hardware. "It clashes with the technological imperative."

This Pentagon adviser noted that he was not pessimistic about ultimately getting a satisfactory command and control system. He volunteered the observation, "Eventually the right thing gets done, but it may be twenty years late and very expensive." The main problem, he feared, was that MILSTAR would be "eating up half of the command and control and communications budget. Is it worth it?"

———

Whatever satellite or radar warning messages—via MILSTAR or other means—are relayed back to the United States, they will have to go somewhere for officials to decide what it all means. NORAD, at present, is the fusion center that carries out attack assessments, and it will continue to play a central role. Its capabilities will be increased, but it will no longer carry this burden alone.

NORAD has undergone several shifts over its almost three decades of existence. Pentagon priorities have changed, technology has changed, Administrations have changed, and not all of this has been in NORAD's favor. The decline of the role of the bomber reduced the importance of bomber defense and, hence, the relevance of much of the early warning mission that NORAD had been carrying out. The increasing attention given to the Soviet submarine threat, on the other hand, led to a decision to send information from the PAVE PAWS radars directly to SAC Headquarters and the Pentagon rather than wait for it to go through NORAD. This also diminished the importance of what went on inside Cheyenne Mountain.

By the 1970s, NORAD found itself losing ground in the bureaucratic pecking order. The job of NORAD Commander in Chief, a prestigious slot that had been filled by a four-star general, was changed to a three-star post. That may not seem like much of a demotion to outsiders, but within the military it was a sign that NORAD had been quietly reassigned from the big leagues to the minors.

NORAD fought back, the result being that the Air Force agreed to establish its new Space Command in Colorado. It also agreed to "dual hat" the NORAD Commander in Chief and make him also the head of the Space Command. His fourth star returned. It happened that Senator Gary Hart of Colorado was the head of a Senate panel on military construction at the time these decisions were made. There was, as Charles Snodgrass, the former Congressional staff member, commented, "some Congressional logrolling thrown in" to the decision to put the Space Command in Colorado under the NORAD umbrella.

The new Space Command will operate the Consolidated Space Operations Center now being constructed near Colorado Springs. In addition to operating future ASAT weapons and ballistic missile defense systems, it will be able to control space shuttle missions—although the necessity for it to do so, given the fact that NASA already has a facility for that purpose, has been questioned—and it will be a backup to the vulnerable Satellite Control Facility in Sunnyvale, California. Its role as a backup is also questioned, but on different grounds. Something surely needs to be done to avoid the catastrophic effects of a Soviet attack, or an earthquake, that could disable the main control center for U.S. military satellites. Colorado Springs, though, is just as easy a target as Sunnyvale, and having two vulnerable facilities instead of one does not greatly increase protection against Soviet dismemberment of the satellite control system.

The upgrades planned for NORAD, in addition to linking it with the Space Command, essentially involve taking out the computer system in Cheyenne Mountain, throwing it away, and putting in a new one. One difficulty with the undertaking is that the current system has to be kept running during the transition. A NORAD official likened the process to changing a black and white television into a color television without shutting the set off. It is difficult to predict how well the computer renovation process will work, since the military, as one government computer expert explained, remains "in a major state of turmoil" about computer technology and how to use it. NORAD, he said, is simply "starting from scratch developing functional specifications" for its new system. What it will ultimately look like, and how well it will work, is anyone's guess.

It is also unclear what difference it will make, whatever is done to upgrade NORAD's computers. Since NORAD, under the system now planned by the Pentagon, will still be dependent on a very small number of vulnerable sensors, the lack of data about Soviet missile launches to put into the computers, rather than their degree of computational sophistication, will remain the limiting problem. The next limiting problem, the very short life expectancy of the Cheyenne Mountain Complex in light of its vulnerability to Soviet SS-18s, also diminishes the value of the new equipment that will be installed. To the extent that the improvements will reduce the danger of NORAD false alerts, they must be considered worthwhile. To the extent that they are intended to increase NORAD's performance under actual attack conditions, they are probably just more "Band-Aids on a dead horse."

With NORAD and other fixed installations in the strategic command system so vulnerable to direct attack, the Pentagon acknowledges the need to use mobile facilities as backups. There is a good deal of confusion about how best to do this. NORAD proposes to have a flying version of itself created. It has wanted such a plane for years. SAC wants to have "smarter" versions of Looking Glass and Kneecap created, ones that can be hooked up directly, via satellite, with the early warning sensors, thereby taking over some of the attack assessment functions of Cheyenne Mountain. SAC is also giving attention to upgrading its headquarters emergency relocation team, which at the moment would be unable to assemble officers, operational plans, and authentication documents very swiftly following the loss of Offutt and Looking Glass. A SAC communications consultant said that the present team would probably have nothing more sophisticated in the way of computing equipment than hand-calculators when they finally set up their emergency headquarters.

Hundreds of millions of dollars are being spent on outfitting the existing airborne command posts with new equipment, although most of it will go for increased EMP protection and communications gear and will not enhance the planes' attack assessment capabilities. On the Looking Glass EC-135s, in particular, there is simply no room for the additional computers and personnel that would be required to analyze the raw data from the early warning satellites. The plane depends on ground stations to do that. If more on-board processing can be done by the warning satellites, on the other hand, Looking Glass may be able to receive and make use of the results.

The Pentagon, however, is trying to shift away from airplanes, since even with a good bit more lubricating oil for their engines, airborne command posts cannot serve as platforms from which the Pentagon can orchestrate protracted nuclear wars over periods of weeks or months. According to what Mr. Latham told me in Detroit, he is thinking about meeting the need for "enduring" command and control by using ground-mobile command posts. These would involve "shipping container-type boxes that are the standard size shipping container, and inside you could place various types of equipment to perform command functions." These modular units, he said, would have their own battle staffs and would be designed to move about on trucks or ships. They would not all have the same equipment, but would be filled with the different kinds of computers and communications gear required by the Joint Chiefs of Staff, the President, CINCSAC, CINCNORAD, and other commanders.

Ground-mobile units that would alleviate dependence on NORAD or the Pentagon or Kneecap could not possibly have all the capabilities of these existing command posts. As Mr. Latham acknowledged, "There's no way to reconstitute the interior of Cheyenne Mountain"— which has eighty-seven computers at present—within a few shipping containers. Instead, some very "austere" version of the NORAD setup will have to be designed. He is very vague about how that will be done, and so is NORAD.

NORAD declined to say who was in charge of designing mobile centers for it, how many will be deployed, or what the anticipated schedule was. It did acknowledge, "We have a limited command and control backup capability to Cheyenne Mountain." A NORAD consultant chuckled when I asked about this, and said that the NORAD "BUF"—backup facility—consisted of a single video display screen and telephone hookup that had been installed near General Hartinger's residence at Peterson Air Force Base. NORAD also said that it had a mobile unit "called our RAPIER team, which deploys from time to time for training exercises." It did not say what kind of equipment the group took on its drills, or what it was capable of doing.

Mr. Latham's proposed ground-mobile command posts, according to Pentagon consultants, are one of the notable cases in which Pentagon rhetoric is bad but the concept is reasonable. Such command posts, if they were properly designed and deployed, might substantially reduce the risk of a decapitating attack. They would deny the Soviets an easy shot at the present U.S. command system, in other words, if they were built in sufficient number, suitably dispersed, and if the delegation procedures were streamlined so that if the President were killed, the surviving commanders could collaborate to issue an Emergency Action Message.

In a protracted nuclear war, on the other hand, the mobile command posts would have doubtful capability. Their information sources —the vulnerable warning radars and satellites—could be quickly knocked out of commission. Another "desperately important" problem they would face, according to an Air Force consultant, is the risk of giving away their locations when they send out messages. There were various technical ways around this, he said, as well as different operational procedures that could be used. Still, there were real limits to what could be done to keep their location secret for any extended period of time.

Mr. Latham gave me this explanation of how to make the mobile ground centers function in a prolonged war: "If you're emitting and you have a lot of activity at some particular place, why, it's possible that he could find you. So you'd have to develop an operations strategy that says that if you have such a facility as this, you only operate in a given facility like that for some period of time. Then you move by some means to another set of facilities like that. Either you physically move those [mobile command posts] or you move the battle staffs. Now all that's going to be part of the operations concept."

Mr. Latham did not mention the difficulties of how one would move the vans around the country after successive Soviet nuclear attacks had occurred. Nor did he comment on how his alternative, moving the battle staffs, could be done safely through all the lethal fallout that might be around. He did admit that there was one "practical problem" in that "you're not going to find that you have enough highly trained, cleared people to operate all these simultaneously or even have some of them stand by and some active. You will end up having a few battle staffs, and you move them between facilities or something like that. You can't do everything. That's why when I say you can only reconstitute a small piece of [the command system] the same thing's true of having enough available surviving people. Your primary battle staff may have been wiped out in some fixed site, gets blown away, and you've got to reconstitute your secondary battle staff in one of these facilities, and then your tertiary, and so on."

Few Pentagon advisers believe that any such ad hoc reconstitution of central control can be accomplished. They conclude that the mission of the mobile command posts is best limtied to improving the reliability of a basic U.S. retaliatory response; their proposed use as the organizing centers for protracted nuclear conflicts should be shelved.

As it turns out, however, the entire program is more or less just sitting on the shelf. Despite the short-run benefits they offer in correcting some of the most pronounced vulnerabilities of the present command system, ground-mobile command posts have nothing like the "brickbat" priority assigned to the multibillion dollar MILSTAR satellite. The mobile command post program, Mr. Latham said in a recent interview, "is fairly low key." The Pentagon was "examining options, not actually producing any equipment. It's just a concept sort of effort —mostly being done in-house and with a little help from MITRE." Possible versions of mobile command posts existed "on paper," but he could not provide any details, he said, about where the program was going, how it would be funded, and when it would produce results.

_____

A Reagan Administration official who would speak about the details of the mobile command post program noted that the main problem with it was that such facilities need to be more than just "führer bunkers, a place to keep somebody alive." They require various types of computers and communications equipment, and once the various Pentagon offices finished with the specifications for the equipment that would be needed, "the whole thing became uncontrollable." The procurement bureaucracy, that is, could not come up with any suitably "austere" command post. By the time the new command posts that were on the drawing boards had acquired all the satellite terminals, nuclear-explosions detectors, portable toilets, cooking facilities, and crew members that were proposed, they would no longer be mobile. "The gimmick is in trouble," this Pentagon expert said.

_____

The final element in the Administration's strategic command and control program is a set of improvements for the communications systems used to broadcast retaliatory orders to the forces. SAC Headquarters, Looking Glass, Kneecap, the Pentagon, and, if they ever come into existence, ground-mobile command posts will be outfitted with several new means of issuing the go codes.

Some of the new communications equipment has already been deployed. An inspection of Minuteman launch control centers shows that something has been added to the aboveground "antenna farm" that provides their key links with the outside world. The new feature is a white, cone-shaped device. It is about three feet wide and two feet high, sits on a concrete platform, and looks like the top of a rocket protruding out of the ground. It is not. It is the protective cover for a small satellite terminal that will allow Minuteman launch orders to be relayed via AFSATCOM, the Air Force Satellite System. (AFSATCOM receivers are also being added at all SAC ground command posts as well as to SAC bombers and airborne command posts.) Instead of having to be relayed over land-lines that are susceptible to EMP, orders from the Pentagon or SAC Headquarters can be issued using the AFSATCOM system.

The use of this satellite hookup is an obvious way around the problem of depending on leased telephone lines. However, the AFSATCOM system, which was designed to permit day-to-day messages to Air Force bases around the world, is a less than reliable wartime communications system. There are only a few AFSATCOM stations in orbit (they are actually not independent satellites but relay equipment carried aboard "host" satellites, such as the Navy's Fleet Satellite Communications System). They operate at UHF, are easily jammed, and have no ability to withstand the kind of direct or indirect attacks that can be made against them. Unless satellites are specially hardened, for example, nuclear detonations even thousands of miles away in outer space can destroy or incapacitate them. AFSATCOM satellites have no such hardening.

Nor does the AFSATCOM system offer the kind of redundancy that would give it the ability to function despite Soviet attacks—using space mines, for example—on some of its components. An unclassified SAC description of the system showed that of the four AFSATCOM satellites in geosynchronous orbit, only one is within range of the Minuteman launch control centers and the fourteen SAC bomber bases in the United States. This satellite is stationed at one hundred degrees west longitude, which would put it over the equator not far from the Galapagos Islands. The disabling or jamming of that satellite would cut the heart out of the new system for broadcasting emergency messages to all SAC bases in the continental United States. The four ground control stations that manage the operation of the AFSATCOM system—at Offutt, Barksdale, March, and Anderson (Guam) Air Force Bases— could also be destroyed quite readily as a way of interrupting the flow of messages through this satellite network.

MILSTAR, which is a decade away from operation, is expected to take over from the AFSATCOM system. It will have anti-jamming features, nuclear and EMP hardening, and other enhancements. It will also be as susceptible to space mines and other ASAT weapons as the less advanced satellites it will supplant. It will be a better (if vastly more expensive) Band-Aid on the existing command system than AFSATCOM, but a Band-Aid nevertheless.

The Pentagon does recognize that its space-based communications system may have handicaps, and so further work, now in the experimental stage, is being done to provide an alternative. The main approach is to use a new kind of radio system to build what is, in effect, a radio version of the telephone network. Instead of land-lines, low frequency radio waves will be used, ones designed to stay close to the ground, not to bounce off the ionosphere. The frequencies will be in the 150 to 190 khz range, which is just off the standard AM radio dial.

The Ground Wave Emergency Network (GWEN), as it is called, will use what look like the same kind of transmitting antennas as commercial AM radio stations. However, in addition to an aboveground, three- or four-hundred-foot antenna, there will be a buried antenna with spokes extending for five hundred feet or so from its base. Moreover, the GWEN antennas will be for both receiving and transmitting. Each GWEN antenna installation—or "node"—will have a range of only a few hundred miles. However, other GWEN stations are supposed to be built within that range. They will pick up and relay the messages from one GWEN facility to another.

Instead of operators and switchboards, new automated systems will be used to route messages. The GWEN installations will be unmanned, and computers at each node are being developed to shunt messages through the system. The technology of "packet switching" will be used —in which messages are broken up, transmitted over different paths, and then reassembled at their point of destination. The computers that run the GWEN system will have to recognize message priorities, sort out the most urgent traffic from other communications, and make sure that what comes in to each node goes out to the right users.

Dozens of GWEN installations will have to be built for a minimal system to connect the Pentagon and SAC Headquarters with the various missile and bomber bases. Hundreds or thousands of such antennas will be needed for a survivable system—one that can still function after heavy Soviet attack. The construction of large numbers of nodes is intended to promote survivability, in that with a minimum number of nodes surviving, the computers at them can bypass damaged nodes and find alternate routes for every urgent message. The system is also supposed to be designed to incorporate several forms of protection against EMP.

The GWEN system, Donald Latham says, is an example of how the Pentagon can make great strides when it dedicates itself to a given program. He fought off the "wish lists" of additional specifications that the services wanted to add, he said, and has moved within two years from the original concept, in 1981, to the completion, at the end of 1983, of a ten-node trial network. (GWEN installations are located in Pueblo and Aurora, Colorado; Omaha and Ainsworth, Nebraska; Manhattan and Colby, Kansas; Fayetteville, Arkansas; Canton, Oklahoma; and Clark, South Dakota, with three commercial radio antennas also used in the testing program.) An additional fifty-node test system is now being constructed by RCA, and the Pentagon schedule sets July 1985 as the deadline for making a decision on building a full-scale GWEN network of several hundred nodes.

The GWEN program is regarded by the experts as one of the most sensible initiatives the Administration has taken. The only reservations expressed about it have nothing to do with the concept itself or its technical feasibility. The issue is simply the ability of the Pentagon to manage all the new technology involved, especially the establishment of the complex computer system that is at the heart of the GWEN radio network. A further question, which has nothing to do with the GWEN program per se, is whether there will be any surviving command posts to feed the retaliatory orders into the new communications systems. Unmanned relay stations do not by themselves make a command and control system.

"Fixing this problem is not going to be easy," Donald Latham told a Congressional committee in 1983. "It will take quite a while, no matter what we do to expedite procurement or what have you. Command and control and communications and intelligence is quite different than buying a plane or a jeep or something like that. There are so many procedural and people considerations involved in getting systems into place."

It will be many years, in some cases more than a decade, before the program planned by the Administration is completed. There is a lot that can happen to sidetrack or delay it, as the history of many Pentagon initiatives has shown. Lieutenant General Brent Scowcroft commented in October 1981, when the President announced the new priority on command and control, "It remains to be seen whether or not it will be carried through." He added that "study groups in the past" had "pointed out many of the problems that we're all aware of, and everybody nods, and yet things change only interceptibly."

The traditional Pentagon budget battles are one major threat to the planned command and control upgrade, as the Navy's attempted diversion of funds for the new TACAMO planes suggests. Another illustration of how easily priorities can be shifted is the collapse of the program for building ground-mobile command posts. When the Strategic Modernization Program was announced in October 1981, Lieutenant General Hillman Dickinson identified this program as one of the highest priority undertakings. Dickinson was attending the symposium at the MITRE Corporation, where he responded to the criticism that money for planning mobile command posts was not enough—that development and acquisition funding was also required. "In developing the recommendations in that [command and control] package, we certainly gave higher priority to those [items] that do have the longest endurance," General Dickinson replied. "For example, there are very substantial additional resources for ground mobile command posts." Two and a half years later, the resources that were supposed to be committed to that undertaking had somehow disappeared. Many such shifts in the command and control budget, and many future struggles among the services for the funds for their favored programs, can be confidently predicted.

Funding, however generous and stable, will not by itself lead automatically to a satisfactory overhaul of the strategic command and control system. "There seems to be one small problem left," Richard DeLauer, the Under Secretary of Defense, said to the experts at the MITRE Corporation after explaining the Pentagon's eighteen billion dollar command and control program. "That's how in the hell do we manage this?" In reply to his own question, he added, "I haven't got an answer today. You're all pretty bright people. I'll accept any suggestions you might have. Put 'em on a piece of paper, send 'em on in."

Actually, there already were quite profound suggestions on the management reforms that have to be made—ones that the Pentagon had been very slow to accept—such as setting up a central office that is *in charge* of command and control programs. A member of the 1978 Defense Science Board panel that recommended this step noted that a further difficulty was that the services were still oriented toward weapons, not communications systems, and that career advancement for command and control specialists remained bleak. Until this changes, he said, and the Pentagon develops the "culture, allegiance, and career

paths in the services for command and control people," there will be
no way that this vital part of the country's defenses can be properly
managed, no matter how much money is spent.

The overall Pentagon track record in managing major procurements, not just communications devices, is perhaps the most fundamental reason for skepticism about how soon a new, high-performance
strategic command and control system can be brought into being. As
Mr. DeLauer himself said at a 1981 seminar at Harvard, shortly before
assuming his post as Under Secretary of Defense, the Pentagon "gets a
lot of money to buy things [but] when they do buy them, chances are
about one in five that the results will really be useful." This caveat
should perhaps be stamped on every Pentagon budget request, the way
the Surgeon General's warning about smoking is put on cigarette packs
—although Congress is no more likely to heed it than smokers are to
defer to the advisory that is given to them. The legislators, it should
be noted, other than raising questions about a few components of the
Administration's command and control package, such as the OTH-B
radars, have yet to look deeply at the undertaking or to evaluate the
alternatives to it.

———

Even if the entire Administration program goes ahead as planned, the
ultimate issue is what overall difference it will make in the performance
of the command and control system. The specialists who have looked
at the undertaking note that most of the initiatives are designed to provide more information to decision-makers planning offensive actions,
not greater assurance in launching a basic retaliatory strike. Thus, the
new DSP satellites and communications gear such as MILSTAR may
provide an abundance of detailed information needed for the rapid
retargeting of U.S. missiles against the Soviet leadership and Soviet
strategic forces. But none of these systems provides any increase in the
physical protection of the President or key decision-makers in the event
the *Soviets* strike first.

The Pentagon has done an internal study that shows how little net
improvement in U.S. retaliatory capability will be achieved by the
Administration's various command and control programs. According
to the unpublished Pentagon analysis, the present system could be
effectively disabled by fewer than fifty Soviet weapons and would survive, at best, for only six to twelve hours after a Soviet attack. (Under

worst-case assumptions, connectivity may last for as little as thirty minutes or so.) The upgraded strategic command and control system, on the other hand, will hardly be much more survivable. It will be able to function only up to about seventy-two hours after an attack, the Pentagon estimates, and it can be effectively disabled by two hundred to two hundred and fifty Soviet weapons.

"Given the number of warheads that the Soviets have," Desmond Ball commented, "the fact that you have to move from fifty to two hundred odd doesn't really increase the survivability of the system dramatically." With their eight thousand warheads, that is, planning a crippling attack on the new U.S. command system will be about as trivial a challenge as knocking out the fragile network that exists today.

Hair triggers, as Daniel Cullity pointed out to me, usually have adjustment mechanisms. There's a little screw that can be used to change the amount of pressure it takes to set them off. He showed me how to do this on the Schuetzen rifle, using what he called a "Howard Hughes screwdriver"—a long nail on his little finger. The Administration's eighteen billion dollar program will allow similar minor adjustments to be made to the firing mechanism for U.S. nuclear weapons. The mechanism itself will not be replaced, only modified, and will remain, for some time to come, a hair trigger.

"We've got the mandate, we've got the bucks, but nothing's come out of it," one officer lamented during lunch in a Pentagon cafeteria. Former Air Force Colonel John Boyd, now a Pentagon consultant, joined us at the table and talked about the Administration's hit-or-miss attempts to achieve enhanced military capability based on Hans Mark's principle of more of everything for each service. The defect of that approach, he said, was stated very well in an old Chinese work, Sun Tzu's *The Art of War*. Boyd took me into a Pentagon bookstore after lunch so I could buy a copy. He opened the book and pointed to a statement of this military strategist of the fourth century B.C.: "And when he prepares everywhere he will be weak everywhere."

The civilian overseers of the Administration's Strategic Modernization Program have tried to prepare for all the hypothetical contingencies they think might arise during a protracted nuclear war. They have been so concerned with how to retarget U.S. missiles in successive salvos against the USSR that they have overlooked the more basic requirement of stable deterrence: a command system that can survive an initial Soviet attack and make it unnecessary for the U.S. to resort to preemptive strikes in a serious crisis. All the preparations for carrying out an extended conflict, and for knocking out the Soviets in the third or fourth or fifth round, come to nothing if the new, supersophisticated U.S. command and control system cannot make it through round one. The Pentagon has not published its analysis of the future command and control system's glass jaw, nor has it yet figured out what to do to develop a better system. This has not, however, stopped the flow of funds toward command and control equipment destined to be just about as vulnerable to Soviet attack as the hardware it supplants.

Charles Zraket of the MITRE Corporation, speaking at its symposium in 1981, commented on the goals of the eighteen billion dollar program that had just been announced. "Well, the last thing I want to do is criticize the package, because I think it's an outstanding one," he said. "I think the point is valid, though, that by no stretch of the imagination will that package give us a fully enduring capability.

"To develop and deploy all these kinds of command, control, communications, and intelligence capabilities will be a very formidable undertaking," Zraket explained, his awareness of the difficulties based on MITRE's close involvement in the execution of the proposed programs. "It will cost tens of billions of dollars over the next ten years, over and above what we're currently spending. If we expect to address the conflict management phase, it would certainly take another ten years. Even after doing all of this, it's not clear how long such a system would endure, because of the uncertainties associated with nuclear war."

Just raising the survivability of the present command system to several hours or a few days would be difficult enough, Desmond Ball said in an interview. The notion of "enduring" command and control was "a bottomless pit that you can throw money into." Like Zraket, he had no objection to practical steps that could make the existing system less hair-triggered. But the Administration's undertaking was different. "What they haven't done is sit down and define what command and control and communications they want, other than to say: 'Throw money at it and that will solve the problem.' "

With the strategic command system expected to remain incapable of functioning for very long after a Soviet attack, this leaves the Pentagon with a major problem in implementing the nuclear war-fighting strategy that calls for the ability to carry on nuclear salvo after nuclear salvo for weeks and months. "I don't agree to building command, control, communications, and intelligence capability toward supporting protracted nuclear war because I don't think we can do it," Richard Garwin said. "I also don't think it's desirable, but really I wouldn't know how to go about it."

"We'd certainly appreciate advice, assistance, suggestions," General Hillman Dickinson told the experts gathered at the MITRE symposium. "We don't have the answers . . . to all the enduring problems for the longer haul. We need bright ideas. We need help."

EPILOGUE

The present strategic command and control system, one of the Pentagon's senior advisers commented, should be a clue to the military's real thinking about nuclear war. The fact that the apparatus for responding to Soviet attack has serious flaws is not an indication of colossal incompetence, he said. It reflects, instead, the feeling of "at least nine out of ten people in the military planning system—and I'm talking about the hawks—that strategic war wouldn't occur. That belief affects their thinking on command, control, and communications requirements."

Pentagon priorities, he continued, are determined more by service traditions, technological imperatives, and the natural desire of the military bureaucracy for more money than by any strongly perceived need to prepare for an imminent showdown with the USSR. The Soviets are viewed as a dangerous but cautious adversary, unlikely to make any frontal assault or even to provoke lesser confrontations that would create the risk of a major war. Why, therefore, should the services cut back their main programs to spend money on command and control systems they don't expect to have to use?

There is also strong military tradition that influences Pentagon planning, a deep-seated bias that provides further reason for deemphasizing the command and control systems suited for striking back at the Soviet Union. Down through the ages, commanders have always favored offense over defense, seizing the initiative rather than ceding it to the enemy, looking for the opportunity to land a Sunday punch instead of waiting for the other side to let go with theirs. Permitting the United States to be destroyed by the Soviets, and then retaliating, is a completely unmilitary notion. The common operating premise among U.S. war planners, therefore, is that the United States would never permit itself to be hit first.

Civilian analysts have said many times that surprise is no longer a factor in the nuclear age. Jacob Viner, of the University of Chicago, one of the leading early interpreters of the meaning of the atomic bomb, said at a 1946 conference, "The atomic bomb makes surprise an unimportant element of warfare. Retaliation in equal terms is unavoidable and in this sense the atomic bomb is a war deterrent, a peacemaking force."

That is not exactly how the military looks at it. Deterrence is accepted, but this does not rule out pushing the button first in a grave crisis if deterrence wobbles and appears to be failing. The entire history of conventional conflict shows that surprise carries with it a large advantage. The effects of a nuclear "second strike" may seem sufficiently devastating to cancel out the hypothetical gain from getting in the first blow, at least in the minds of many civilians. But this "fact," which is supposed to dominate thinking about warfare in the nuclear age, does not reflect the military's established outlook. As George Orwell wrote, "Traditions are not killed by facts," and there is, in any event, enough narrow military logic behind the existing first-strike plans that it is unlikely they will ever be abandoned so long as weapons fit for this purpose are in military hands.

The apparent "defects" in U.S. retaliatory capability, in this context, are a by-product of the military's unstated reliance on the major first-strike option it has always included in the S.I.O.P. Looking Glass has been allowed to have a key antenna that falls off and other shoddy arrangements have been tolerated, Desmond Ball said, because "down inside, they don't really believe that this stuff's going to be of any use" in the type of war the United States would end up fighting. The Strategic Air Command simply does not plan to be in a retaliatory mode, and if U.S. leaders want to push the button first, they do not need to use

cumbersome antennas or other such devices. They can just pass along
their orders over the telephone lines the Pentagon leases from AT&T.

Psychoanalyzing the military, like trying to affix motives to anyone's behavior, is a tricky business. Ball's statement and those of other
observers on what happens "down inside" the psyche of the Strategic
Air Command can be accepted or ignored. Less readily dismissed are
the documents written by General Holloway and other statements by
SAC officials on "the tremendous advantage" of striking first. And no
one who analyzes the type of missiles being added to the U.S. arsenal
can doubt the offensive role they are designed to play. Weapons with
the technical attributes of the MX and the Trident D-5 have an inherent
first-strike capability—their accuracy, destructive power, and speed
make possible pinpoint attacks that would destroy Soviet underground
command posts and missile silos before the Soviets have a chance to
act. Once the MX and D-5 are deployed later in this decade, they will
create an inescapable temptation for the United States, in a dire crisis,
to use them before the Soviets used their SS-18s.

The awesome power and accuracy of the new U.S. missiles, the
Pentagon may argue, is a manifestation of the country's technological
prowess, a natural step in missile development, not the result of any
offensive planning. Even if retaliation were the only purpose the Pentagon originally had in mind, means and ends tend to interact. What
we become capable of doing we often become interested in doing, and
if the military has offensive weapons it is likely to adopt offensive
plans. It is clear in this instance, though, that the new missiles are not
father to the plans; they will merely make it easier to execute the major
first-strike option on which SAC has relied for the past three decades.

Thus, the coming together of the diverse factors that influence
strategic war planning—traditional ways of thinking, new weapons
technology, and the technical difficulty of launching retaliatory strikes
—keeps first-strike options firmly entrenched in the S.I.O.P. The public,
however, is oblivious of the nation's dependence on contingency plans
for going on the offensive. Congress has not inquired about them. Our
Presidents, with few exceptions, never bother to probe the details of
how the nuclear trigger is set. Everyone leaves the arcane issue of
nuclear strategy to the specialists. Discussion and debate on the true
nature of the S.I.O.P.—and on its dangerous implications—are long
overdue.

The main risks created by the first-strike component of the S.I.O.P. are latent in peacetime. So long as both sides maintain their customary wariness about engaging in direct confrontation, no one in either military establishment will be nervously fingering any buttons. There are, moreover, layers upon layers of inhibit switches, procedural controls, and other safeguards to quash any unauthorized action or correct any technical glitch that could cause the nuclear firing mechanism to go off. From a peacetime point of view, the existing command and control systems are superbly well designed to head off serious nuclear accidents.

There is no fail-safe system, however, to make peace a permanent state of affairs, especially given the extremely vigorous arms race and the anxieties it creates. However blue the sky may seem, storm clouds can gather quickly, and while no one seriously worries about a "bolt from the blue," the two nations must worry about what Churchill called "a bolt from the grey"—a war arising out of a tense situation. Nations, he emphasized, are not simple pieces on a chess board but more like "planetary bodies" that cannot approach each other "without giving rise to profound magnetic reactions."

In particular, once something happens to make today's leaders sense the danger of an attack, all of the peacetime safety catches on their nuclear firing mechanisms—the precautions from which so much comfort is normally derived—must necessarily be eased. If a nation is in danger, it may have to use its weapons and cannot do so if they are totally locked up. As a crisis deepens and safeguards are consecutively removed, each side broadcasts frightening signals to the other. As all of this happens, more or less automatically, political leaders on both sides may not want war, but they may be unable to stop the others, or themselves, from pushing the button. Like captains of giant vessels, they may be unable to bring their war machines to an immediate halt although they recognize that they are on a potential collision course. They may even be forced to decide, if they have to hit at all, that the lesser of two evils is to ram the enemy at full speed.

In addition, in weighing the decision to attack, the new missile-guidance technology that is available—and which permits U.S. and Soviet missiles with an inherent first-strike capability to be deployed—will put a thumb on the scale. For the choice between using one's own first-strike weapons or waiting for the other side to use theirs is not, in military terms, one that calls for extended deliberations. Instead of both sides, as in peacetime, being deterred from attacking the other, they could both feel prompted to commence hostilities as soon as possible. The only question in such an unstable situation will be who will fire first.

The tremendous drawbacks of depending on an offensive nuclear strategy and on nuclear forces with inherent first-strike roles do not appear to have registered in the minds of Pentagon planners. The technocracy focuses mainly on deploying the latest gadgetry and fails to see, and sometimes does not wish to see, the larger implications. It is routine enough for the weapons procurement bureaucracy to exploit every new advance in strategic missile design that comes along. But like calm streams that come together to form dangerous rapids, the business-as-usual approach toward missile development results in an overall strategic posture that has terrifying flaws. The whole slide toward an offensive, nuclear war-fighting posture has this kind of happenstance to it. No one, if asked, would recommend a posture that encourages both sides to make first strikes in a crisis—presumably this is exactly what we want to prevent—yet, unhappily, this is the net result of the current S.I.O.P. and the plans to deploy the MX and D-5 missiles.

The Soviets, to be sure, have acted in a similar manner in formulating their war plans and building up their own nuclear arsenal. Scholars of Soviet military doctrine find ample evidence that they also favor an offensive strategy to one of pure deterrence. They are likewise just as vigorous in keeping up with the technological advances that give their missiles a first-strike capability. The Soviets are by no means innocent victims of U.S. strategic machinations. Through the correspondingly provocative strategic posture they maintain, they are full partners with U.S. war planners in creating the conditions that will pull the rug out from under mutual deterrence in the event of a major confrontation.

Yet there are decisive measures the United States and the Soviet Union could take to extricate themselves from the present war plans and war machines that could propel them into an unintended nuclear war. Neither side's military leaders are going to submit to lobotomies that stop them from thinking in traditional terms about the advantages of first strikes. Arms control negotiations that curb deployment of first-strike weapons, on the other hand, can make the issue moot: they can get rid of the tools that make offensive action an attractive and potentially feasible alternative in a crisis.

If the Nixon Administration had not bungled the SALT I Treaty and had included a ban on MIRVs, this goal would already have been largely achieved. (Without MIRVs, neither side would have the key technical advantage that permits several warheads to be aimed at each of its opponent's missile silos, thereby permitting, at least in theory, a successful knockout blow against the other's ICBM force.) Still, it is not too late to try to change course. A U.S.–Soviet agreement that phased out MIRVed ICBMs and replaced them with single-warhead missiles would be a giant step in defusing current first-strike war plans.

Even without formal arms control agreements, the United States could, with great benefit to itself, back off from the provocative strategic posture it has adopted. It is feasible for the United States to do this without waiting for any new technology or arms control breakthroughs. Our nuclear submarines, with their clumsy (but nevertheless effective) fail-deadly communications system, offer today and for the foreseeable future an invulnerable retaliatory force that can negate any military advantage the Soviets might hope to derive from attacking the United States in a crisis. An S.I.O.P. that puts the priority on submarine attack-response plans would provide the basis for a deterrent posture most consistent with long-term U.S. security.

At present, however, the deterrent value of submarines is undermined not by any Soviet action but by our own ill-conceived policies. The priority assigned in the S.I.O.P. to using our ICBMs in a preemptive attack encourages the Soviets to do the same. This option must be stricken from the war plan and the Soviets must be given plain evidence that it has been. To demonstrate the switch to a purely retaliatory S.I.O.P., U.S. fixed land-based Minuteman missiles with multiple warheads must be phased out and replaced—if at all—only by mobile, single warhead missiles that do not pose a first-strike threat. The second factor undermining the stable deterrence submarines can presently assure is the plan to deploy the D-5 missile on future Trident submarines. This program, which converts these submarines into potential first-strike weapons, must be cancelled if there is to be any hope of preserving the major contribution submarines can make to maintaining the peace.

It may seem paradoxical that getting rid of some of our most advanced weapons is the best way to improve our security, but until the wisdom of this course of action is appreciated, there will no way that mutual deterrence can be preserved in major crises. We must somehow learn to see that we cannot feel safe from Soviet attack in a crisis unless they feel safe from an attack by us, and that first-strike weapons will not deter them but only provoke them to lash out against us. As Roger Fisher of the Harvard Law School observed, the United States and the Soviet Union have to remember that they are in the same boat when it comes to a nuclear showdown. "You can think of that physically," he added. "There is no way we can make our end of the boat safer by making the other end more likely to tip over." Removing first-strike weapons from our arsenal is thus by no means a gratuitous concession to the Soviets. It is a necessary step to keep us both from drowning.

A further step in rectifying the weaknesses in the U.S. deterrent would be building a more robust command and control system, thereby eliminating a window of vulnerability that could make the Soviets think there was much to gain from a first strike. Various technically sound proposals to repair the present command and control system have been advanced—such as the deployment of simple, highly redundant satellite communications systems to improve the transmission of retaliatory orders. However, the command and control improvement program now underway appears to have little chance, by the Pentagon's own estimates, of doing this. For the Pentagon has subordinated basic improvements intended to enhance U.S. retaliatory capability in favor of programs for fighting protracted nuclear wars. We ought to be protecting our own jugular, but the real priority in the Administration's Strategic Modernization Program is to develop better means to cut the other side's.

Instead of doing something fundamental to change the provocatively supercharged U.S. war machine, the Pentagon's civilian hierarchy has merely fine-tuned the official "strategic doctrine" in a way that will supposedly reduce the risks of a cataclysmic war. Rather than replacing the first-strike weapons that make it possible for all-out war to develop out of a major crisis, the civilian strategists have proposed that the military follow certain rules of the road in the event that conflict occurs —a policy of controlled escalation. The merits of this policy are supposedly demonstrated in "war games," exercises that simulate the possible circumstances that could lead to nuclear war. These sessions routinely produce optimistic results, since it's hard to design a nuclear war that makes sense when each prospective participant realizes how it will end up destroyed along with its opponent.

"The good news is it's terribly hard even in a [war] game with fairly bloodthirsty players on both sides, terribly hard to get anybody to use nuclear weapons in a crisis and terribly hard to get anybody to contemplate any use of nuclear weapons except a diffident, shy, cautious use," Thomas Schelling, the Harvard economist and nuclear strategist, said. "That's the good news. The bad news, of course, is that we still don't know how that war might come about. I think all we know is that it will come about by ways we probably can't describe in detail."

In fact, a study of how each side's nuclear trigger is set shows quite clearly how nuclear war can come about: through complex crisis dynamics that force leaders to choose preemptive attacks to forestall the other side from the same thing. Brinksmanship is not just dangerous rhetoric from the 1950s but an *inherent* feature of opposing strategic forces that are programmed for first strikes. The proponents of controlled escalation do not appear to appreciate the military and technological imperatives involved—how loaded the dice are, on both sides, in favor of offensive action and how weak, on both sides, are the means to stop automatic, reflex, military precautions that could inadvertently produce all-out war. "People don't seem to realize that that's the kind of situation we have on our hands," John Steinbruner said. Given the offensive weaponry and first-strike plans on which it depends, trying to indoctrinate the Strategic Air Command about controlling escalation is like thinking a Dutch uncle talk can keep a hot rodder from flooring it when the red light yields to green.

The strategists who have advocated the controlled-escalation theory, disregarding the hair triggers on the opposing war machines, envision the superpowers bargaining sensibly in a major crisis. This would involve making correct interpretations of each other's behavior, such as distinguishing defensive maneuvers from offensive ones. Yet the line between the two is so fuzzy that it is absurd to expect that this can be done in a reliable way. A good example of the uncertainty and unpredictability of such judgments was Professor Schelling's comment in a recent interview about one decision that might have to be made. With the President so vulnerable to attack, should he stay in the White House or go aboard Kneecap, his emergency airborne command post, and carry on negotiations from aloft? "The President's leaving Washington would not in itself be an inflammatory thing to do," Schelling concluded. By the time a crisis had reached its peak, he explained, the National Guard would already be called out in every city, all normal television and radio broadcasts shut down, and the President's departure would be seen by the Russians as just one more precaution.

On the other hand, when this same subject was discussed by a senior military officer, Lieutenant General Brent Scowcroft, his evaluation of the implications of the President's departure from the White House was quite different. "I think you could assume that the President would want to stay in the White House during a crisis until the last possible minute," Scowcroft said. "His leaving the White House would in itself be a signal. . . . Therefore he may stay too long and not survive."

The American professor and the American general view the situation differently, but how would the Russians—separated by an even greater cultural divide—regard such a step in the middle of a crisis? Few experts on the Soviet Union offer much encouragement about the ability to predict Soviet responses. "The more we study the Russians, the less we understand them," a senior Soviet analyst at the Central Intelligence Agency told me, adding, "There's an old saying in the intelligence community based on how often our predictions are wrong —'You're not a good analyst until you've not only eaten crow but you've learned to like it.' "

But unless there is confidence that the United States can predict Soviet behavior during a crisis—and especially their reaction to our threats or actual use of nuclear weapons—no strategy of controlled escalation can be implemented. Actions that were intended to bring them into submission might only serve to provoke them. It is no wonder, with all the uncertainties about Soviet reactions, that the military has no interest in limited nuclear options and prefers, if it has to fight, to launch a major first strike.

It is also no wonder that despite all the emphasis placed on controlled escalation by the civilian strategists in the Pentagon, this is not actually incorporated in the war plan prepared by the Joint Strategic Target Planning Staff in Omaha. "There is no provision in the S.I.O.P. for controlled escalation," a senior officer who has worked on it told me. "The S.I.O.P. is essentially a set of fixed plans." Of course, the President can try to negotiate with the Soviets if he wants, but the military options in his black book are not designed with any step-by-step bargaining process in mind. The main option at the moment is the kind of attack outlined in General Holloway's memorandum: a first strike whose goal is to kill Soviet leaders, and thereby paralyze their command and control system, as well as attacking the Soviet nuclear forces before they can be used.

Few U.S. national security experts have focused on the risk that our offensive war plan could merely encourage the Soviets to go on the offensive themselves, although U.S. strategists are aware of some of the other conundrums posed by the conflicts between the requirements of controlled escalation and the provisions of the S.I.O.P. Thus, at a MITRE Corporation symposium, Lieutenant General Scowcroft noted, "There's a real dilemma here that we haven't sorted out," in that the use of "controlled nuclear options" to force concessions from the Soviets "presume[s] communication with the Soviet Union. And yet, from a military point of view, one of the most efficient kinds of attack is against leadership and command and control systems. . . . This is a dilemma that, I think, we still have not completely come to grips with."

Scowcroft did not say when, or how, U.S. strategists were going to resolve this question, although the lack of an answer has not stopped the United States from moving ahead with developing and deploying the weaponry for making a first strike on the Soviet leadership. The question whether it is better to plan to kill Soviet leaders or to keep them around to negotiate with has simply been left open. The subject is treated in the way it is customary for Pentagon planners to handle other important problems about nuclear-war fighting that they are unable to resolve. The official attitude is that we will fall off that bridge when we come to it.

NOTES

Foreword

PAGE

12 ... as Winston Churchill noted ...
Winston S. Churchill, *The World Crisis 1911–1914* (Thornton Butterworth Limited, 1923), p. 166.

15 Just like King Arthur ...
Sir Thomas Malory, *Le Morte D'Arthur* (Washington Square Press, 1963), p. 7.

15 ... the President has been said to have ...
United States Air Force, "SAC Underground Command Post" (Strategic Air Command Fact Sheet 82–09, August 1982), p. 2.

16 The Roman centurion ...
Matthew VIII: 8, 9.

16 Key portions of the ...
Harvard University, *Seminar on Command, Control, Communications, and Intelligence* (Incidental Paper, Center for Information Policy Research, 1981), p. 27. [The Center also held seminars on this subject in 1980 and 1982; the transcripts of these sessions are referred to hereafter as Harvard Seminar plus the date.]

Chapter 1

PAGE

20 A fact sheet that NORAD gives ...
North American Aerospace Defense Command, "NORAD Cheyenne Mountain Complex" (NORAD Public Affairs Office, October 1983), p. 7.

21 NORAD replied to my subsequent written ...
Letter from K. Cormier, NORAD Headquarters, to the author, February 14, 1984.

PAGE
21   I spoke with General Wagoner again . . .
     Telephone interview with Brigadier General Robert Wagoner, April 13, 1984.
22   "I'll give you a little bit of . . ."
     Interview with Daniel Cullity, June 9, 1983.
24   "We've got to realize the implication . . ."
     Interview with John Steinbruner, June 14, 1983.
25   The Pentagon's view on this subject . . .
     Interview with Lieutenant General Robert Herres, June 14, 1983.
26   William Perry, the Under Secretary . . .
     William J. Perry, "Technical Prospects," in Barry M. Blechman et al., *Rethinking
     the U.S. Strategic Posture: A Report from the Aspen Consortium on Arms Con-
     trol and Security Issues* (Ballinger, 1982), p. 129.
26   "When the services found out . . ."
     Interview with Rear Admiral Paul Tomb, June 15, 1983.
26   "perhaps the weakest link . . ."
     Hearings before the House Committee on Armed Services, *Military Posture and
     H.R. 1872, Department of Defense Authorization for Appropriations for Fiscal
     Year 1980* (February, March, and April 1979), Part 3, Book 1, p. 233.
27   "I know of no other President . . ."
     Robert Rosenberg, "The Influence of Policy Making on C³I," in Harvard Seminar
     1980, p. 60.
27   "It may be relatively simple and . . ."
     Hillman Dickinson, Harvard Seminar 1982, p. 15.
28   President John Kennedy . . .
     Interview with Jerome B. Wiesner, October 25, 1984.
28   "I think we would all like to be . . ."
     "Reducing the Risk of Inadvertent War," transcript of a Conference on Crisis
     Management (Lyndon B. Johnson School of Public Affairs, University of Texas
     at Austin, February 24, 1983), Volume I, p. 60 [hereafter referred to as LBJ
     School of Public Affairs].
28   The warning system, for instance, "begins . . ."
     Ibid., p. 66.
29   A brief in the case prepared . . .
     General Counsel of the Department of Defense, "Department of Defense Anal-
     ysis of the Impact of the Department of Justice–American Telephone and Tele-
     graph Company Antitrust Suit Settlement Agreement Upon the Provision of
     Telecommunications Services to the Department of Defense," April 20, 1982,
     pp. 3–4.
30   "If somebody says there's a . . ."
     Tomb interview.
31   The bomb went off at 11:02 A.M. . . .
     Frank W. Chinnock, *Nagasaki: The Forgotten Bomb* (World Publishing Com-
     pany, 1969), p. 89.
31   The present command system "works" . . .
     Perry, in Blechman, op. cit., p. 150.
31   "five hours down to thirty minutes"
     Interview with General Bennie L. Davis, June 1, 1983.
31   In 1957, General Omar Bradley . . .
     Speech at St. Alban's School, Washington, D.C., November 5, 1957.
31   "The way the warning systems work . . ."
     Interview with Desmond Ball, September 1, 1983.
32   U.S. leaders, William Perry noted . . .

Perry, in Blechman, op. cit., p. 147.

32 Vice Admiral Gerald Miller . . . told Congress . . .
Testimony before the House Committee on International Affairs, *First Use of Nuclear Weapons: Preserving Responsible Control* (March 1976), p. 71.

33 "Would the President of the United States . . ."
Henry Kissinger, "The Future of NATO," *Washington Quarterly*, Autumn 1979, p. 7.

34 He told Secretary of Defense James Forrestal . . .
Walter Mills, ed., *The Forrestal Diaries* (Viking, 1951), p. 458.

34 The Strategic Air Command, during most of this period . . .
Fred Kaplan, *The Wizards of Armageddon* (Simon and Schuster, 1983), p. 131.

35 . . . about as likely to blow up on the launching pads . . .
Paul Bracken, *The Command and Control of Nuclear Forces* (Yale University Press, 1983), p. 213; see also Robert Berman and John Baker, *Soviet Strategic Forces* (The Brookings Institution, 1982), p. 49.

36 A capability to launch some or all . . .
Richard L. Garwin, "Launch Under Attack to Redress Minuteman Vulnerability?" *International Security*, Winter 1979–80, pp. 117–139.

36 Having a reliable means . . .
Interview with Richard Garwin, June 27, 1983.

37 In April 1983, however, an Air Force . . .
Hedrick Smith, "Colonel Stirs Questions on MX-Firing Doctrine," *New York Times*, April 8, 1983, p. D15.

37 "It is our policy not to explain . . ."
Ibid.

38 "It would be a hair-triggered . . ."
Ibid.

39 "They will revenge themselves . . ."
Niccolo Machiavelli, *The Prince* and *The Discourses* (Modern Library College Editions, 1953), pp. 8–9.

39 "a command and control structure developed . . ."
Bobby Inman, Harvard Seminar 1981, p. 199.

39 The problems are also discussed in an . . .
Desmond Ball, "Can Nuclear War Be Controlled?" (The International Institute for Strategic Studies, Autumn 1981), Adelphi Paper 169.

40 "These and other key facilities . . ."
John Hamre et al., *Strategic Command, Control, and Communications: Alternative Approaches for Modernization* (Congressional Budget Office, October 1981), p. 13.

41 Western analysts believe that some . . .
Desmond Ball, "Soviet Strategic Planning and the Control of Nuclear War" (The Strategic and Defence Studies Centre, Australian National University, November 1983), Reference Paper No. 109, p. 8.

41 "Lack of centralized control is not . . ."
Interview with Frank von Hippel, May 24, 1984.

41 The U.S. submarines on patrol have . . .
General Accounting Office, "An Unclassified Version of a Classified Report Entitled 'The Navy's Strategic Communications System—Need for Management Attention and Decisionmaking' " (Report to Congress, May 2, 1979), PSAD-79-48A, Chapter 1; see also the remarks of Rear Admiral Paul Tomb at the MITRE Corporation National Security Issues Symposium (MITRE Corporation, 1981), pp. 108–109 [hereafter referred to as MITRE 1981 Symposium].

PAGE
43   The U.S. war plan itself is supposed . . .
     United States Air Force, "Joint Strategic Target Planning Staff" (Strategic Air
     Command Fact Sheet 83–8, April 1983).
44   "I'm very familiar with the popular terms . . ."
     Davis interview.
44   In part, the low state of readiness . . .
     Berman and Baker, op. cit., Chapter 3.
45   The Soviets have also put some of . . .
     Ibid., p. 20.
45   According to Donald Latham, . . . the Soviets . . .
     Interview with Donald Latham, May 29, 1983.
45   Barry Blechman of the Institute for . . .
     LBJ School of Public Affairs, p. 54.
45   "It's not as though the computer . . ."
     Davis interview.
46   General Bennie Davis, in May 1983 . . .
     Hearings before the Senate Committee on Armed Services, *MX Missile Basing
     System and Related Issues* (April 18, 20, 21, 22, 26; May 3, 1983), p. 417.
47   Under questioning by Senator Nunn . . .
     Ibid., p. 418.
47   "Unfortunately, a preemptive attack . . ."
     John Steinbruner, "Nuclear Decapitation," *Foreign Policy* 45, Winter 1981–82,
     p. 19.
48   "One of the most destabilizing things . . ."
     General Richard Ellis, Harvard Seminar 1982, p. 8.
49   Thus, among the contingency plans . . .
     Herres interview.
50   The recent work of two psychologists . . .
     Philip Boffey, " 'Rational' Decisions Prove Not to Be," *New York Times*, De-
     cember 6, 1983, p. C1; see also Daniel Kahneman and Amos Tversky, "Choices,
     Values, and Frames," paper presented at the National Academy of Science Sym-
     posium, Knowledge in Social and Behavioral Science, November 29, 1983.
51   "That's the strongest . . ."
     Steinbruner interview; see also John Steinbruner, "National Security and the
     Concept of Strategic Stability," *Journal of Conflict Resolution*, Vol. 22, No. 3,
     September 1978, p. 424.
51   Like the peacemakers who . . .
     Churchill, op. cit., p. 201.
52   "The machine was there; and because it . . ."
     Robert Musil, *The Man Without Qualities*, translated by Eithne Wilkins and
     Ernst Kaiser (Perigee Books, 1980), Vol. I, p. 265.
52   "the automatic phase of the war"
     Lieutenant General Brent Scowcroft, MITRE 1981 Symposium, p. 94.
52   "It was now minutes before seven . . ."
     Barbara Tuchman, *The Guns of August* (Bantam Books, 1976), p. 101.
53   "What you're really talking about . . ."
     Herres interview.
54   The difficulty of shifting people's basic ideas . . .
     Max Planck, *The Philosophy of Physics* (Norton, 1936), p. 90.

Chapter 2

PAGE

56 "The whole thing was invisible . . ."
Bruce Catton, *A Stillness at Appomattox* (Simon and Schuster, 1953), p. 93.

56 "[t]he commanders behind the lines . . ."
Ibid., p. 95.

57 As the Japanese armada approached . . .
Richard K. Betts, *Surprise Attack* (The Brookings Institution, 1982), pp. 42–50.

57 "It is proper to suggest that . . ."
Report of the Committee on the Investigation of the Pearl Harbor Attack, *Investigation of the Pearl Harbor Attack* (79th Congress, 1946), p. 264.

58 Admiral Noel Gayler, the former . . .
Interview with Noel Gayler, May 24, 1984.

58 Even when unambiguous warnings were . . .
Betts, op. cit., p. 49.

59 There are fifteen steel buildings . . .
North American Aerospace Defense Command, op. cit., p. 1.

59 The stunning surprise attack against . . .
Betts, op. cit., pp. 65–68.

60 The Missile Warning Center has a . . .
Cormier, op. cit.

60 Its video screens are programmed by . . .
Interview with Major Robert Walden, October 23, 1983.

61 Some twenty-two thousand miles . . .
Desmond Ball, "Code 647: Australia and the U.S. Defense Support Program" (The Strategic and Defence Studies Centre, Australian National University, July 1982), Reference Paper No. 82; see also *Aviation Week & Space Technology*, December 2, 1974, p. 16.

61 (The missile bases stretch across . . .)
Berman and Baker, op. cit., p. 14.

62 The classification of the missiles . . .
Report of Senator Gary Hart and Senator Barry Goldwater to the Senate Committee on Armed Services, *Recent False Alerts from the Nation's Missile Attack Warning System* (October 9, 1980), p. 2.

63 "Anything that receives . . ."
Herres interview.

64 Thus, turning on or repositioning . . .
Interview with Colonel Gerald May, October 23, 1983.

64 "within bazooka range of a highway"
Atlanta Journal & Constitution, September 21, 1980, p. 1.

64 Unclassified Pentagon testimony . . .
Statement by Donald C. Latham, Deputy Under Secretary of Defense, before the Subcommittee on Strategic and Theater Nuclear Forces of the Senate Committee on Armed Services (March 18, 1983), p. 3.

64–65 The importance of the Sunnyvale . . .
General Accounting Office, "Consolidated Space Operations Center Lacks Adequate DOD Planning" (Report to Congress, January 29, 1982), MASAD-82-14, p. 4.

65 Precisely what would happen . . .
Tomb interview.

65 Desmond Ball estimated that the . . .
Ball interview.

PAGE
66   A key part of the communications setup . . .
      Ball, Reference Paper No. 82; see also Desmond Ball, *A Suitable Piece of Real
      Estate: American Installations in Australia* (Hale and Iremonger, 1980); State-
      ment to the Australian Parliament by the Prime Minister, Robert J. Hawke,
      "Arms Control, Disarmament, and Australia" (June 6, 1984), pp. 11–15.
66   "Since relatively few fixed installations . . ."
      Hamre et al., op. cit., p. 13.
67   "A lot of things were overlooked . . ."
      Harvard Seminar 1982, p. 5.
67   Another official, General Robert . . .
      Ibid., p. 102.
67   The routing of military . . .
      Major General Vaughn O. Lang, "Interoperability—The Key to C 3 Systems in
      Support of USPACOM," *Signal*, February 1984, p. 27.
      NORAD informed me that the "situation" . . .
      Cormier, op. cit.
68   (Nurrungar is equipped with an AN/MSC . . .)
      Ball, Reference Paper No. 82, p. 22; see also Lang, op. cit., p. 26.
68   In addition, there is the problem . . .
      General Accounting Office, MASAD-82-14, op. cit., pp. 7–8, 33.
68   The DSCS WESTPAC satellite merely . . .
      Telephone interview with Major General Vaughn O. Lang, November 27, 1984.
69   As Major General J. C. Pfautz . . .
      Quoted in John H. Cushman, *Command and Control of Theater Forces* (Harvard
      University, Program on Information Resources Policy, April 1983), pp. 7–19.
73   The radar has a range of about . . .
      Hamre et al., op. cit., p. 10.
74   "The early warning radars are supposed . . ."
      Garwin interview.
75   I asked NORAD why this set of . . .
      Cormier, op. cit.
75   (Brigadier General Wagoner confirmed . . .)
      Wagoner interview.
76   U.S. missile experts estimate . . .
      Kurt Gottfried et al., *Space-Based Missile Defense* (Union of Concerned Scien-
      tists, 1984), p. 14.
76   These AN/FPS-115 radars were all designed . . .
      Carmen Alatorre and John Dymond, "Early Warning," *Raytheon Magazine*,
      Summer 1981, pp. 1–3; see also United States Air Force, "PAVE PAWS" (Stra-
      tegic Air Command, May 1982).
78   "All that information comes in to . . ."
      Harvard Seminar 1982, p. 5.
78   The type of computer problem that . . .
      Hart and Goldwater, op. cit., pp. 5–7; see also, Hearings before a Subcommittee
      of the House Committee on Government Operations, *Failures of the North
      American Aerospace Defense Command's Attack Warning System* (97th Con-
      gress, 1st Session, May 19–20, 1981) [hereafter referred to as House hearings,
      Warning System Failures]; General Accounting Office, "NORAD's Missile Warn-
      ing System: What Went Wrong?" (Report to Congress, May 15, 1981), MASAD-
      81-30, pp. 13–14.
79   The circuit board, which was designed . . .
      Cormier, op. cit.

PAGE
79   "Everybody would have told you . . ."
     LBJ School of Public Affairs, p. 101.
80   At a 1981 symposium, another . . .
     Warren Anderson, transcript of unpublished remarks of MITRE 1981 Symposium.
80   NORAD consultants, such as the MITRE . . .
     General Accounting Office, "NORAD's Information Processing Improvement
     Program—Will It Enhance Mission Capability" (Report to Congress, September
     21, 1978), LCD-78-117, p. 20.
80   One report by the Congressional General Accounting . . .
     Ibid., pp. iii and 7.
80   A 1978 study by a blue-ribbon panel . . .
     E. L. Dreeman et al., "National Security Team Report" (Federal Data Processing
     Reorganization Study, President's Reorganization Project, October 1978) p. 11
     (reprinted in House hearings, Warning System Failures, p. 353).
80   The Air Force Finance Center . . .
     Twenty-third Report by the House Committee on Government Operations,
     NORAD Computer Systems Are Dangerously Obsolete (97th Congress, 2d Ses-
     sion, 1982), p. 18.
81   . . . the Pentagon dismissed the protest . . .
     Letter from General Seth McKee to General John Ryan, August 12, 1970.
81   It also dismissed a report by the General . . .
     General Accounting Office, "Problems in the Acquisition of Standard Computers
     for Worldwide Military Command and Control System" (Report to Congress,
     December 29, 1970).
81   Congressman Jack Brooks of Texas . . .
     House hearings, Warning System Failures, p. 267.
82   The Air Force Inspector General . . .
     Inspector General of the Air Force, "Special Management Review of USAF
     Support to the Tactical Warning/Attack Assessment System," September 1980.
82   The Congressional auditing agency . . .
     General Accounting Office, "The Worldwide Military Command and Control In-
     formation System—Problems in Information Resource Management" (Report to
     Congress, October 19, 1981), MASAD-82-2, p. 9.
82   Assistant Secretary of Defense . . .
     Letter from Gerald Dinneen, Assistant Secretary of Defense, to Elmer Staats,
     Comptroller General of the United States, November 19, 1979, p. 1.
83   A few months later, however, the . . .
     General Accounting Office, "The Worldwide Military Command and Control
     System—Evaluation of Vendor and Department of Defense Comments" (Report
     to Congress, June 30, 1980), LCD-80-22A, pp. 26–27.
83   Dr. Dinneen, who is now a vice . . .
     Science, March 14, 1980, p. 1184.
84   Known as the Enhanced Perimeter Acquisition . . .
     Hamre et al., op. cit., p. 10.
84   Thus, within a minute of sending . . .
     Interview with Colonel Mario Masciola, October 21, 1983.
85   "What you've got out there is . . ."
     Harvard Seminar 1982, p. 5.
85   . . . some five thousand and twenty-six items . . .
     Computer printout, NORAD Space Surveillance Center, October 23, 1983.
85   . . . which happened, for example . . .
     General Accounting Office, MASAD-81-30, p. 3.

PAGE
85   The computers in the Space Surveillance . . .
     May interview.
86   "The map is up there . . ."
     Walden interview.
86   "I have confidence in the integrity . . ."
     New York Times, May 29, 1983.
87   "People have not yet learned how . . ."
     Charles Zraket, "The Impact of Command, Control, Communications and In-
     telligence on Deterrence," paper presented at the annual meeting of the American
     Association for the Advancement of Science, Detroit, Michigan, May 29, 1983,
     p. 6.
88   During this March 1979 episode . . .
     Daniel F. Ford, *Three Mile Island* (Penguin, 1982), Chapter 5.
88   (A special red light . . .)
     Ibid., p. 101.
88   On March 31, 1979, when . . .
     Ibid., p. 159.
88   "Our people don't shock . . ."
     Wagoner interview.
89   "One of the things we have discussed . . ."
     Harvard Seminar 1981, p. 70.
89   Bill Gulley, the former Director . . .
     Bill Gulley (with Mary Ellen Reese), *Breaking Cover* (Simon and Schuster,
     1980), pp. 178ff.
90   In remarks omitted from the . . .
     Anderson, op. cit.
92   While the White House has refused . . .
     Letter to the author from Robert B. Sims, Special Assistant to the President and
     Deputy Press Secretary for Foreign Affairs, March 13, 1984.
92   The *New York Times* reported . . .
     New York Times, October 16, 1983.
93   . . . a statement of his in May 1982 . . .
     New York Times, October 22, 1984.
93   Richard Garwin explained the basic . . .
     Garwin, op. cit., p. 133.

Chapter 3

PAGE
96   "It's never there when it's . . ."
     Ball interview.
96   The Pentagon belatedly acknowledges . . .
     Air Force Magazine, July 1979, p. 36.
97   "It was amazing . . ."
     Tomb interview.
97   Major General Winston Powers . . .
     MITRE 1981 Symposium, p. 100.
98   General Curtis LeMay, who would . . .
     New York Times, September 21, 1945, p. 4.
98   . . . Senator Edwin Johnson of Colorado . . .
     John L. Gaddis, *The United States and the Origins of the Cold War* (Columbia
     University Press, 1972), p. 245.

PAGE

99   Historians have jested . . .
     William H. McNeill, *The Pursuit of Power* (University of Chicago Press, 1982),
     p. 258.

99   "I went overseas . . ."
     Harvard Seminar 1982, p. 20.

100 The announced U.S. nuclear weapons . . .
     For a lucid survey of these policies, see Lawrence Freedman, *The Evolution of
     Nuclear Strategy* (St. Martin's Press, 1981); another valuable treatment is pro-
     vided by Kaplan, op. cit.

101 There are many subtleties . . .
     Freedman, op. cit., p. 308.

102 "the extent to which the leading . . ."
     Interview with Paul Bracken, September 29, 1983.

103 The Soviets, moreover, do not . . .
     Ball, Reference Paper No. 109; Freedman, op. cit., Chapter 17.

103 Secretary of Defense James Schlesinger . . .
     Hearing before the Subcommittee on Arms Control, International Law and
     Organization of the Senate Committee on Foreign Relations, *U.S.-U.S.S.R. Stra-
     tegic Policies* (March 4, 1974), p. 19.

104 The physicist Richard Garwin . . .
     Garwin interview.

104 Kahn wrote that . . .
     Herman Kahn, *On Escalation* (Penguin Books, 1965), p. 211.

104 Garwin comments that . . .
     Letter to the author, March 19, 1984.

105 A few months after . . .
     Freedman, op. cit., p. 76.

105 "Mere prattle without . . ."
     William Shakespeare, *Othello* (I,i).

106 The basic Air Force attitude . . .
     Freedman, op. cit., p. 129.

106 Instead, the Air Force position . . .
     D. A. Rosenberg, "A Smoking Radiating Ruin at the End of Two Hours," *Inter-
     national Security*, Winter 1980–81, p. 27.

106 When a member of a blue-ribbon . . .
     Kaplan, op. cit., p. 133.

106 In a 1968 book, LeMay . . .
     Curtis E. LeMay (with Dale O. Smith), *America is in Danger* (Funk & Wag-
     nalls, 1968), pp. 82–83.

107 "We have never as a matter of . . ."
     John Steinbruner, remarks at the American Association for the Advancement
     of Science Annual Meeting, Detroit, Michigan, May 29, 1983.

107 "For ever, really, the . . ."
     Interview with Barry Blechman, June 16, 1983.

107 "This nation has always . . ."
     Davis interview.

108 SAC's success in keeping . . .
     Hearing before the Senate Committee on Foreign Relations, *Nuclear War Strat-
     egy*, (96th Congress, 2nd Session, September 16, 1980), p. 18.

108 The Air Force refers to its . . .
     Whiteman Air Force Base, Wing Mission Briefing, May 31, 1983.

108 "rival groupings of officers . . ."

PAGE

McNeill, op. cit., p. 160.

109   Nations do not wage war "by halves" . . .
Tuchman, op. cit., p. 136.

109   When the subject of limited . . .
Garwin interview.

109   "If the U.S. [limited nuclear . . ."
Freedman, op. cit., p. 381.

110   "We have built a whole cottage . . ."
Interview with Jon Boyes, June 15, 1983.

113   There are, as Desmond Ball . . .
Ball, Adelphi Paper 169, op. cit., p. 6.

114   The Truman Administration took a . . .
Frank G. Klotz, "The U.S. President and the Control of Strategic Nuclear Weapons" (Ph.D. thesis, Oxford University, 1980).

114   It is noteworthy that the Soviets . . .
Bracken, op. cit., p. 23.

115   "[T]he idea of turning over . . ."
Quoted in Klotz, op. cit., p. 176.

115   By the early 1950s, the military . . .
Bracken, op. cit., p. 180.

115   The protocols for transferring . . .
Ibid.

116   Some of the junior-size . . .
Thomas Cochran et al., *Nuclear Weapons Databook: U.S. Nuclear Weapons and Forces*, Vol. I (Ballinger, 1983).

117   Simple PALs had four-digit codes . . .
Ibid., Table 2.1.

119   "As far as the United States . . ."
Davis interview.

119   "People who talk about accidental . . ."
Ball interview.

119   "Without proper authority, it would . . ."
House testimony, *First Use of Nuclear Weapons*, p. 94.

120   "It isn't as if just any . . ."
Steinbruner interview.

120   "Navy commanders take it as . . ."
Garwin interview.

120   Herbert York, another physicist . . .
House testimony, *First Use of Nuclear Weapons*, p. 96.

Chapter 4

PAGE

122   Soviet strategists have written . . .
Ball, Reference Paper No. 109, p. 6.

123   "Under conditions of a nuclear war . . ."
Ibid., pp. 9–10.

123   Aiming the limited Soviet . . .
Steinbruner interview.

123   Robert Berman and John Baker . . .
Berman and Baker, op. cit., pp. 117–118.

124   "By attacking the U.S. forces . . ."

PAGE

Ball, Reference Paper No. 109, op. cit., p. 3.

124   Soviet awareness of the potentially . . .
Norman Polmar, "Soviet C³," *Air Force Magazine*, June 1980, pp. 58–66.

124   To protect their own high officials . . .
Director of Central Intelligence, *Soviet Civil Defense* (Central Intelligence Agency, July 1978), p. 8; see also Harold Brown, *Department of Defense Annual Report Fiscal Year 1981* (Department of Defense, 1980), p. 78.

125   "We must operate on the theory . . ."
MITRE 1981 Symposium, p. 93.

125   A secret study by the MITRE . . .
MITRE Corporation, *Proceedings of the MITRE Seminar on Survivability of Command and Control Systems, May 16–17, 1961* (October 1, 1961), Supplement No. 1.

126   "the loss of the command function . . ."
Richard B. Foster et al., *National Strategic Command-Control-Communications Requirements to 1975, Final Summary Report*, Volume I (Stanford Research Institute and Bell Telephone Laboratories, 1962; reprinted December 1981), p. 1.

126   "For example, it requires only 17 . . ."
Ibid., pp. 87–88.

126   "was sharply mitigated in reality . . ."
Steinbruner, "Nuclear Decapitation," op. cit., pp. 21–22.

126   In addition to providing greater protection . . .
Ball interview.

128   "We don't even consider such a . . ."
Interview with Donald Latham, June 13, 1983.

128   Leon Sloss, the Pentagon official . . .
Leon Sloss and Marc Millot, "U.S. Nuclear Strategy in Evolution" (mimeograph, December 12, 1983), p. 14.

128   The Congress was informed of the . . .
Desmond Ball, "Targeting for Strategic Deterrence" (The International Institute for Strategic Studies, 1983), Adelphi Paper 185, p. 31.

128   General Holloway, in a March 31 . . .
Letter from Bruce Holloway to Dr. Francis X. Kane, TRW, Inc., March 31, 1980.

131   Its opposition had "an edge . . ."
Blechman interview.

131   "I think a fundamental issue here . . ."
Davis interview.

131   Colin Gray, a participant . . .
Colin S. Gray and Keith Payne, "Victory Is Possible," *Foreign Policy*, Summer 1980, pp. 14–27; see also James Lardner, "The Call of the Hawk's Hawk," *Washington Post*, May 14, 1982.

132   "[i]t is generally presumed . . ."
Ball, Adelphi Paper 169, p. 14.

132   The amount of warning . . .
Ibid.

132   "It's even worse than that . . ."
Garwin interview.

134   "If we go ahead with sea-launched . . ."
Paul Warnke, "Which Comes First, Arms Control or Security?" *New York Times*, March 21, 1982.

134   The Soviets are reportedly developing . . .

PAGE

Drew Middleton, "U.S. Seeks Ways to Bolster Air Defense," *New York Times*, January 10, 1984.

134   At a distance of one thousand . . .
Henry W. Kendall, "Radar Coverage" (unpublished technical note, January 9, 1984).

134   ICBM warheads, which on standard . . .
Ashton Carter, *Directed Energy Missile Defense in Space* (Office of Technology Assessment, April 1984), Figure 2.2, p. 9.

136   Under Secretary of Defense Perry . . .
Ball, Adelphi Paper 169, op. cit., p. 15.

136   According to Donald Latham . . .
Charles Mohr, "President's War Jet Is to Be Based Farther Inland," *New York Times*, September 24, 1983.

137   . . . Senator Daniel Quayle of Indiana . . .
Press release, "Quayle Announces Grissom, AFB New Base for NEACP" (Office of Senator Dan Quayle, September 24, 1983).

138   Thus, according to reports . . .
Desmond Ball, "Strategic Nuclear Targeting" (The Strategic and Defence Studies Centre, Australian National University, August 1981), Reference Paper No. 98, pp. 58, 66, 69, 72, 80–81, 91.

139   Some of the most important U.S. . . .
Desmond Ball, "The Rhyolite Programme" (The Strategic and Defence Studies Centre, Australian National University, November 1981).

139   The Rhyolites function . . .
Ibid., p. 3.

139   Detecting the latter is an "extremely . . ."
Ibid., p. 16.

140   "if there are differences . . ."
Steinbruner interview.

140   "Prudence dictates that . . ."
Davis interview.

140   In addition, as Lieutenant General Scowcroft . . .
MITRE 1981 Symposium, p. 95.

141   Scowcroft himself said . . .
Anderson, op. cit.

141   "Well, there are contingency plans . . ."
Interview with Donald Latham, May 29, 1983.

141   Thus, an Eisenhower Administration . . .
Klotz, op. cit., p. 362.

141   "This is probably one of the . . ."
Ball interview.

142   The Carter Administration initiated . . .
Presidential Directive 53, November 15, 1979, and Presidential Directive 58, June 30, 1980.

143   In fact, according to the transcript . . .
Raymond Tate, Harvard Seminar 1980, p. 43.

143   "If the President should for . . ."
Steinbruner interview.

144   With the control arrangements now . . .
Bracken, op. cit., pp. 196–204.

144   "In my view, an irrelevant . . ."

PAGE

Davis interview.
145   "So if all else goes . . ."
Tate, op. cit.
146   William Perry told Congress . . .
Senate Armed Services Committee, *Department of Defense Authorization for Appropriations for Fiscal Year 1980*, Part 1 (January–February 1979), p. 350.

Chapter 5

PAGE
147   Every eight hours . . .
United States Air Force, "Post Attack Command and Control System" (Strategic Air Command Fact Sheet, August 1981).
148   SAC will not officially acknowledge . . .
SAC Briefing, June 1, 1983.
148   A documentary film produced . . .
KRON-TV, "First Strike" (Chronicle Publishing Company, San Francisco, 1980).
149   Looking Glass has no direct . . .
SAC Briefing, June 1, 1983.
149   Looking Glass, in theory . . .
Ibid.
153   The four relay stations, which . . .
SAC Headquarters, "Backdoor PAS and PACCS Access" (undated slide used in ibid.).
154   The test designated *Starfish* . . .
Ball, Adelphi Paper 169, op. cit., p. 11.
154   The launch control centers are . . .
Ball interview.
159   "Chips and this low-power . . ."
Harvard Seminar 1982, p. 7.
160   (more than a hundred million . . .)
DMS, *Market Intelligence Report*, January 1983.
161   "The one continuing weakness . . ."
Hamre et al., op. cit., p. 35.
163   The plane flies at a normal . . .
SAC Briefing, June 1, 1983.
164   If the plane were located . . .
Garwin interview.
164   Looking Glass can fly for eleven . . .
SAC Briefing, June 1, 1983.
165   As one study of the Looking . . .
Ball, Adelphi Paper 169, op. cit., p. 18.
166   "Well, there are many ways . . ."
Davis interview.
166   Lieutenant General William Hillsman . . .
LBJ School of Public Affairs, p. 106.
167   The policy is exceedingly dangerous . . .
Bracken, op. cit., p. 233.

Chapter 6

PAGE

169   The first three planes . . .
      Hamre et al., op. cit., Note 6, pp. 25–26.
169   Dr. Gerald Dinneen, the Assistant . . .
      Ball, Adelphi Paper 169, op. cit., p. 17.
169   "If you think we're in trouble . . ."
      Harvard Seminar 1982, p. 2.
170   "The obstacles are not financial . . ."
      Harvard Seminar 1981, p. 96.
170   "For the typical senior commander . . ."
      Cushman, op. cit., p. ES-3.
172   "I think it is hard to make the . . ."
      Harvard Seminar 1981, pp. 129–133.
172   The present Pentagon procurement bureaucracy . . .
      Telephone interview with James M. Osborne, January 30, 1984.
172   "Finally, we deliver the equipment . . ."
      Harvard Seminar 1981, p. 18.
172   At the AFCEA convention, I spoke . . .
      Boyes interview.
173   However, some of the messages . . .
      Tate, op. cit.
174   A special Congressional panel . . .
      Report by the Command, Control, and Communications Panel to the House
      Committee on Armed Services, *Review of Department of Defense Command,
      Control, and Communications Systems and Facilities* (February 18, 1977), p. 26.
175   "I think we are not well organized . . ."
      Harvard Seminar 1982, p. 24.
175   "If there is a World War III . . ."
      General Accounting Office, "Better Planning and Management of Threat Simu-
      lators and Aerial Targets Is Crucial to Effective Weapons Systems Performance"
      (Report to Congress, June 23, 1983), MASAD-83-27, p. 2.
175   "Many military commanders . . ."
      Harvard Seminar 1981, p. 134.
176   "[p]eople saw it then (and . . ."
      Harvard Seminar 1982, p. 3.
176   "The Navy's basic view . . ."
      Ball interview.
177   Lieutenant General William Hillsman . . .
      LBJ School of Public Affairs, pp. 77–78.
177   "Now, try telling a tactical . . ."
      Harvard Seminar 1982, p. 104.
177   "That's real money you're . . ."
      Ibid., p. 25.
178   "As soon as there is a whiff . . ."
      New York Times, December 3, 1983, p. 25.
178   General John Vessey, Jr., the . . .
      LBJ School of Public Affairs, p. 99.
178   "We're caught up in a lot . . ."
      Boyes interview.
178   The government auditors were . . .

PAGE

General Accounting Office, MASAD-83-27, p. 21.

179 There is a strong feeling of "us" . . .
Cushman, op. cit., pp. 3–12.

179 "Look at the [NATO] European . . ."
Boyes interview.

180 "Everything is so single-interest . . ."
Harvard Seminar 1982, p. 151.

180 "Well, it really boils down . . ."
Harvard Seminar 1981, p. 4.

181 "The problem is, everything . . ."
Harvard Seminar 1982, p. 149.

182 A 1982 review of current . . .
Ellis Rubinstein, ed., *Technology in War and Peace* (Institute of Electrical and Electronics Engineers, 1982), p. 49.

182 "We try to evaluate the needs . . ."
Harvard Seminar 1982, pp. 13–15.

182 Once a decision is nominally . . .
Ibid., p. 151.

182 Even the President . . .
Ibid., p. 19.

183 To correct this resource allocation . . .
S. J. Buchsbaum et al., *Report of the Defense Science Board Task Force on Command and Control Systems Management*, July 1978, p. v.

183 "It's very difficult to get the . . ."
Harvard Seminar 1982, p. 28.

183 The University of Chicago . . .
McNeill, op. cit.

183 "patterns of both naval and . . ."
Ibid., p. 232.

184 The naval arms race of the early . . .
Ibid., p. 289.

184 A Congressional panel that reviewed . . .
House report, *Command, Control, and Communications.*

184 James Osborne said . . .
Osborne interview.

186 "No military officer whose goal . . ."
Harvard Seminar 1980, pp. 40–41.

186 "military commanders do not fully . . ."
General Accounting Office, MASAD-83-27, p. 12.

187 The DSCS II program did not proceed . . .
House report, *Command, Control, and Communications*, pp. 16ff.

187 "The various unique requirements . . ."
Ibid., p. 17.

189 The set of instructions that tell . . .
Rubinstein, op. cit., p. 53.

189 The scorecard for Operation *Prime* . . .
General Accounting Office, LCD-80-82, p. 51.

189 After additional exercises in 1980 . . .
General Accounting Office, MASAD-82-2, p. 56.

189 A General Accounting Office . . .
Ibid.

PAGE
190   In a keynote speech at the 1983 . . .
      Major General D. L. Evans, "C⁶: Command, Control, Communications, Com-
      puters, Community, and Contractors," speech at the Armed Forces Communica-
      tions and Electronics Association, Sheraton Washington Hotel, June 15, 1983,
      pp. 5ff.

                                   Chapter 7

PAGE
191   He has observed "what the African . . ."
      Harvard Seminar 1981, p. 83.
192   "We need everything . . ."
      Michael Heylin, "Nuclear Arms Race Gearing for Speedup," *Chemical and
      Engineering News*, March 16, 1981, p. 28.
192   Winston Churchill, who was a . . .
      Churchill, op. cit., p. 37.
193   "Fearing to be taken advantage . . ."
      Tuchman, op. cit., pp. 19–20.
193   "Bismarck had warned . . ."
      Ibid., p. 20.
193   Former Secretary of Defense . . .
      Melvin Laird, "Not a Binge, but a Buildup," *Washington Post*, November 19,
      1980, p. A17.
193   James Osborne, the defense . . .
      Osborne interview.
193   "You know, the problem becomes . . ."
      Boyes interview.
194   . . . the Pentagon's neglect of likely . . .
      Richard DeLauer, "The Force Multiplier," in Rubinstein, op. cit., p. 37.
196   The Navy, for example, has already . . .
      Thomas Sweeney, *C³I: Market Study and Forecast* (DMS, Inc., December 1983),
      p. I–i.
197   "There are a few command . . ."
      Ball interview.
197   "Very often people will say . . ."
      Garwin interview.
198   "Well, the concept is . . ."
      Interview with Donald Latham, May 29, 1983.
198   "The thing that bothered me . . ."
      Interview with Donald Latham, June 13, 1983.
201   Advanced Defense Support Program . . .
      Sweeney, op. cit., pp. I–27, 28.
203   As an alternative to the vulnerable . . .
      Garwin interview.
205   "I wish I had thought through . . ."
      Elizabeth Drew, "An Argument over Survival," *The New Yorker*, April 4, 1977,
      p. 100.
206   "We expect a large, permanent . . ."
      George C. Wilson, "Soviets Reported Gaining in Space Weapons," *Boston Globe*,
      March 3, 1982.
208   The DEW Line, as it is called, . . .

PAGE

Major General Bernard P. Randolph, presentation to the Strategic and Theater Nuclear Forces Subcommittee of the Senate Committee on Armed Services (March 18, 1983), p. 3.

209 "Early on in our study . . ."
Buchsbaum et al., op. cit., p. 7.

209 Rear Admiral Paul Tomb explained . . .
Tomb interview.

211 The threat posed by the two hundred . . .
U.S. Department of Defense, *Soviet Military Power* (Second Edition, March 1983), pp. 24–25.

212 As Air Force General Bernard Randolph . . .
Randolph, op. cit., p. 10.

212 "This program has taken just . . ."
DMS, *Market Intelligence Report*, April 1983.

215 MILSTAR will have a variety . . .
Sweeney, op. clt., p. I–95.

216 "All it is really doing . . ."
Ball interview.

218 There was, as Charles Snodgrass . . .
Harvard Seminar 1981, p. 133.

219 A NORAD official likened the process . . .
Sweeney, op. cit., p. III–38.

222 The mobile command post program, Mr. Latham . . .
Telephone interview with Donald Latham, February 21, 1984.

224 An unclassified SAC description . . .
SAC Headquarters, "AFSATCOM FLTSAT Connectivity" (undated slide used in SAC Briefing, June 1, 1983).

225 The GWEN system, Donald Latham . . .
Larry Waller, "The U.S. attacks the C³I problem," *Electronics*, December 15, 1983, p. 107.

226 (GWEN installations are located . . .)
DMS, *Market Intelligence Report*, September 1983.

226 "Fixing this problem . . ."
Sweeney, op. cit., Overview, p. 2.

226 Lieutenant General Brent Scowcroft . . .
MITRE 1981 Symposium, p. 94.

227 "In developing the recommendations . . ."
Ibid., p. 90.

229 "Given the number of warheads . . ."
Ball interview.

229 Hair triggers, as Daniel Cullity . . .
Cullity interview.

229 "And when he prepares . . ."
Sun Tzu, *The Art of War*, translated by Samuel B. Griffith (Oxford University Press, 1963), p. 98.

230 "Well, the last thing I want . . ."
MITRE 1981 Symposium, pp. 89–90.

231 "I don't agree to building . . ."
Garwin interview.

231 "We'd certainly appreciate . . ."
MITRE 1981 Symposium, p. 113.

Epilogue

PAGE
234   Jacob Viner, of the University . . .
      Kaplan, op. cit., p. 26.
234   "Traditions are not killed . . ."
      George Orwell, *The Road to Wigan Pier* (Harcourt Brace Jovanovich, 1958),
      p. 113.
234   Looking Glass has been . . .
      Ball interview.
236   Nations, he emphasized . . .
      Churchill, op. cit., p. 45.
239   "You can think of that . . ."
      Roger Fisher, "Can We Negotiate With the Russians?," remarks at the Confer-
      ence on Nuclear Arms Control, First Parish Church, Weston, Massachusetts,
      November 14, 1981.
240   "The good news is it's . . ."
      LBJ School of Public Affairs, p. 244.
241   "The President's leaving Washington . . ."
      Interview with Thomas Schelling, May 23, 1983.
241   "I think you could assume . . ."
      MITRE 1981 Symposium, p. 95.
242   "There's a real dilemma here . . ."
      Ibid.

INDEX

ABOUT THE AUTHOR

DANIEL FORD is an economist and writer specializing in nuclear-policy questions. A graduate of Harvard College and former executive director of the Union of Concerned Scientists, he has worked on a variety of studies related to nuclear power plant safety. His most recent work is *The Cult of the Atom*: The Secret Papers of the Atomic Energy Commission (Simon and Schuster, 1982). He is also the co-author of six technical volumes on nuclear power and national energy policy, including *Energy Strategies* (with Henry Kendall and Steven Nadis), which was named one of the best energy books of 1980 by *Library Journal*. Mr. Ford also writes for *The New Yorker*. He lives in Cambridge, Massachusetts.